# THE THREE FACES OF REVOLUTION

# THE THREE FACES OF REVOLUTION

by

**Dr. Fred Schwarz**

THE CAPITOL HILL PRESS
WASHINGTON, D.C.

THE THREE FACES OF REVOLUTION

Copyright © 1972 by Prospect House, Inc.

Library of Congress Catalog Card Number: 72-83849

ISBN: 0-88221-003-3

First Printing October 1972

Printed in the United States of America

The Capitol Hill Press
—a division of—
Prospect House, Inc.
1825 Connecticut Ave., N.W.
Washington, D.C. 20009

# Contents

This book is dedicated to my wife
Lillian whose love and loyalty know no
limits.

# PREFACE

The world has changed dramatically during the past decade. When my previous book, *You Can Trust The Communists (to be Communists),* was first published in 1961 international communism presented a united front to the world - though there were reports of difficulties between the communists of the Soviet Union and China. Within the United States, Marxism and communism were the only doctrines commanding any popular following which taught the necessity of overthrowing the American economic and political system. A few communist and communist-inspired organizations were the only major forces working to achieve this goal.

How different the situation is now. Internationally, communism is fragmented. The reverberations of the Sino-Soviet split are felt everywhere throughout the world. Wihtin the United States the revolutionary movement is split asunder as violent revolutionaries, who acknowledge neither Marx nor Lenin, work to destroy the stability and vitality of the nation. Both the doctrines and practices of many of these new revolutionaries seem bizarre and strange, with new life-styles accompanying new revolutionary methods.

Today, there are three primary faces to revolution—communism, anarchism and sensualism. The time has come to take a new and careful look at these three forces on the revolutionary scene and attempt to clarify the confusion. The purpose of this book is to explain these three doctrines which teach violent revolution and to describe the organizations associated with them. Both the points of agreement and dispute between the various doctrines will be considered. In addition, I have described how activities of the various organizations complement or cancel each other.

This is the age of ideology. Ideas are incarnate in individuals, organizations and activities. Unlike some currently popular theories, this analysis does *not* ignore the doctrinal motivations of the revolutionaries. Once American citizens understand the ideas that

recruit individuals into the revolutionary organizations, they can more accurately interpret the activities of these organizations, predict their future actions, and combat their plans.

It would be tragic for mankind if the system which has preserved unequalled individual liberty, while producing and distributing material well-being in an unprecedented manner, were destroyed. Conservation and, where necessary, reformation form the path to human progress and happiness. I hope the thoughts in this book will guide America along that path.

# INTRODUCTION

Violent revolution is the subject of this book. This type of revolution was described clearly by Frederick Engels, the alter ego of Karl Marx.

> Have these gentlemen [the antiauthoritarians] ever seen a revolution? A revolution is certainly the most authoritarian thing there is; it is an act whereby one part of the population imposes its will upon the other part by means of rifles, bayonets and cannon—authoritarian means, if such there be at all; and if the victorious party does not want to have fought in vain, it must maintain this rule by means of the terror which its arms inspire in the reactionaries.*

The term revolution as it is used here means violent activity designed to overthrow the government, while "revolutionary" means an individual who is consciously and actively promoting the violent overthrow of the government.

The history of the past decade is the history of the rise of revolutionary rhetoric and activity within the United States. Not too many years ago, the present chaos within the United States would have been inconceivable. Who would have predicted that major university campuses would be scenes of violence, bloodshed, arson, bombing, kidnaping and murder? Who could have imagined that a group of the most brilliant students of America's most prestigious universities, the children of wealthy parents, would form themselves into a terroristic underground and engage in an orgy of bombing and arson in order to weaken the U.S. Government?

The country is ringing with revolutionary rhetoric accompanied by the bursting of bombs and flames or arson. Kidnapings, riots in the ghettos, riots on campus, riots in the prisons, and mutiny in the armed forces show that the revolutionary words of yesterday have been followed by the revolutionary deeds of today.

*V. I. Lenin, The Proletarian Revolution and the Renegade Kautsky (Moscow, Foreign Languages Publishing House, 1947) p. 27.

## INGREDIENTS FOR THE REVOLUTIONARY BOMB

Who sows the seeds of revolution? How do they germinate? How do they grow?

A revolution is complex. It involves people, ideas, organizations, social forces and weapons. I have developed a diagram to depict the relationship among these ingredients of revolution. This diagram places these various revolutionary ingredients in perspective, and I call it "The Revolutionary Bomb."

The Bomb

This bomb consists of a destructive core surrounded by a mass of flammable material which ignites when the appropriate stimulus is given to it.

The core consists of those individuals who adhere to a specific doctrine which declares that modern, capitalist society is intrinsically evil and must be destroyed.

The Core

All their energies, therefore, are directed to the consummation of destruction. Every cause they support, every demonstration they organize, and every alliance they form must be made to serve this purpose. They call themselves RADICALS, but the name "DESTROYERS" is more appropriate.

The body of the "Revolutionary Bomb" consists of those individuals who are prepared to partake in illegal, disruptive and even violent activity in pursuit of some specific cause or because of some emotional condition. In the core are the destroyers; in the body are the needy.

Most of the destroyers adhere to one of the three doctrines: Communism, Anarchism or Sensualism. Each of these three groups believe American society is evil and must be destroyed. This is their major point of agreement. But they are not always in agreement on the techniques of destruction, and they disagree violently on what should be done after destruction is achieved.

All three groups differentiate between the "people" and the "State". They accept the Marxist doctrine that society is class society and that the people are divided into antagonistic classes, one of which is dominant and suppresses the others. The State is, to them, the instrument of suppression. In the words of Lenin, "The state is a special organization of force. It is an organization of violence for the suppression of some class."*

The State consists of the entire governmental and cultural apparatus. It includes the legislature, executive, and judiciary of federal, state, and local governments, and extends into the educational sphere through the ruling bodies such as the regents or trustees of the colleges and universities.

According to this theory, the army, the national guard, and the police are the instruments of State violence against the "people". They are the enemy of the "people" because of their class relationship. Modern theory of the State emphasizes the sinister power of the so-called Military-Industrial Complex.

The revolutionaries agree that the State must be destroyed. However, the Communists, Anarchists, and Sensualists each have differing doctrines, organizations, methods and final objectives. These will be considered in more detail in later chapters.

## HOW MANY DESTROYERS?

The number of those committed to destruction is not very great. Fortune magazine† conducted a survey of the revolutionaries

---

*V. I. Lenin, The State and the Revolution (New York, International Publishers Company, 1932) p. 41.
†January, 1969

among campus youth on the eve of the 1970 decade. The magazine stated the number of hard core activists was less than 30,000. This figure is only approximate but the number of radicals is no doubt small relative to those involved in violent activity from time to time. In recent years, for instance, radicals have rallied, occasionally, as many as several hundred thousand people for a series of demonstrations. The significance of 30,000 destroyers is much more than mere numbers might indicate.

Those who have investigated the membership of the core of the "Revolutionary Bomb" have made a remarkable discovery. The so-called generation gap plays little or no part in the motivation of young radicals. In fact, there is a rather pronounced identification with the preceding generation. The destroyers are actually following the tradition of their parents!

Eugene Lyons refers to the years 1930–1940 as the "Red Decade".* This tumultuous decade was characterized by the Great Depression, the rise to power of Hitler in Nazi Germany, the persecution of the Jews, the Spanish Civil War, and culminated in the Second World War. As a reaction to these events, many intellectuals joined the Communist Party and the membership of the Communist Party rose to about 300,000, while many more became sympathizers.

Where are those erstwhile Communist Party members and sympathizers today? Most of them have long since severed their formal links with the Communist Party. This is obviously so, since the membership of the Communist Party has been reduced to between 10,000 and 15,000. Many ex-members, however, have retained their radical philosophy while they have prospered in bourgeois life. They have become successful professional men such as doctors, lawyers, educators or businessmen. However, many of them have also developed a guilt complex because of their reconciliation with the comforts of bourgeois life and their past association with Stalinism. Their children learned radical anti-capitalist doctrines at the breakfast table. It is no wonder that they have picked up the torch of revolution which their parents laid down. Many of these parents are not passive and observe the actions of their off-

*Eugene Lyons, Red Decade (New Rochelle, N.Y., Arlington House, 1971).

4

spring with admiration, pride, and awe. They keep their checkbooks ready to help when money is needed.

It is probable that a big percentage, if not the majority of the hard-core revolutionists, come from a radical background. Well-known examples are Mrs. Bettina Aptheker Kursweil, who is the daughter of Herbert Aptheker, the leading theoretician of the American Communist Party, and the 6 radical sons of radical attorney Vincent Hallinan of San Francisco. It is with good reason, then, that these second generation destroyers are sometimes called Red Diaper babies.

Thus the generation gap has little significance at the core of the bomb, but, as we shall see later, plays a significant role in the body of the bomb.

## THE BODY OF THE BOMB

The body of the bomb consists of numerous individuals who surround the core and who can be ignited in support of revolutionary causes. The individuals in the body of the bomb are motivated primarily by material or psychological need. This need may drive them to illegal, irrational, or violent activity which the skillful destroyers try to exploit in order to produce a desired explosion. Sometimes, but not always, their efforts are crowned with success.

Those in the body of the bomb can be divided into three major groups. These groups are not mutually exclusive and an amount of overlapping takes place. However, most individuals in the body of the bomb would fit rather naturally into one of these groups. These groups may be called: 1) Partisans, 2) Reformers, 3) Alienated.

# THE THREE FACES OF REVOLUTION

## THE PARTISANS

The partisans are those individuals and groups who are concerned with one special objective above all others. In fact, they want one thing so much that they tend to lose perspective. They are so eager to achieve their objective that they are willing to engage in illegal and violent activity. This violent activity may become destructive, but their motivating purpose is really achievement, not destruction. When they are denied what they yearn for and to which they believe they are justly entitled, their frustration may lead to an emotional destructiveness.

Partisans come from a variety of sources, including: national minority movements, labor groups, "peace" groups, religious groups, women's liberation organizations, homosexuals, military dissidents, and prisoners.

It must be emphasized that not all in these groups are considered to be in the revolutionary bomb. Only those who can be stimulated to violence are included. Let's take a closer look.

*National Minority Groups:* Among these would be organizations of blacks, Mexican-Americans, Puerto Ricans, and American Indians. Sometimes small groups or Orientals such as the Chinese, Japanese, Indians, and Koreans are also involved. On the university campus, these groups may unite into one organization such as the Third World Liberation Front.

*Labor Groups:* A typical labor group would consist of disaffected teachers who are willing to join with the students to promote campus demonstrations and disruption. They may be motivated by genuine economic or professional objectives such as increased pay or more privileges, but they may also be expressing an inner resentment because they have not experienced the success in academic life to which they believe their merits entitle them. Behind rebellious students almost invariably there stand rebellious members of the faculty.

*Peace Groups:* The so-called "peace" groups contain many and varied elements. They include genuine pacifists, conscientious opponents of a particular war such as the one in Vietnam, and also supporters of the communist enemy who desire peace by victory for the communists. Their activities are often confined to picketing and peaceful protest. Some in the "peace" movement have en-

6

gaged in violent fights. Strange things indeed are done in the name of peace!

*Religious Groups:* Various religious individuals and groups have now adopted violence as "a Christian method" of producing social change. Organizations advocating violence have sprung up within the Catholic Church as well as in Protestant denominations. Their rationale is that the status quo is maintained by violence, so those who react violently are the victims, not the instigators, of violence.

*Women's Liberation Groups:* These consist of women who believe that women are an oppressed majority who must be liberated. They claim that women constitute the largest oppressed group of the nation. Some devote their energies to the improvement of conditions of employment and the removal of artificial barriers to the full participation of women in national life. Extreme groups, however, which war against essential femininity spring up from time to time. One such group called itself the "Women's International Terrorist Conspiracy from Hell" or WITCH. This group regarded marriage as a form of slavery and whoredom. They picketed bridal fairs and beauty competitions under the slogan "Picket the Whoremongers". Starry-eyed young girls, ecstatically surveying the dresses and beauty aids offered to make their coming weddings occasions to treasure have been bewildered when confronted by a group of bedraggled females carrying picket signs and screaming obscenities.

*The Homosexuals:* Recently, various homosexual groups have become militant. Some have embraced Marxism and consider themselves part of the revolutionary movement.

*Servicemen:* Military men, particularly in the lower ranks, have grievances and personal problems. Resentment against officers by enlisted men is common, and, of course, conflict between black and white servicemen exists as in society. Various radical groups have formed organizations to exploit this discontent within military ranks. One such organization is the American Servicemen's Union which advocates the organizing of GI's to do battle against "white racism and imperialist war."

It should never be forgotten that it was revolution in the army that finally resulted in the communist dictatorship in the Soviet Union.

*The Prisoners:* The grievances of prisoners are numerous and

7

genuine, but revolutionary organizations including the Muslims and the Black Panthers are attempting to channel prisoner resentment into revolutionary destruction. Revolutionary groups are being formed in prisons from coast to coast.

## ⫯ THE REFORMERS

The reformers are the second basic category of people who are in the body of the Revolutionary Bomb. This group includes student idealists who are very concerned because of injustices that still exist within the American system. They have lost patience because democratic methods seem to work so slowly and have succumbed to the temptation to substitute direct action for persuasion and due process.

These students have the idealism of youth and the arrogance of intelligence untempered by the humility of experience. They are exceedingly sensitive to the evil in the society that surrounds them and remarkably insensitive to the evil within themselves. They survey the existing situation and find much of it intolerable. They cannot resign themselves to the fact that poverty continues to exist in a country with the productive capacity and affluence of the United States of America. They believe that the continued existence of poverty must be due to the cynicism and corruption of the older generation, and they are quite convinced that if they and their chosen representatives were granted political power, the defects would be remedied in short order indeed.

Many of these experienced a great surge of enthusiasm for the presidential candidacy of Senator Eugene McCarthy. They went "clean for Gene" and worked energetically and unselfishly to have him nominated as the Democratic presidential candidate in 1968. His defeat was a traumatic emotional experience.

They could not believe it was simply the consequence of the working of the democratic processes that more people preferred Hubert Humphrey. They believed the defeat of McCarthy was brought about by power politics and this tended to cause them to lose faith in the democratic process itself. Consequently, some of them succumbed to the temptation to step outside the democratic system and use extraparliamentary methods in order to achieve quick results.

The problem here is not one of good will but one of humility. They have little sense of history and the historical achievements of the democratic society. They fail to realize that the dramatic solution of one problem may create others so that the final outcome is worse than the original situation. They look at a glass of water and protest because it is one-tenth empty while they ignore the fact that it is nine-tenths full.

Most of these reformers will become very fine citizens. However, during a time of crisis, their youthful exuberance, impatience, and intolerance may lead them into some outburst engineered by the destroyers.

## THE ALIENATED

The alienated are a third basic category in the body of the Revolutionary Bomb.

The alienated were well described by Carl Davidson in 1967 when he was Vice President of Students for a Democratic Society. He describes 85 per cent of the members of SDS as follows:

> They are usually the younger members, freshmen and sophomores, rapidly moving into the hippie, Bobby Dylan syndrome, having been completely turned off by the American system of compulsory miseducation, they are staunchly antiintellectual and rarely read anything unless it comes from the underground press syndicate. They have never heard of C. Wright Mills or even Bob Moses, nor do they care to find out. In one sense, they have no politics. But they come to the meetings, for awhile anyway. They turn out regularly for the demonstrations. They are morally outraged about the war, cops, racism, poverty, their parents, the middle class and authority figures in general. They have a sense that all those things are connected somehow and that money has something to do with it. They long for community and feel their own isolation acutely, which is probably why they stick with SDS.*

They are the uprooted young of America. They have lost the roots which attach individuals to the traditions, culture, and moral values of their society. There is no nutrient stream flowing

*National Guardian, April 15, 1967, p.5.

to them from their community. Consequently, they suffer from moral malnutrition and cultural instability and are at the mercy of every emotional breeze that blows.

Some of the roots that have been torn up are: The family root, the religious root, the patriotic root, the economic root, and the intellectual root.

*The Family Root:* In the past, most Americans grew up as members of a family with emotional ties, responsibilities, and duties to parents, brothers, and sisters. These family ties were strong and endured for a lifetime. Each child was required to contribute his share of work towards the maintenance of the family. It was accepted as a matter of course that members of the family stood by each other in trouble. While they had their internal conflicts, they presented a united front against the outside world. Often there was a unity of generations as aged grandparents lived with their children and grandchildren. While there was often a scarcity of food and clothing, there was usually an abundance of love.

This situation has changed during the past couple of generations. Where there is an abundance of food and clothing, there is often a scarcity of love. Divorce and family breakdown have become widespread, and many children grow up in broken homes. Their parents are too busy indulging in their own interests to bestow the personal attention for which the child craves. The child comes to regard his parents as hypocritical, demanding one standard from him while they practice something quite different. The protests of parents about the danger of such drugs as marijuana, LSD and amphetamines are ineffective when they themselves are dependent on alcohol and tranquilizers.

As soon as the child completes high school, he hastens to a college as far away from home as possible. He is now on his own, free to choose his own morals, and decide his own course of action. This separation is often a relief to both parents and child. The emotional umbilical cord is now severed. However, financial support continues to flow.

Many children, who have been allowed to grow up without adequate guidance and discipline, bear a deep resentment towards their parents. They are convinced that their parents did not love them sufficiently to guide them adequately. As

Carl Davidson says, "They are outraged about their parents."

*The Religious Root:* The students no longer believe in God or in the faith of their fathers. They thus lose all links with the past and the future and life is robbed of continuity and meaning. It becomes temporary, purposeless, and absurd. Each individual is isolated, cut off from outside sources of help, and left to his own devices.

This loss of meaning in life is shattering. It is described in the words of the English poet, James Thompson, in his poem "The City of Dreadful Night":

> The sense that every struggle brings defeat,
> Because fate holds no prize to drown success;
> That all the oracles are dumb or cheat,
> Because they have no secret to express;
> That none can pierce the vast dark veil uncertain,
> Because there is no light beyond the curtain;
> That all is vanity or nothingness.

This attitude is translated by the alienated as: "If you are traveling on the Titanic, you may as well go first class." There may be feasting and dancing and laughter, but ahead there lies the iceberg and the ocean grave. They rationalize that the present is all you have; therefore, claim from it every possible sensory experience. Indeed, the alienated are convinced, "Eat, drink and be merry for tomorrow we die". Life thus becomes a quest for sensation, governed by the motto, "never postpone until tomorrow what you can enjoy today."

Even here disappointment lies in store for them. They eat, and they drink, but they are not merry. The quest for pleasure is the quest for the end of the rainbow.

*The Patriotic Root:* The hearts of the alienated do not burn with pride when they think of their own native land. They are ashamed of their country and its history. They regard American history as a record of bestial cruelty stretching from the massacre of the Indians to the war in Vietnam. The tremendous contributions to human welfare such as the emphasis on the well-being and liberty of the individual, limited constitutional government, the growth and distribution of food, and defeat of disease, are overlooked.

This attitude to their homeland results in a sense of guilt and justifies to them dropping out of society and indulging in violent and destructive impulses against society.

*The Economic Root:* The desire to save enough money to marry and establish a home and family has always been a stabilizing influence on impulsive youth. They longed for the day when they could make a down payment on a car, a piece of land, or a house. Adolescent and early adult life were guided towards this objective. The desire to make money was as natural as the desire to breathe.

A remarkable change in the psychology of many students has taken place. It is revealed in the *Fortune* survey mentioned before. This survey reports that 40 per cent of students show a lack of concern about making money. This is a startling number! *Fortune* classifies them as the "forerunners" of the student population which totals 8 million.

This contemptuous attitude towards making money is not due to idealism alone. It is partly due to the affluent society. These are privileged students who have always lived in an environment where money is readily available. Thus, they tend to regard it as one of the basic comforts of life, like running water. It is not exciting. The challenge for a life purpose, they believe, must be sought elsewhere. With alienation, this attitude may turn into hostility towards a money economy. They have a vague sense that money lies at the root of most of the things that outrage their peculiar moral sense.

When the incentive derived from the desire to make money disappears, it leaves a vacuum. This vacuum may be filled by unselfish service or selfish indulgence. Unfortunately, the alienated choose the latter.

*The Intellectual Root:* One of the saddest features of the attitude of the alienated is their loss of faith in reason and intelligence. As Carl Davidson states, "They are staunchly anti-intellectual and rarely read anything unless it comes from the underground press syndicate."

This loss of faith in reason is partly due to their loss of religious faith. Life is reduced to an absurdity. It is also due in part to their revulsion from the conditions created by applied intelligence.

Most of the conditions that outrage them are the product of the human intellect. Australia's greatest medical scientist, Sir McFarlane Burnet, recently stated his view of the three greatest dangers confronting mankind. They are: 1) The hydrogen bomb, 2) The population explosion, and 3) The availability of leisure time to those morally ill-equipped to use it.

All these major problems have been created by human intelligence. Even the invention of the lifesaving drugs such as penicillin, the sulpha drugs, and the antibiotics threatens to curse mankind. They have defeated the major infectious diseases such as pneumonia, malaria, tuberculosis, and bubonic plague, but a side effect has been the population explosion which menaces civilization. The alienated, in citing problems caused by human intellect, do not look to the problems *solved* by intellect before rejecting the necessity for rational application of intelligence. In fact, they often seem oblivious to the fact that their own survival is dependent on applied reason and intellect.

Disillusionment with reason leads to the exaltation of sensuality and the quest for emotion. The new morality exalts anything that produces pleasurable feeling. This includes the taking of drugs and limitless sexual indulgence. The result is the hippie cult.

Instead of producing happiness and excitement, the hippie mode of life produces sadness and boredom. This is obvious to even the casual observer. Folksinger Joan Baez has said she has never met a happy hippie.

One block on the Sunset Strip, Los Angeles, was hippie territory in the late 1960's. Each evening the sidewalks were jammed by so-called flower people. They appeared to lack the normal energy of youth. Most gatherings of young people are characterized by noise. This was not true of the hippies. They were on display and there was very little conversation and less laughter. They seemed de-energized. Maybe they validate the Freudian teaching that, when you indulge in every carnal impulse immediately and without restraint, there is no energy left for the constructive activities of life.

As a bored, unhappy group, they crave excitement and community. Demonstrations are often exciting so they often turn out regularly for the demonstrations. They long for community, and having lost the community of home, school, church, and society, they seek it in radical groups.

Because of their hunger to find meaning in life, they tend to give

*13*

temporary allegiance to any philosophy that promises meaning. This explains their partiality to astrology, transcendental meditation, Zen Buddhism, and similar fads.

## TRIGGERING THE BOMB

Having described the structure of the bomb, the natural question is "How can the inner core of destroyers detonate it? This requires both the right conditions and organizational skill.

The members of the core, the destroyers, are well aware that for any explosion to be effective, it must involve large numbers from the body as well as those in the core. This can be brought about in two ways:

First, the radical destroyers promote a confrontation on a popular issue which escalates until it involves many people.

Second, the radicals support a conflict that has been caused by the demands of a group of partisans and try to usurp leadership, enlarge the conflict and redirect it to create maximum discord and destruction. When this is achieved, the goal originally sought by those who precipitated the dispute becomes secondary.

Examples of these two mechanisms are the strike at Harvard in 1969 and the strike at the University of California at Berkeley that same year.

The crisis at Harvard was precipitated by the action of a group of SDS militants who were a tiny minority of the institution's 15,000 students. They used the issue of opposition to militarism with the specific demand being the elimination of R.O.T.C. courses from the curriculum.

Only about 300 of Harvard's 15,000 students belonged to the SDS chapter and the "hard core" consisted of a minority of those members. Nevertheless, they were able to plan and carry out a program that led to a confrontation with the Harvard Administration and police intervention. The decision to seize a university hall was made by a few leaders without notifying the members who had previously declined to authorize an immediate invasion.

The immediate objective is to involve the police. The radicals know that the psychology of many students and professors is such that police intervention will immediately polarize both the student body and faculty and win many of the hesitant and indifferent to active participation.

The authorities are confronted with a dilemma. If they do not call the police, they may deny the rights of other students and cooperate in the destruction of property. There is the possibility that the conflict will enlarge as other groups are drawn into the battle and that police force will ultimately be required on a much larger scale than would have been the case if early action had been taken.

This lesson was learned by the President of Harvard University. When the students there illegally occupied buildings and denied other students their rights, he immediately called the police who removed the trespassing students. He was appalled at the consequences. A large number of both faculty and students immediately sided with the disrupters in protest of his action.

Whether the police are called early or late, their involvement constitutes a victory for the disrupters. Their objective of producing a confrontation and thereby rallying many more to their cause has been achieved. The dilemma confronting the university authorities is difficult to resolve.

The second method of triggering the bomb is illustrated by the strike at the University of California at Berkeley in March, 1969. In this case the conflict originated in the body of the bomb, and the destroyers from the core attempted to usurp leadership.

The strike at Berkeley was promoted by a group calling itself the Third World Liberation Front (TWLF), and the principal demand was for a college of "Third World Studies."

The "Third World" refers to the noncommunist countries of Asia, Africa, and Latin America. Those who use this terminology divide the world into camps: 1. "The Imperialist Camp," or the Free World led by the United States. 2. "The Socialist Camp" led by the Soviet Union and Communist China. 3. "The Third World" which the other camps seek to influence and recruit.

(In the U.S., the "citizens" of the Third World are mostly Mexican-Americans, Puerto Ricans, and blacks—though there are a few Filipinos, Koreans, and members of other Asian nationalities.)

The white radicals supported the strike and tried to shift the emphasis to a confrontation with the police. The issues of leadership and tactics were never completely resolved and the strike finally collapsed, leaving the leadership of the Third World Liberation Front with considerable bitterness towards the white radicals. The *Guardian* newspaper of March 29, 1969 reported:

> "A majority of TWLF leadership puts the main blame on white students in general for not rallying in large numbers to the cause. They have several criticisms of the support they did get from white students. They say the white strikers constantly refused to follow the TWLF's tactical leadership, often continued demonstrations after the TWLF had ordered them ended and carried demonstrations to a level of militancy that third-world leaders felt was inappropriate. . - .
> 
> *"In addition the TWLF feels the white leadership failed to keep the focus clearly on the demand for a third-world college rather than on resisting police occupation of the campus.* Finally, third-world leaders have expressed disappointment at the white leadership's inability to mobilize strike supporters, refusing to accept their argument that the TWLF's toning-down of the strike had turned off many white militants."

## THE OBJECTIVES OF THE RADICAL DESTROYERS

The objectives may be listed in order of escalation: 1. Confrontation with the police. 2. Radicalization of the participants. 3. Destruction of the Institution. 4. Destruction of the state.

1. *Confrontation with the police:* We have already discussed the fact that the immediate objective of the destroyers is to provoke a confrontation with the police. Whatever the outcome of the confrontation may appear to be, they regard the fact of the confrontation as a victory in itself. This confrontation will compel the police to use force. Even if this force is the absolute minimum demanded by the situation, it will be deeply resented by those against whom it is directed. This resentment will result in a psychological transformation and may lead to the attainment of the second objective, the radicalization of those against whom the force is used.

2. *Radicalization of the participants:* This is the term used for

*16*

the conversion of one of the Partisans, Reformers, or Alienated into a Destroyer. The best instrument of conversion is a policeman's nightstick. The individual who has felt the force of this instrument on his own body is likely to develop an enduring hatred for the police. This hatred may be transferred with relative ease to the society which the policeman is protecting. He is easily convinced that this society is vicious and evil and must be detroyed. His emotional state leads to a ready acceptance of this central doctrine of the Destroyers. From a mere participant in an action designed to attain a specific objective, he is transformed into a radical with the objective of the destruction of society.

Thus, every confrontation results in an increase in the number of radicals or an enlargement of the core. This constitutes a victory.

Human nature being what it is, individuals tend to grow weary in the battle and give up the struggle. There is constant defection and, if the ranks of the radicals are to grow, there must be constant confrontations so that recruits may outnumber defectors. This is the key to the strategy of confrontation.

3. *Destruction of the Institution:* The object of most recent attacks has been the University. The cry, "Shut it down," rings out from the radical camp. Society must be attacked at its weakest point, and the radicals believe the universities constitute this point of weakness. Resolute action by the authorities is difficult because of legal restraints against the dismissal of radical faculty members and the expulsion of radical students. This is compounded by the fact that while the majority of students and faculty may oppose the actions of the radicals, they may also oppose strong measures being taken against them. If they take strong action, the administrators fear the unpleasant possibility of a faculty and student strike and the necessity to close the institution.

If the institution is closed, an angry and idle student body will be cast into the community along with a frightened and frustrated faculty. Again the ranks of the radicals are likely to increase. Fortunately the campus scene has been much more peaceful in recent days.

4. *Destruction of the State:* This is the ultimate goal. The radicals believe that the universities are essential to the functioning of the State. They believe that universities are necessary to provide

17

the trained and skilled recruits for industry and the military. The radical theorizes that if the source of skilled managerial and professional help is dried up, the consequences will soon be apparent in the community at large. Economic and moral disintegration will prevail in all areas. Torn by internal strife and lacking a united will, the State will be paralyzed and impotent against both external and internal subversive forces. The radical objective will have been reached.

As I hope this introduction has made clear, the ingredients of revolution are many and their relationships with each other rather complex.

The body of the revolutionary bomb contains so many diverse elements—the Partisans, the Reformers, the Alienated—that it is certainly not an easy proposition to keep tabs on them all. In any case, there are more vital considerations. For the "body" of the bomb is only the fuel of revolution; these elements would pose no serious long term threat to society if it were not for the hard-core radicals—the Destroyers.

And so it is to the core of the revolutionary bomb—the spark which directly results in the explosion—that this book will be devoted.

Accordingly, let us now turn our attention to what is undoubtedly the dominent force in the revolutionary bomb of the 1970's —Communism.

# PART I:
# COMMUNISM

# ESSENTIALS OF COMMUNISM      1

**W**hat essential qualities must an organization possess before it can be classified as communist? To answer this we must consider the nature of communism and look beyond the dictionary meaning of the name. In this imperfect world, complex organizations select words to serve as labels, and "communism" is simply a label. In fact, the original meaning of the word has very little to do with the content of communism. For instance, there is a radical political party in California known as the "Peace and Freedom Party," yet, of course, not everyone who desires peace and freedom supports that party. Plainly, a name is a label and the contents are not always revealed by labels.

There is a world communist movement. It is represented by the communist parties of the world. These are not figments of the imagination. There are fifty million people in the world who claim to be communists and they govern more than one billion people. These communists cite Karl Marx and Lenin as their mentors and call themselves Marxist-Leninists. Thus, a better name for communism is Marxism-Leninism. In this book then, communism and Marxism-Leninism are synonymous.

There are six essential elements of communism. If an individual or a party is communist, it will meet these six qualifications. Communism has 1) a diagnosis; 2) a philosophy; 3) a party; 4) a program; 5) a promise and 6) a prognosis.

## DIAGNOSIS

The communist diagnosis of capitalist society was originally made by Karl Marx. Marx claimed that he had discovered the forces which generated the characteristics of a society and which created the mind and personality of the people who lived within that society. This discovery was that the mode of production created the institutions of a society and the emotional and mental qualities of the citizens. "Human nature", Marx claimed, was merely a product of those environmental forces. Frederick Engels, lifelong collaborator and interpreter of Marx, and co-author of the Communist Manifesto, gives credit to Marx for this discovery.

"The Manifesto being our joint production, I consider myself bound to state that the fundamental proposition, which forms its nucleus, belongs to Marx. That proposition is: that in every historical epoch, the prevailing mode of economic production and exchange, and the social organization necessarily following from it, form the basis upon which is built up, and from which alone can be explained, the political and intellectual history of that epoch; that consequently the whole history of mankind has been a history of class struggles."*

The basic doctrine of Marx, according to Frederick Engels, was the creative power of the mode of production.

Life exists in a struggle to obtain food, clothing, shelter, and transportation. Marx teaches it is the developments of this struggle which determine the changing institutions of society and the changing morals, ideas, and being of man.

Stalin expresses this teaching of Marx in these words:

*Karl Marx, and Frederick Engels, Manifesto of the Communist Party (Moscow, Progress Publishers, 1969) p. 63.

"Whatever is the mode of production of a society, such in the main is the society itself, its ideas and theories, its political views and institutions.

"Or, to put it more crudely, whatever is man's manner of life, such is his manner of thought."*

Marx and Engles stated that the family was created by the capitalist mode of production.

"On what foundation is the present family, the bourgeois family, based? On capital, on private gain. In its completely developed form this family exists only among the bourgeoisie. But this state of things finds its complement in the practical absence of the family among the proletarians, and in public prostitution.

"The bourgeois family will vanish as a matter of course when its complement vanishes, and both will vanish with the vanishing of capital.

"The bourgeois clap-trap about the family and education, about the hallowed co-relation of parent and child, becomes all the more disgusting, the more, by the action of Modern Industry, all family ties among the proletarians are torn asunder, and their children transformed into simple articles of commerce and instruments of labor."†

Marx taught all men are economically created, or economically generated, beings. This concept enabled him to interpret all past societies in terms of the mode of production and to diagnose the ills of the capitalist system. Examining the capitalist system, Marx discovered what he considered a basic flaw within it. This flaw was a conflict between the mode of production and the relations of production.

What is meant by relations of production? A clear exposition is given by Stalin:

> But the productive forces are only one aspect of production, only one aspect of the mode of production, an aspect that expresses the relation of men to the objects and forces of nature which they make use of for the production of material values. Another aspect of production, another aspect of the mode of production, is the rela-

*J. Stalin, Problems of Leninism (Moscow, Foreign Languages Publishing House, 1968) p. 732.
†Marx, op. cit., p. 69.

tion of men to each other in the process of production, men's relations of production. Men carry on a struggle against nature and utilize nature for the production of material values not in isolation from each other, not as separate individuals, but in common, in groups, in societies. Production, therefore, is at all times and under all conditions social production. In the production of material values men enter into mutual relations of one kind or another within production, into relations of production of one kind or another. These may be relations of cooperation and mutual help between people who are free from exploitation; they may be relations of domination and subordination.*

He predicted that because of this flaw, the development of capitalism would inevitably lead to the destruction of the capitalist system; that the capitalist system would create its own gravediggers, as stated in the "Communist Manifesto."

Who will be the gravediggers of capitalism? In Marxist theory, capitalist society exists where there are a few who own the means of production while the majority sell their labor for wages. Those who own the means of production Marx called bourgeoisie and those who sell their labor for wages, the proletariat. He discovered conflict of interest between these two groups. The owners of the means of production are motivated by the desire for profit but those who sell their labor for wages are motivated by the desire for higher wages. If wages go up, profits come down. This creates irresolvable conflict which Marx called the class war. This class war is the dynamic of capitalist society.

Marx claimed to discover certain laws which operated within capitalism. One was that because of competition within the capitalist system, monopoly would inevitably develop, and the bourgeoisie would become a progressively smaller class. When two factories compete, the one that could extort the most profit from its workers, by paying them lower wages and working them longer hours, would put the other one out of business. The bankrupt ex-owners would be forced down into the proletariat. Thus, the proletariat would become larger and larger, while the bourgeoisie would become smaller and smaller, and the conflict between them would become more acute. Marx called this unavoidable develop-

*Stalin, op. cit., p. 731.

ment the law of increasing misery. This increasing proletarian misery would generate a revolutionary consciousness. When proletarianization developed sufficiently, revolution would break out just as when the temperature of water reaches a certain point, it begins to boil. This revolution would destroy capitalism.

From this it appears that capitalism is incurably diseased and is doomed. It is creating its own gravediggers—the workers; the proletariat. The dilemma of capitalism is: to operate it must create a proletariat, yet the proletariat must destroy capitalism.

In modern jargon, the experiences of workers in industry should program them to be revolutionaries. But while there are convincing elements in this theory, it obviously does not match with known facts. Let me elaborate.

Karl Marx taught that experiences as a worker in a mine or a factory program an individual to be a revolutionary. But this basic doctrine of Marx is wrong, for history has proven it false. The workers are not and never have been revolutionary. They will fight for higher wages, shorter hours, and fringe benefits but they do not want to overthrow capitalism. Clearly the doctrine that their experiences as workers automatically generates a revolutionary consciousness is untrue.

There are some who accept the fact that the working class today is not revolutionary. The truth is, it never was revolutionary. Some may ask "What about the workers in Russia? Didn't they revolt against capitalism?" No, they revolted for capitalism. The slogan of the Bolshevik Revolution, the slogan that Lenin presented to the Russian workers to induce them to support the Bolsheviks was, "Bread, Peace, and Land." Lenin won their support by offering them land ownership, which is the core of capitalism.

In the "Communist Manifesto", however, Karl Marx and Frederick Engels say, "The theory of the communists may be summed up in the single sentence: Abolition of private property."

In one of history's great frauds, the followers of Marx and Lenin came to power in Russia by the creation of private property. They bribed the workers to support them temporarily by granting them their capitalistic desire, ownership of their own land. The same thing happened in China. This confused many alleged experts who observed the actions of the Chinese Communists and said they could not be communists because while communism teaches the abolition of private property, the Chinese Communists were creating private property in land. Consequently, they were not communists; they were agrarian reformers.

Obviously, these observers did not understand that the communists see no inconsistency in approaching their goal by steps, and no inconsistency in approaching their goal by going away from it. Often, descent into a valley is necessary to climb a mountain. Marxism is definite capitalism is doomed. The workers, the communists say, are the revolutionaries who will destroy it.

## THE PHILOSOPHY

The philosophy of communism is called "Dialectical Materialism" and all communists accept it though few may understand it. Consideration of the doctrines and applications of this philosophy will be undertaken when the teachings of Mao Tse-tung are discussed.

## THE PARTY

Communism always operates through a party. The concept of the party is one of the contributions of Lenin to communism. He wrote the book "What is to be Done" in which he proposed that an elite should be organized into a unified party. This party, Lenin said, would become the instrument to create and conduct the revolution, and to impose and operate the dictatorship of the proletariat after the revolution.

Following Lenin's lead, every communist operates, not as an individual, but as a member of a party. A communist who does not belong to a party is a contradiction in terms. As a matter of fact some of the radicals who have denounced Leninism in recent years do so because it demands the creation of an elite party. Above all else, it is the role of the party which differentiates communism from other revolutionary and radical forces.

The party is organized in accordance with a principle of "Democratic Centralism". This means that the party must be disciplined and united so that it has a single mind, a single will, and a single program. Democratic Centralism is so important to the communists that one of the reasons given by the Russian Communist Party, for instance, to justify the invasion of Czechoslovakia in 1968 was the claim that the Czechoslovak Communist Party was about to depart from Democratic Centralism. A letter was sent to the Central Committee of the Communist Party of Czechoslovakia on July 18, 1968, from the parties of the Soviet Union, Bulgaria, Hungary, Poland, and East Germany in Warsaw which stated:

"You are aware of the understanding with which the fraternal parties treated the decisions of the January plenary meeting of the central committee of the Communist Party of Czechoslovakia, as they believed that your party, firmly controlling the levers of power, would direct the entire process in the interests of socialism and not let anti-communist reaction exploit it to grind its own axe. We shared the conviction that you would protect the Leninist principle of democratic centralism as the apple of your eye."*

Democratic Centralism demands that a loyal party member must identify himself intellectually and emotionally with any decision of the Party which comes from a higher Party organ. The Party is accordingly built like a pyramid. At the bottom of the pyramid are the party members organized in local groups who elect their representative to the district committee. But the representative is not instructed by his local group. At the district committee, they debate a given issue. Once the vote is taken, it is unanimously binding on every member of the committee and binding on everyone below it. This principle applies to the entire pyramid of party power. Towards the top of the pyramid, there are the state committees and finally the central committee which is theoretically the highest authority. Absolute truth emerges from the verdict of the central committee. Thus everyone in the Party is completely bound by whatever the central committee decides.

In practice, the central committee is a large body which does not meet very often so an executive of the central committee which can handle day to day affairs is needed. This executive is usually called the Politbureau and it is, "de facto", the highest authority.

The Politbureau decisions are submitted to the central committee whose members then pass them unanimously. From the cen-

*Daily World (July 19, 1968), pp. 1, 2.

tral committee, directives go down to the next level where instructions and ideas which come down from above must be accepted completely. This means acceptance in thought and emotion as well as in execution. A very instructive statement on Democratic Centralism was made by Henry Winston, Chairman of the Communist Party, USA at that party's 1969 national convention:

> "Democratic Centralism is indivisible. It must apply to all policies, all decisions without exception. Some comrades who disagree with the Party's position on the events in Czechoslovakia have asked why we cannot demand unity on domestic questions but allow disagreement on international questions. These comrades fail to see the oneness of Party policy. They fail to see that it stems from one body of theory, one set of principles. Differences on international questions are therefore quickly reflected in differences on domestic questions . . . Democratic Centralism, if it is to be effective, is also inseparable from the constant practice of criticism and self-criticism . . . Comrades, factionalism is a most destructive force. It is incompatible with membership in our Party. It must be rooted out of our ranks, firmly and without hesitation."*

Can a communist exercise academic freedom? Since they are bound by Democratic Centralism, this is impossible. The Academic Senate of the University of California recognized this when it stated in 1950: "No person whose commitments or obligations to any organization, communist or other, prejudice impartial scholarship and free pursuit of truth will be employed by the University. Proven members of the Communist Party, by reason of such commitments to that Party, are not acceptable as members of the faculty."

Since a communist is bound by party discipline, he is not free to follow the truth wherever it leads. Why not? Because it is conceivable that an honest search for truth might lead to the following conclusions:

1. The retention of private property is in the interests of mankind.
2. The investment of American capital in underdeveloped countries is in the interest of the people of those countries.

*World Marxist Review, September, 1969, pp. 61–62

3. Classes are being abolished in America.
4. Class cooperation is preferable to class conflict.
5. Intellectual freedom should be granted to the university professors in communist countries.
6. Full political and intellectual freedom should be granted to the people of Czechoslovakia.
7. A personal God exists and is the Creator of mankind and moral law.
8. The Dictatorship of the Proletariat is tyranny.

Every communist must reject these statements. For the Party has spoken and members must believe and obey.

Liu Shao-chi was once President of Communist China and Secretary of the Communist Party of China, but he was dethroned during the "Great Cultural Revolution." However, a generation of Chinese Communists was reared on his book, 'How to be a Good Communist.' Discussing the subjection of the individual to the Party, he wrote:

"In accordance with this principle, every Party member must completely identify his personal interests with those of the Party both in his thinking and in his actions. He must be able to yield to the interests of the Party without any hesitation or reluctance and sacrifice personal interests, end even one's life, for the Party and the proletariat and for the emancipation of the nation and of all mankind—this is one expression of what we usually describe as 'Party spirit', 'Party sense' or 'sense of organization'. It is the highest expression of communist morality, of the principled nature of the party of the proletariat, and of the purest proletarian class consciousness."*

Mao Tse-tung repeatedly stresses the subordination of the individual communist to the collective will:

A communist should have largeness of mind and he should be staunch and active, looking upon the interests of the revolution as his very life and subordinating his personal interests to those of the revolution, always and everywhere he should adhere to principle and wage a tireless struggle against all incorrect ideas and actions

*Liu Shao-chi, How to be a Good Communist (Peking, Foreign Language Press, 1951) p. 47.

so as to consolidate the collective life of the Party and the masses; he should be more concerned about the Party and the masses than about any individual and more concerned about others than about himself.*

Do all communists measure up to these standards? Of course they don't. No machine works perfectly. Communists are people with human weaknesses. Some lives approach the ideal. Those that fail are frequently expelled from the party. The communists expect this. Lenin operated in accordance with the slogan "fewer, but better".

## UNITY AND DIVERSITY

As I have indicated, the Communist movement in the United States has become fragmented since the relatively unified days of the 1950's. There are now at least four communist parties and a considerable number of minor sects, all claiming to be the genuine article.

The Communist Party—USA is the largest with a membership of about 15,000. It acknowledges allegiance to the Communist Party of the Soviet Union. The Party's General Secretary is Gus Hall, and its youth group is called the Young Workers Liberation League. It publishes the DAILY WORLD, a daily newspaper on the East Coast; and the PEOPLES WORLD, a weekly on the West Coast. It also publishes a theoretical journal, POLITICAL AFFAIRS, each month.

Although the American Communist Party is the strongest of the communist parties numerically, it is also probably the weakest of the communist groups on the college campus.

The second Communist Party is the Socialist Workers Party. Its members follow the communist line of Leon Trotsky; the youth group is the Young Socialist Alliance. While the numerical strength of the Socialist Workers Party is considerably lower than that of the American Communist Party, they are much more effective on the university campus. They have shown remarkable

*Mao Tse-tung, Combat Liberalism, Selected Works Vol. II (San Francisco, China Bks, 1965) p. 33.

skill in exploiting the peace issue and control the Student Mobilization Committee and the National Peace Action Committee. They also have organized sedition in the army most effectively.

The third communist party is the Progressive Labor Party. It was formed by two communists who were expelled from the American Communist Party for taking the side of the Chinese Communists in the Sino-Soviet dispute. Until 1970, the Progressive Labor Party was generally referred to as the communist party affiliated with the Chinese Communists. But changes in the policies of communist parties are often dramatic. The Progressive Labor Party changed its allegiance when leaders repudiated the Chinese Communist Party and accused it of joining the ranks of the Social Imperialists and the Revisionists. In their judgement, Mao Tse-tung has betrayed the revolution. The reason? Progressive Labor dogma now alleges that China practices "Great Nation Chauvinism," which means placing the interests of the nation-state ahead of the interests of the international proletariat. The visit of President Richard Nixon to Communist China has confirmed them in this conviction.

Progressive Labor, like the Socialist Workers Party, has also been very effective on the college campus, and in 1969 the group captured the once-powerful Students for a Democratic Society (SDS), although, as we shall soon see, this victory was something of a hollow triumph. Progressive Labor's youth organization is called the Student Worker Alliance (SWA).

There is a fourth Communist Party, the Black Panther Party. I classify it as communist with some hesitation because it meets all the criteria of a communist party except one. It claims to be a communist party and its organization is Marxist-Leninist. There is however, one basic Marxist doctrine which is accepted by all other communists which the Panthers reject. They do not regard the working class as the present instrument of revolution. They believe it has been displaced by the "lumpen proletariat," i.e., the chronically unemployed, unemployables, criminals, etc. They claim this is not a repudiation of Marxism but the application of Marxism to modern society. This deviation will be discussed in some detail later.

The complexity of the present communist situation is illustrated by Students for a Democratic Society in its death agony. SDS flourished for a short season last decade before internal dissension caused it to break up into three warring factions. The three groups into which it divided were called: 1) "The Weatherman" or Revolutionary Youth Movement I (RYM I); 2) Revolutionary Youth Movement II (RYM II); and 3) The Progressive Labor-Student Worker Alliance (PL-WSA) faction. The formal break-up occurred at the SDS national conference in Chicago in 1969, where Progressive Labor, by superior organization, had a majority of the delegates present. By the process of democratic vote, Progressive Labor could have taken over the entire organization. When the officers of SDS realized this, they performed a remarkable "democratic" operation. The office-holders, led by secretaries Bernadine Dohrn and Mike Klonsky, walked out of the meeting hall and reconvened the SDS convention in another building. This new convention then passed a motion expelling PL-SWA from SDS. Incredibly, the minority had democratically expelled the majority. It was a strange democratic procedure, but in this case, it was effective because the minority possessed the keys to the office and the safe. Thus the minority had control of the SDS treasury and membership lists. Democratic power, for radicals, apparently can consist of having merely the keys to the appropriate doors. The original SDS convention, of course, continued under Progressive Labor control. The group that had walked out then split into two, the Weatherman and RYM II. These three groups each went their own way attacking each other viciously, with the Weatherman members soon becoming notorious for their terrorist activities.

What is the difference between these groups? Let's ask a spokesman for each group, "What do you believe and propose?"

At the time of the split, the Progressive Labor spokesman would have replied: "Our position is perfectly clear. We're communists, we're Marxist-Leninists, we're followers of Mao Tse-tung. We are the only genuine communists. All others are imposters."

To the same question, Mike Klonsky, leader of RYM II, would have replied in much the same way: "It's perfectly clear; we are Marxist-Leninists, we are followers of Mao Tse-tung. We are the only genuine communists; all others are imposters."

And the spokesman for the Weatherman would have replied with perhaps more violent rhetoric but the same content.

We have, thus, three groups, all claiming the identical ideology yet fighting each other to the point of mutual extermination.

Shortly after this convention, the Black Panthers organized a "Conference for a United Front Against Fascism" in the Civic Auditorium of Oakland, California. They stated that everybody was welcome except the anti-communists and Progressive Labor. Progressive Labor didn't take their exclusion gracefully, and representatives went to one of the park meetings and tried to distribute literature. The Weathermen attacked them and reported exultantly in the official publication of SDS, NEW LEFT NOTES, "We sent ten of them to the hospital."

This illustrates how they feel toward each other and yet they all claim to be communists!

# THE COMMUNIST PROGRAM    2

Communist programs are designed to fit existing social and economic conditions. In general, they can be divided into three categories: 1) Pre-revolutionary, 2) Revolutionary, and 3) Post-revolutionary. The programs are numerous and diverse, but the aim is that they should all minister to the goal of seizure and retention of power by the communists.

If we accept the words of the Communist Manifesto, the program of communism is the abolition of private property. However, most programs advocated by communists seem to deviate a long way from this objective since they appear to be highly pragmatic. Programs advocated with equal zeal may be mutually contradictory. This has led many to accuse modern communists of forsaking Marx. However, this accusation is based on failure to recognize that the philosophy of Marx teaches retreat as well as advance en route to the communist objective.

A survey of communist history is illuminating. In 1921, many

Kremlinologists informed the world that communism had died, as Lenin had supposedly discovered that communist economics would not work and so he had returned to capitalism. What had happened? In 1921, Lenin initiated the New Economic Policy (NEP) which fostered capitalist enterprise. It restored private trading in grain and permitted small business enterprises. Feeling betrayed, some of his fanatical followers found these changes very hard to accept and committed suicide in protest. Of course, the NEP was only a temporary tactical maneuver, though many alleged experts failed to realize this at the time. The NEP period ended in 1928 when forced collectivization took its place.

As another example, in 1931 Joseph Stalin delivered a speech on wages. To many, it contradicted the wage equalitarianism supposedly inherent in Marxism.

What is the cause of the heavy turnover of labor power?

The cause is the wrong structure of wages, the wrong wage scales, the 'Leftist' practice of wage equalization. In a number of our factories wage scales are drawn up in such a way as to practically wipe out the difference between skilled and unskilled labour, between heavy and light work. The consequence of wage equalization is that the unskilled worker lacks the incentive to become a skilled worker and is thus deprived of the prospect of advancement; as a result he feels himself a 'visitor' in the factory, working only temporarily so as to 'earn a little' and then go off to 'seek his fortune' elsewhere. The consequence of wage equalization is that the skilled worker is obliged to wander from factory to factory until he finds one where his skill is properly appreciated.

In order to put an end to this evil we must abolish wage equalization and discard the old wage scales. In order to put an end to this evil we must draw up wage scales that will take into account the difference between skilled and unskilled labor, between heavy and light work. We cannot tolerate a situation where a rolling-mill hand in a steel mill earns no more than a sweeper. We cannot tolerate a situation where a locomotive driver earns only as much as a copying clerk. Marx and Lenin said that the difference between skilled and unskilled labor would exist even under socialism, even after classes had been abolished; that only under communism would this difference disappear and that, consequently, even under socialism 'wages' must be paid according to work performed and not according to needs. But the equalitarians among our business executives and trade union officials do not agree with this and believe that under our Soviet system this difference has already disappeared. Who is right, Marx and Lenin, or the equalitarians? We must take it that it is Marx and Lenin who are right. But if that is so, it follows that whoever draws up wage scales on the 'principle' of wage equalization, without taking into account the difference between skilled and unskilled labor, breaks with Marxism, breaks with Leninism.

In every branch of industry, in every factory, in every shop, there is a leading group of more or less skilled workers whom it is our immediate and urgent duty to retain in industry if we really want to secure for the factories a permanent labor force . . . But how can we retain them in the factories? We can retain them only by promoting them to higher positions, by raising the level of their wages, by introducing a system of wages that will give the worker his due according to qualification.

And what does promoting them to higher positions and raising their wage level imply as far as unskilled workers are concerned? It implies, apart from everything else, opening up prospects for the unskilled worker and giving him an incentive to rise higher, to rise to the category of a skilled worker . . . In order to build up cadres of skilled workers, we must provide an incentive for the unskilled workers, provide for them a prospect of advancement, of rising to a higher position. And the more boldly we do this the better; . . . To economize in this matter would be criminal, it would be going against the interests of our socialist industry.*

In this speech, Stalin certainly sounds like a capitalist. How can he be a consistent communist with such a program? This illustrates the great flexibility of the communists. The rule is, "Use whatever works."

The program of communism can be summed up very simply as "attain and retain power." To attain power, the support of many people is needed. To gain their support, a program to fulfill their immediate needs is necessary. Thus, the program of communism in any pre-revolutionary situation can be expressed by the formula, "find out what people want, promise it to them, and go to work to get it for them so that you can come to power over them."

To the communists, this is being scientific. They claim they are

*Stalin, op. cit., pp. 463–465.

practitioners of the science of Marxism-Leninism. A scientist is one who multiplies his individual power by harnessing and using existing natural forces. The sailor harnesses and uses the wind; the aeronautical scientists harness and use the weight of the atmosphere. Archimedes, the ancient Greek scientist, said, "give me a lever long enough and somewhere to stand, and I'll move the earth."

The communists see themselves as scientists harnessing and using social forces. They don't create these social forces, they harness and utilize them. A social force is something that will motivate masses of people. It may be a desire, an emotion, or a grievance shared by a group of people. The working people want higher wages, so the communists become great advocates of higher wages. National minorities want national liberation, so communists are advocates of national liberation. If certain religious groups want religious freedom, the communists become advocates of religious freedom for these groups. Capitalists want higher profits, so the communists become advocates of trade to increase profits. They become all things to all men so that they can harness them for revolutionary purposes.

The fact that the program that they are advocating in one place contradicts the program that they are advocating elsewhere is to them an indication of scientific efficiency not hypocrisy. They do whatever will help them attain and retain power.

The force the communists have used most effectively to attain power is love of private property. The desire to own land is almost universal and this is the desire which they have used with great effectiveness. For instance, by creating little capitalists, the communists attained power in both Russia and China. In Russia the slogan was, BREAD, PEACE, AND LAND; in China they were Agrarian Reformers.

The pre-revolutionary program is designed to prepare for the revolution. Before a revolution can take place, a revolutionary situation must develop or be created. Such a revolutionary situation is characterized by: 1) Massive public discontent, 2) The existence of a functioning communist party to plan or coordinate mass actions growing out of this discontent, and 3) A crisis of will in the existing authority.

During the preparatory phase, the communist program is:

1. Strengthen and develop the communist party.
2. Gain the support of the masses by working actively to secure for them those things they desire.
3. Undermine existing authority.

During this pre-revolutionary stage, the general directive to communists is: "Find out what people want; promise it to them; work hard to get it for them so that you can lead them to revolution."

## THE REVOLUTION

Communists propose a revolution to seize power.

They believe this revolution will need to be violent in most cases and that it must be actively supported by masses of people. However, the communists are flexible and believe the possibility of a peaceful transition to socialism via the ballot box is still an option is some countries. They do not strictly follow the teachings of Lenin on this point since he stated categorically that "the suppression of the bourgeois state by the proletarian state is impossible without a violent revolution."*

Marx had maintained that there was a possibility that power could be seized in England and America without violence. Lenin claimed that the conditions which had led Marx to this conclusion no longer existed, so there was no longer any alternative to violent revolution in England and America.

Lenin's argument is:

> Marx excluded England, where a revolution, even a people's revolution, then seemed possible, and indeed was possible, without the preliminary condition of destroying the 'ready-made state machinery'.
>
> Today, in 1917, in the epoch of the first great imperialist war, this qualification made by Marx is no longer valid. Both England and America, the biggest and the last representatives—in the whole world—of Anglo-Saxon 'liberty', in the sense that they had no militarist cliques and bureaucracy, have today completely sunk into the all-European filthy, bloody morass of bureaucratic-mili-

*V.I. Lenin, The State and Revolution (Moscow, Foreign Languages Publishing House, 1951) p. 37.

tary institutions which subordinate everything to themselves and trample everything underfoot. Today, in England and in America, too, 'the preliminary condition for every real people's revolution' is the smashing, the destruction of ready-made state machinery.*

Lenin developed a theory of revolution and applied it successfully in practice. He claimed three objective factors were necessary before a revolution could be successful. These factors are:

1) A revolutionary mood caused by a grievance felt by a large percentage, if not the actual majority of the people.
2) A disciplined party to organize and lead the revolutionary masses and
3) A crisis of will in the existing authority.

If a widely felt grievance was adequate to create a revolution, most countries would be in a constant revolutionary state. Grievances are common if not universal. Poverty has been the fate of the majority of mankind since the dawn of history. Oppression has likewise been a common human condition. However, intolerable conditions of life do not, of themselves, generate a revolution. Mass starvation may actually impede a revolution. There is obviously much truth in the Leninist analysis of revolutionary potential.

The revolutionary forces need leadership. To the communists this is the specific role of their party. Mao Tse-tung expresses it thus:

> If there is to be a revolution there must be a revolutionary party. Without a revolutionary party, without a party built on the Marxist-Leninist revolutionary theory and in the Marxist-Leninist revolutionary style, it is impossible to lead the working class, the broad masses of the people, in defeating imperialism and its running dogs.†

The third condition, a crisis of will in the existing authority, is also essential before a successful revolution can be carried out. This is becoming increasingly true with the increasing power of modern weapons. No unarmed mass can survive against a machine-gunning plane. Where there is hesitation in the leadership,

* *Ibid.*, p. 63.
†Mao Tse-tung, op. cit., Vol IV, p. 284.

mass revolution becomes possible. It is one of the tasks of the communists to cause such hesitation.

These conditions also apply to revolution by the people against a communist government. The question is frequently asked "Why don't the people revolt against the communists if conditions are unbearable."

The communists try to prevent the creation of any organization to lead the revolution and any indecision in their own ranks. They employ a large internal espionage network so that they can detect any potential opposition leadership in its embryonic phase and destroy it. They strive to prevent any internal crisis of will by the strict appliance of Democratic Centralism.

Despite all such precautions sometimes an internal crisis in the Communist Party has resulted in the development of a revolutionary situation. Such was the case in Hungary in 1956 and Czechoslovakia in 1968. In these circumstances the Soviet Army stepped in.

In review, then, the communist program during the revolution is 1) stimulate and lead the masses, 2) maintain the internal discipline, authority and clear vision of the Communist Party, and 3) direct military and paramilitary activity.

## THE POST-REVOLUTIONARY PROGRAM

Following a successful revolution, the communists do not immediately create a society of communism. They consider it necessary to pass through an intermediate, or "First Phase," which they call "Socialism." For instance, the initials, U.S.S.R., stand for the Union of Soviet Socialist Republics.

The slogan of Socialism is "from each according to his ability, to each according to his work."

The government during Socialism is called "The Dictatorship of the Proletariat." Its first task is to smash all vestiges of the residual bourgeois state. Lenin writes, "Briefly: the dictatorship of the proletariat is the rule—unrestricted by law and based on force —of the proletariat over the bourgeoisie, a rule enjoying the sympathy and support of the labouring and exploited masses."*

*Joseph Stalin, Foundations of Leninism (New York, International Publishers, 1070) p. 53.

Lenin realized that because of its size, the proletariat could not rule directly. However, this presented no problem for him. Fortunately, history had selected and created a brain for the proletariat. The brain of the proletariat was the Communist Party. The proletariat was the body, and this brain made the decisions for the body. Therefore, the Communist Party should rule over the proletariat and all other inhabitants of the communist empire.

The dictatorship of the proletariat must complete the smashing of the bourgeois state. Fidel Castro, communist conqueror and dictator of Cuba, understood this well. He studied "The State and Revolution" thoroughly. When he seized power in Cuba, he abolished the army and created the People's Militia. He abolished the judicial system and every justice of the Supreme Court became a refugee. Furthermore, he dismissed the teachers and trade union officials and created new educational and labor institutions. He smashed the apparatus of the bourgeois state thoroughly.

The communists in the U.S.A. do not plan to elect the President, to win a majority in Congress or to appoint the Justices of the Supreme Court. Instead, they plan to abolish the presidency, Congress and the Supreme Court. The communists will create whatever institutions are needed to carry out the dictatorship of the proletariat. Finally, they do not desire to appoint the defense chiefs; they wish to abolish the U.S. Army and create their own Red Army.

How does the dictatorship of the proletariat operate? It operates through the power of monopoly. It establishes the most total monopoly conceived by the human mind. The Communist Party monopolizes the executive, legislative, and judicial power; it monopolizes the economy and becomes the sole employer; it monopolizes the education system; it has monopoly power over the cultural system, the police force, and the army; it governs all communications.

In the light of this, it is strange that the communists appear so outraged by the alleged monopolies that operate in the U.S.A. Some years ago I was in a television studio in Los Angeles to debate Ben Dobbs, the Executive Director of the Communist Party of Southern California. Present in the studio was Dorothy Healy, at that time Chairman of the Communist Party of Southern

California. Dorothy Healy said to me, "But Dr. Schwarz! What about the dreadful monopolies in America?"

I looked at her and said, "Did I hear you correctly? Did you say monopoly? A communist talking against monopoly! It's a wonder the word doesn't shrivel in your throat. That's like Al Capone talking against crime. That's like Hitler talking against bigotry."

The Communist Party imposes a monopoly beyond anything conceivable in the capitalist system.

This monopoly gives them awesome power. They can starve any individual of whom they disapprove.

During the debate, Ben Dobbs said to me: "What's wrong with communism? We communists believe in full employment, what's wrong with that? We communists believe in medical care for the sick and the elderly, what's wrong with that? We communists believe in the end of war for all time, what's wrong with that? We communists believe in universal peace and human brotherhood, what's wrong with that?" He turned and he said to me, "Don't you believe in these things, Dr. Schwarz?"

I thought for a moment and I said, "That reminds me of the mackerel swimming by off the coast as it sees a succulent piece of fish floating towards it. It says to itself, 'High protein content! What's wrong with that? Delicious aroma, what's wrong with that? Just the right size, I can take it in one mouthful, what's wrong with that?' " I replied, "What's wrong with it is that there's a hook in it, and what's wrong with the present communist program is that is contains the hook of communist monopoly, dictatorship, and universal tyranny."

I then said to him, "Can you answer a question which is perplexing me and which I've asked many people who are communists and for which I can't get an answer? Where did Boris Pasternak get his food? Did Boris Pasternak starve to death?" Pasternak was one of Russia's greatest writers. During an alleged thaw in the Cold War he wrote the book '*Dr. Zhivago*' which is mildly critical of communism. He was applauded throughout the world and given the Nobel Prize, but the communist monopolistic dictators of the Soviet Union did not like him. His book was not published in Russia and has not been published there to this day. He was expelled from the Union of Soviet Writers and he was not allowed to leave Russia to accept the Nobel Prize. But Pasternak was not arrested, imprisoned, tortured, sent to Siberia or put in an insane asylum. This supposed lack of harsh treatment confirmed the ideas of some that communism had mellowed. However, because Pasternak had been expelled from the Union of Soviet Writers he could no longer make a living as an author. There is only one employer in the Soviet Union, the communist state. If Pasternak couldn't earn any money, how would he be able to support himself? Ben Dobbs' answers to these questions were brief. "He'd been well paid. He'd translated Shakespeare."

Well, let's assume Pasternak had practiced "thrift" and saved his money, keeping it in the bank. What bank? The State Monopoly Bank directed by the Communist Party. If the Communist Party issues orders that this man's funds are frozen, he cannot withdraw any money. Assume he says, "I'll take you to court." What court? The court set up by the Communist Party with judges chosen by the Communist Party to administer laws written by the Communist Party. The laws do not apply to the Communist Party because the "Dictatorship of the Proletariat" is unrestricted by law. The courts are instructed to rule against him.

What now? He looks around his dwelling and sees a piece of furniture. He thinks, "If I could sell this, I could eat for some time." How does he sell it? Put an advertisement in the paper? The only press that exists is the communist monopoly press, and it does not accept advertisements, certainly not his. Should he take it to the store? What store? The monopoly store controlled by the Communist Party? He is face to face with the most complete monopoly conceived by the mind of man.

Perhaps the communists did not starve Pasternak to death. But once the state has the power and people know it has the power, it will need to be used only infrequently.

Despite ridicule from certain quarters, I continued to raise the question of how a dissident in a monopoly society secures food.

In a February 21, 1966 newsletter, I wrote, "Communism may be defined as government by potential starvation. I have frequently tried to illustrate this power by the case of Boris Pasternak, the Russian author, who wrote the book *Dr. Zhivago.* For this he earned the displeasure of the communist state. I have repeatedly raised the question of whether he starved to death. For doing this I have been ridiculed and abused but my arguments have never been answered. I have never stated that the communists did starve him to death but have insisted that their system gave them the power to starve him and have questioned whether they did so. The same power controls all employment, all banks, all stores, all law courts, and all communications. The plight of an individual who falls foul of this power is obvious. Once dismissed from his job, he cannot secure another; if he has savings in the bank, he cannot withdraw them; he has no prospect of legal redress; he cannot sell his possessions; and he has no free press to publicize his condition. He retains the freedom to starve."

There is now evidence from his own statements that Pasternak himself was vitally concerned with this possibility. This evidence is presented in a book, *Moscow Under the Skin,* written by an Italian journalist, Viro Roberti, who interviewed Pasternak several times during his ordeal. He describes the sequence of events leading to the death of Pasternak:

1. Pasternak wrote the novel *Dr. Zhivago.* He submitted it to the Soviet Publishing House, Novy Mir, which refused to publish it.
2. He submitted it to an Italian publisher believing that he had the agreement of the Soviet authorities to do this. Consequently, the book was first published in Italian.
3. In October, 1958, he was awarded the Nobel prize. The Soviet authorities were irate at the award and stated that if Pasternak chose to go to Stockholm to accept the award, he would be allowed to go. However, he would not be permitted to return to Russia.
4. On October 28, Boris Pasternak was expelled from the Union of Soviet Writers.
5. On October 31, the Moscow branch of the Union of Soviet Writers unanimously passed a resolution asking the government to deprive Boris Pasternak of Soviet citizenship and to expel him from U.S.S.R. territory.
6. On May 30, 1960, Boris Pasternak died, allegedly of cancer of the lung, preceded by a long period of increasing debility.

Roberti was in Moscow when the announcement of the award of the Nobel prize to Boris Pasternak was made. He managed to interview Pasternak on the day of the announcement, October 23, 1958, and several times thereafter until the poet's death.

On the evening of October 23, 1958, I telephoned to my newspaper a short interview I had with Boris Pasternak. Fear of the Censor has made my colleagues Nicolas Chatelain, Michel Tatu and myself describe our meeting with the poet in a matter-of-fact way. It was easy to guess that the award to Pasternak of the Nobel Prize for Literature would anger the Soviet leaders and the guardians of the so-called Soviet 'realism'. It was the first time that a major international literary award had been given to a Russian author resident in the Soviet Union.

Nicholas, Michel and I were the only ones who managed to reach Pasternak's 'dacha' at Peredelkino. We had gone on the electric train; the other correspondents who had ventured in their cars along the Minsk road were turned back by the police before reaching the Peredelkino crossroads.

"Here is the dispatch I sent to my newspaper. The words in italics and in parenthesis are those that did not pass the Censor. I still have the original copies with the Censor's stamp on them.

"Pasternak shakes our hands and invites us to sit down. He had kept us waiting because he had wanted to change. He apologises and says he has been for his daily walk. 'There is something wrong with my right knee and the doctor has advised me to walk for at least an hour every day'."

'I haven't received the official confirmation yet,' he replied to a question of mine, (*'and I shall defer my decisions until the Soviet authorities let me know their intentions'*). I cannot tell you therefore whether I shall go to Stockholm.' *

Roberti again visited Pasternak on October 30. His report to his newspaper was totally censored by the Soviet authorities. However, he kept a copy and he reports Pasternak as saying:

" 'The Union of Soviet Writers has expelled me,' he said, 'and today they have sent three doctors to check on my health. They are waiting over there. Why? I just do not understand!' Then after a pause he added: 'Why did they cover me with mud from head to toe? It isn't true that I'm a superfluous person, a poisonous creature, an emigrant in my own country, a petty philistine and a traitor. My goodness, such insults and lies. Now today they have sent three doctors to see me, but everyone knows I suffer from a

*Viro Roberti, *Moscow Under the Skin* (London, Geoffrey Bles, 1961) pp. 212–213, 215–216

mild form of sinovitis. Why? I must go and see them now; please wait here for me.'

A horrible thought came to me and I asked Boris Leonidovich whether he wanted me to be present at the examination. He replied: 'Thank you, but I think it would be better if you waited here.' I tried to insist and suddenly the poet realised what was in my mind. He turned pale and with a deep sigh, put a hand on my shoulder and said gently, 'Thank you, thank you! I understand your concern but what can I do now? I am already dead!'

After about twenty minutes he returned and exclaimed: 'They found nothing wrong with my health!*

His report of his final meeting is as follows:

On March 15, 1960, I met Boris Pasternak for the last time. A common friend had told me that he would be pleased to see me. I went to Peredelkino on the electric train again. It was very cold. The countryside was still covered with snow.

"Pasternak was a ghost of his former self. He was much thinner. There was no expression in the eyes of his pale emaciated face. He talked to me about his sadness and his anguish, 'I have no strength left to work and I sit for hours without any thoughts entering my poor head. Perhaps I am paralysed and do not realise it yet. I cannot even reply to the letters from friends which are piled up on my table . . .

'I have been expelled from the Union of Soviet Writers so that I shall starve. No one publishes my poetry or my translations anymore, which was my daily bread. The first payments from my editor have been confiscated by order of the authorities . . .'

Suddenly his eyes lit up and in a harsh voice he exclaimed: 'They have taken away this money in the hope that I will go down on my knees and disown my novel and my poetry. But nothing will ever make me yield . . . I yield only to death!'

Two days later the same friend, whose name I cannot reveal, came to see me at the Central Telegraph Office and told me that Boris Pasternak was 'gol kak sokol' (hungry as a hawk), extremely poor and had to borrow money to exist. 'All his works have been ostracised. Boris Leonidovich is unaware that his brother Alexander helps him and seeks help for him from

*Ibid, p. 222.

his friends. If he knew this he would rather starve to death. He is also very ill!'*

The power of the Dictatorship of the Proletariat is based on the power to starve.

Once the power to starve is built into the system, it may operate spontaneously and without malice. Illustrations of the actual use of this power are now coming from the communist press. The communist press is not given to sensationalism. When a particular incident is reported, it is usually because it is typical of a general situation which needs attention. For this reason it is probable that the following is not an isolated instance:

A United Press International report from Moscow, dated February 2, 1966, gives a report by the communist youth newspaper "Komsomol Pravda" of how a young girl was driven to suicide by starvation. The paper reported that a Galina Ozornina had worked at a textile factory in the Tadzhikistan capital of Dushanbe when the factory, finding its plan unfulfilled, ordered her and other girls to work nights.

"Teen-agers are not allowed to work nights," the paper said. "The factory administration knew about this law but its plan was failing."

When the girls failed to show up, the shop foreman, Mrs. E. Chetverikova, went to the girls dormitory, scolded them and fired Galina. Galina then became caught in a vicious circle of red tape that ended in her death.

The factory demanded that she be cleared by the factory library, personnel department and dormitory before she could collect her pay. But she could not pay her dormitory rent until she got her pay. And her internal passport—which she needed to get a new job—had been taken from her until she paid her rent.

Galina wandered around Dushanbe for two months and occasionally crept into the dormitory to sleep. Eventually she killed herself, and the factory (suddenly magnanimous) gave her back pay to her family."

When this monopoly power is fully mature, as it was in the case of Joseph Stalin, the power it gives the individual monopolist is

*Ibid, pp. 225–226.

so great that it is impossible to comprehend. Stalin's power is revealed in Khrushchev's speech on the crimes of Stalin, delivered at the 20th Congress of the Soviet Communist Party in 1956. This is the most awe-inspiring and dreadful speech delivered in the history of mankind. It makes clear that Stalin possessed the power of life and death over every individual within the Soviet Union. At his slightest whim he could order people killed or deported. Khrushchev describes Stalin's conduct during the Second World War:

"I will allow myself in this connection to bring out one characteristic fact which illustrates how Stalin directed operations at the fronts. There is present at this congress Marshal Bagramyan, who was once the Chief of Operations at the Headquarters of the Southwestern front and who can complete and corroborate what I say.

"When there developed an exceptionally serious situation in the Kharkov region, we had correctly decided to drop an operation whose objective was to encircle Kharkov, because the real situation at that time would have threatened our army with fatal consequences if this operation were continued. We communicated this to Stalin, stating that the situation demanded changes in operational plans so that the enemy would be prevented from liquidating a sizeable concentration of our army.

"Contrary to common sense, Stalin rejected our suggestion and issued the order to continue the operation aimed at the encirclement of Kharkov, despite the fact that at this time many army concentrations were themselves actually threatened with encirclement and liquidation.

"We should note that Stalin planned operations on a globe. (Animation in the hall.) Yes, Comrades, he used to take the globe and trace the front line on it. I said to Comrade Vasilevsky:

'Show him the situation on a map; in the present situation we cannot continue the operation which was planned. The old decision must be changed for the good of the cause.'

Vasilevsky replied saying that Stalin had already studied this problem and that he, Vasilevsky, would not see Stalin further concerning this matter, because the latter didn't want to hear any arguments on the subject of this operation.

'I telephoned to Stalin at his villa. But Stalin did not answer the telephone and Malenkov was at the receiver. I told Comrade Malenkov that I was calling from the front and that I wanted to speak personally to Stalin. Stalin informed me through Malenkov that I should speak with Malenkov. I stated for the second time that I wished to inform Stalin personally about the grave situation which had arisen for us at the front. But Stalin did not consider it convenient to pick up the phone and again stated that I should speak to him through Malenkov, although he was only a few steps from the telephone.

After 'listening' in this manner to our plea, Stalin said, 'Let everything remain as it is !'

And what was the result of this? The worst that we had expected. The Germans surrounded our army concentrations, and consequently we lost hundreds of thousands of our soldiers.'*

Stalin was so contemptuous of human life that he would not even pick up a telephone when the lives of hundreds of thousands of men depended upon his response to the message! Khrushchev described another aspect of Stalin's tyranny:

It was determined that of the 139 members and candidates of the party's Central Committee who were elected at the seventeenth congress (1939), 98 persons, i.e. 70 percent were arrested and shot (mostly in 1937–8).

"What was the composition of the delegates to the 17th Congress? It is known that 80 percent of the voting participants of the 17th Congress joined the party during the years of conspiracy before the Revolution and during the Civil War; this means before 1921. By social origin the basic mass of the delegates to the Congress were workers (60 per cent of the voting members).

"For this reason, it was inconceivable that a Congress so composed would have elected a Central Committee, a majority of whom would prove to be enemies of the party.†

This remarkable achievement reveals more than the nature of Stalin. It reveals the nature of communism and the grip that Marxist doctrine retains on communist leaders.

*N. Khrushchev, *The Dethronement of Stalin* (Manchester Guardian, June, 1956) pp. 20–21.
†*Ibid.*, p. 10

The Central Committee of the Communist Party of the Soviet was theoretically the highest communist authority. The members elected Stalin to his secretaryship. If 70 per cent were traitors, it would seem his election was invalid. Nevertheless Stalin executed 70 percent of them and retained his power. What gave Stalin his power? It was the product of democratic centralism and communist dedication to the Party. The Party was idolized as all-seeing and all-wise and all communists must submit to the judgement of the Party. Stalin was selected by the Party and given the power to operate its eyes, mind and hands.

The discussion by Khrushchev concerning the guilt or innocence of those executed reveals how powerful Marxist doctrine remains with the top communists. To determine their guilt, Khrushchev does not discuss their activities, spoken or written words, or even their thoughts. He turns to the basic Marxist criterion of character—the class of social origin. Marxism teaches that class origin determines character. Communists believe that bourgeois class origin produces traitors while proletarian class origin produces loyal communists. Khrushchev argued that since 60 percent of the Central Committee members were of proletarian origin, 70 percent of the members could not have been traitors. If Stalin had limited those executed to 40 percent of the membership, apparently Khrushchev could have found no fault.

This doctrine has never been repudiated by the communists. It leads, during this post-revolutionary phase, to another inevitable development, class liquidation. The ultimate objective of communism is the classless society, and this can only come about after the liquidation or extermination of the bourgeois class. Genocide is not essential to communism but classicide is. In practice, the borderline between genocide and classicide is sometimes hard to determine as Khrushchev reveals when he tells how Stalin deported and practically exterminated entire nationalities within the Soviet Union.

Today, some sects of communism are attempting to link nationality with class. They regard the blacks as proletarians; they regard the population of the underdeveloped nations of the world as the international proletariat. Thus genocide and classicide are very closely related.

Classicide is not only communist theory; it is communist practice. Recently statistics have been compiled giving the numbers killed after the communists conquered power in the Soviet Union and in the Peoples Republic of China. They are awesome.

Robert Conquest, a noted British authority on the Communist world and a man of impeccable academic qualifications has concluded that at least 21.5 million persons have been executed or otherwise killed by Soviet Communism since the revolution.*

The principal source of information used by Mr. Conquest are reports published by the Russian authorities and eye-witness accounts written by survivors of prison camps. He classifies the deaths under Soviet rule as follows:

| | |
|---|---:|
| Executed or died in prison camps during the post-revolution period (1919-23) | 500,000 |
| Executed during the Stalin terror | 2,000,000 |
| Died in camps during the pre-Yexhov period of Stalin's rule (1930-36) | 3,5000,000 |
| Died in forced labor camps during the Stalin-Yexhov terror (1936-38) | 12,000,000 |
| Died in the politically organized famine during the forced collectivization of the thirties | 3,5000,000 |
| TOTAL | 21,500,000 |

Mr. Conquest points out that this is a conservative estimate which is almost certainly too low and that the real figure might very well be 50 percent greater than this.

He does not include in this tabulation the deaths caused by the civil war, 1919-1921. During this war 9 million lives were lost from military action, executions, typhus, and famine while the great famine of 1921, which followed the civil war, cost another 5 million lives.

If these figures were added, *a minimum estimate of human lives lost is 35 million while 45 million is more probable.*

The story of communism in China is equally gruesome.

It is obviously impossible to give precise figures of the number

*U.S. Senate Internal Security Sub-Committee, The Human Cost of Soviet Communism (Washington, D.C., Government Printing Office, 1970) p. 1.

of people murdered by the communists as it is unlikely that the communists have kept the statistics. If they have, they do not publish them. However, reasonable estimates can be made. A lifetime student of Chinese affairs, Professor Richard L. Walker, has prepared a study entitled "The Human Cost of Communism in China" for the Senate Subcommittee on Internal Security.* Professor Walker is Director of the Institute of Internal Studies at the University of South Carolina. It is Professor Walker's estimate, after having studied all the evidence, that communism in China has cost a minimum of 34 million lives and that the total may run as high as 64 million. He presents the following table listing the casualties:

Casualties to Communism in China

| | Minimum | Maximum |
|---|---|---|
| 1. First Civil War (1927–36) | 250,000 | 500,000 |
| 2. Fighting during Sino-Japanese War (1937–45) | 50,000 | 50,000 |
| 3. Second Civil War (1945–49) | 1,250,000 | 1,250,000 |
| 4. Land reform prior to "Liberation" | 500,000 | 1,000,000 |
| 5. Political Liquidation Campaigns (1949–58) | 15,000,000 | 30,000,000 |
| 6. Korean war | 500,000 | 1,234,000 |
| 7. The "Great Leap Forward" and the Communes | 1,000,000 | 2,000,000 |
| 8. Struggles with minority nationalities, including Tibet | 500,000 | 1,000,000 |
| 9. The "Great Proletarian Cultural Revolution and its aftermath | 250,000 | 500,000 |
| 10. Deaths in forced labor camps and frontier development | 15,000,000 | 25,000,000 |
| TOTAL | 34,300,000 | 62,534,000 |

The mass killing has continued from the communist conquest of China in 1949 to the present.

The programs of communism range from serve the people, to enslave the people, to slaughter the people. But they are all justified by communists as steps towards the communist *promise.*

*Washington, D.C. (Government Printing Office; 1971) p. 16.

# THE COMMUNIST PROMISE & PROGNOSIS

# 3

**C**ommunism would never have succeeded in recruiting intelligent and idealistic youth without an attractive promise. The question most frequently asked by those bewildered by communism can be phrased, "I can understand the appeal of communism to the poor, the illiterate, the hungry, and the oppressed; what I cannot understand is the appeal to the privileged, the wealthy, the educated, and the religious. Why do millionaires, college professors, even ministers of religion become communists? This I cannot understand."

This question is based on the failure to understand the nature of communism. Communism, as such, has no appeal to the poor. It has no appeal to the oppressed nor to the working class. Of course, scientific communists have from time to time enticed segments of the working class to take violent action by promising them something they wanted. But not even the Russian revolution was revolution for communism. It was a revolution for capitalism

55

—-the slogan of Lenin was "bread, peace, and land." His promise was to distribute land to the peasants so that each peasant could become a landowner. Surprising as it may sound, private ownership of land, the essence of capitalism, was actually the promise which lured the Russian peasant into supporting the Bolshevik revolution.

Actually, the appeal of communism has always been to the educated and they come mostly from the privileged. Communist theory needs study before it can be understood, and study requires leisure time—a luxury which working classes usually do not have. Hence communism makes its appeal to a literate, intellectual group. To these people communism offers two very attractive promises. The first is that in a communist world, war will end for all time. The second is that they as communists will be able to perfect human nature and end the alienation between man and man, man and society, man and nature. Communists proclaim that they will create people so perfect that when men indulge their own impulses, they will inevitably serve their fellowman.

These two very significant promises come to grips with the most fundamental problems of life. As the poet Robert Burns says, "Man's inhumanity to man makes countless thousands mourn," and war is the ultimate expression of man's inhumanity to man.

Marx developed an extremely persuasive argument concerning the cause of war which is summarized in my earlier book, *You Can Trust the Communists (to be Communists):*

"Marx taught that the Capitalist system does two things: it produces commodities for distribution, and it circulates purchasing power or money. Capitalist society is built upon the production of commodities to be exchanged for money and the distribution of money to secure those commodities. Capitalist society is healthy, according to Marx, when the amount of money available to the people is adequate to buy the commodities produced.

Marx contended that, by the very nature of capitalism, this balance between goods produced and money available cannot be maintained for very long. A certain sequence of events is inevitable. The goods produced have a certain money value. That money is distributed in two ways: the major portion is paid out in wages to the workers who manufacture the goods—to the directors, the supervisors, and all the laborers down to the janitor; a smaller portion is retained as profit by those who own the means of production. During the early stages of the industry, the money paid to the owners as profit goes into circulation, because new capital goods such as buildings and machinery are necessary. Since these capital goods are produced and are not available for purchase by the mass of the people, the wages paid to the workers producing these capital goods are used to buy consumer commodities. During the period of capitalization, there is usually enough money in circulation to buy the consumer goods produced. Eventually the point is reached where there are enough factories and machinery, and there is no longer need for this expenditure. The profit is then retained and accumulated in bank balances, and the only money circulated is the money paid in wages for producing the goods. Since this is never quite enough to buy the goods produced, production inevitably leads to over-production.

At first this over-production is small and almost unnoticeable, but gradually it becomes more significant. The warehouses of the manufacturers become filled with goods, the inventories of the distributors are complete, and the point is reached where the factory has enough goods on hand to supply the demand for some considerable period. When that point is reached, alternative courses of action present themselves. The manufacturers may say, 'Now, the real trouble is that people haven't enough money to purchase these goods. We had better find some way in which people can get more money.' On the other hand, they may say, 'We have enough goods now. We do not need to make any more for a certain period. We had better cease production until our surplus is used up.' The normal process is to follow the latter course and to lay off the workers. When they are laid off, the purchasing power is further reduced, and the situation becomes worse.

According to Marx, this cycle is inevitable. Production leads to over-production which leads to unemployment. This leads to reduced purchasing power, which aggravates the entire situation by accelerating the accumulation of surplus products and leading to further unemployment. The eventual outcome is depression and crises. Warehouses are filled with goods which the people cannot buy. The economy stagnates and grinds to a standstill.

When this happens, a method must be found whereby purchasing power is once again given to the people that the goods may be bought and that the wheels of the economy may begin to roll once again. Historically, one method has always put money in people's pockets without simultaneously creating consumer goods. That method is war. A war breaks out on some pretext or another. Money is found to finance the war; the wheels of industry begin to turn on war production; money is distributed to the peole, and the surplus consumer products are purchased. When the surplus is consumed, normal production begins again, and the cycle goes on, repeating itself again and again. According to Marx, therefore, as long as Capitalism continues, there will be recurrent crises of depression and war.*

This argument sounds so powerful that I'm almost afraid to present it to an audience which is not well versed on communist thought. Whittaker Chambers, ex-communist and author of the magnificent autobiography *Witness*,† stated that Western intellectuals embrace communism because of the problem of war or the problem of recurrent economic crises. These intellectuals turned to communism, he said, because they accepted the Marxist diagnosis of the cause of depression and war, and the Leninst solution that wars and economic crises may be ended by the destruction of capitalism.

However, though the argument may appear convincing, the facts of life now prove that it is fallacious. Fighting has taken place between the forces of the Soviet Union and the Peoples Republic of China on their common border. Obviously capitalism is not the sole cause of war, and the abolition of capitalism does not automatically eliminate war.

Of course, each side tries to cling to the Marxist doctrine, despite the hostilities, by claiming that the other side is no longer socialist. China classifies Russia as "Socio-Imperialist" while Russia claims China is "petty-bourgeois nationalist". However each side acknowledges that the other was socialist at one time. Even if these charges are accepted as true, the facts remain that both nations embraced socialism and later fought. The abolition of capitalism does not mean the abolition of war.

If further evidence is needed of the falsity of these communist doctrines, it was provided by the military invasion of Socialist

*Dr. Fred Schwarz, *You Can Trust the Communists (to be communists)* (New York, Prentice-Hall, 1961), pp. 20–22.
†Whittaker Chambers, *Witness* (New York, Random House, 1952).

Hungary by the forces of Socialist Russia and of Socialist Czechoslovakia by the forces of the Warsaw Pact nations.

The second promise offers a solution to the universal human
dilemma: the disharmony that exists between the indivdual and
his environment. It is a promise to bring the individual and his
environment into complete harmony. This disharmony between
the individual and his environment is expressed in many ways, and
these are included in the general term "alienation", meaning
loneliness, depression, boredom, and misery. Alienation is a very
real and a very vital problem, and quite inescapable because it is
universal. We are not master of our moods and appetites. Most
people acknowledge periodic bouts of apparently causeless depression. Obviously, there is conflict within our natures; communism
promises that it will deal with this by creating happiness and
making each life meaningful and fulfilling. Marx claimed that
alienation is caused by capitalism and his argument may be para-
phrased:

> The economic environment generates the character and person-
> ality. The economic environment of capitalism is based on profit,
> greed and self, therefore it generates people who are greedy and
> selfish. All the evil in human nature is the result of the economic
> environment in which the individual was formed.
> "Actions, attitudes, emotions and ideas emerge from the brain.
> The brain is the storehouse of life's experiences, primarily those
> received as babies and little children. These experiences are pro-
> vided you by the environment which is predominately economic.
> The brain is a complex electronic computer programmed by the
> experiences of childhood and babyhood. The mind is the subjective
> state of thought and emotion which accompanies the energy dis-
> charge of the conditioned reflexes.

Once it is agreed that man is created by his early experiences,
it follows that a selected set of experiences can create a selected
type of character. A selected environment will give a selected set
of experiences which will create a selected individual who will act,
feel, and think in a predetermined fashion. The perfectability of
mankind now becomes an attainable goal.

Once man is perfect, everything evil will be abolished. War,
crime, vice, lust, jealousy, greed, selfishness and malice will disap-

pear so completely that the words for them will disappear from the language. Once man is perfect, government will be unnecessary and will be replaced by the administration of things. Lenin had a vision of a society in which everyone was a universal specialist. The individual in the morning could administer the affairs of state; in the afternoon he could write a symphony; and in the evening he could create a great sculpture.

To achieve this, communists explain that a regenerative environment must be provided. The first step is to destroy the environment that generates evil so the destruction of the capitalist system is essential. This can only be achieved by a revolution. Reforms are futile except as aids to revolution. To try to reform people while they live within the degenerative environment of capitalism is as foolish as taking the towel and trying to dry the baby while it remains in the bathwater. Before it can be dried, it must be removed from the bath. It is just as foolish to expect to reform individuals and society without removing them from the capitalist environment.

Marxist theory says that once the evil environment of capitalism has been destroyed, it is necessary to create the environment which will provide the necessary experiences to create the perfect character. Two problems arise for the communists.

1. How can this environment be created and maintained? There must be some authority with the understanding, power and will to provide the essential environment. This authority is the Communist Party which is all wise and all powerful. Lenin stated that the Communist Party is the mind, the conscience and the morals of our epoch. This party must have unrestricted power. It must exercise the Dictatorship of the Proletariat.

2. The second problem is that the program to create perfection only applies to the babies and the young who are reared in the new environment. It doesn't apply to those whose characters have already been formed by the capitalist environment. While some may be re-educated, many mature, diseased individuals must be controlled, isolated, and, if necessary, eliminated. If allowed unrestrained freedom, they will poison the environment of the young. This will destroy the whole program.

These problems are allegedly solved by setting up the dictatorship of the proletariat and creating a temporary state, based on labor, called Socialism. The term "socialism" has many possible meanings. To communists, however, the meaning is precise. To them it is the state of society formed after the revolutionary destruction of the Capitalist State. It is characterized by: 1) The dictatorship of the proletariat, exercised by the Communist Party; 2) Universal compulsory labor; 3) the liquidation of the residual bourgeoisie; 4) The rise of the New Socialist Man; and 5) the withering away of the State.

During the "socialist" stage, labor is the therapy which will regenerate mankind. The labor of progressively improving individuals will become increasingly productive and will create universal abundance which is essential before communism can come to pass. The slogan of socialism is: From each according to his ability; to each according to his work. The communists maintain that under socialism, babies will be born, not into an environment of labor for profit, but into an environment of labor as its own reward. Labor will be the law of their being. As the children grow to adolescence and the adolescents grow to adults, everyone will work because they love working; everyone will give because it is better to give than to receive; the hand of none will be raised in anger against his brother. Because there exists this pool of skilled, selfless workers, an abundance of everything needed is produced. There is no longer any such thing as theft. Everyone contributes his maximum and takes what he needs from the general wealth. Money is abolished. There is no need for a police force because there is nothing for the police to do. There is no need for an income tax, no need for government or laws so the state as we know it, withers away, and the second phase, the golden era of communism, comes to pass. Human nature is now perfect. The slogan "from each according to his ability to each according to his need," prevails.

With these two promises, many intellectuals were lured into the communist party. As long as there was no society by which to test the validity of the theory, the promises retained their lustre. Today, these two promises have been revealed for the mirage which they are. The dictatorship of the proletariat has existed in the Soviet Union for more than 50 years. The inescapable fact is that Russian youth is no closer to the state of perfection than before. The literature coming out of Russia bears ample testimony to this.

Abundance has not been created; selfishness continues to dominate; prisoners abound and the state shows no signs of withering away.

The deathblow to the idea that selfishness could be eliminated from human character by an environment of pure labor was given by Mao Tse-tung of China when he initiated the Great Cultural Revolution. The G.C.R. was designed, according to Mao Tse-tung and his cohorts, to eliminate self-interest and selfishness from the minds and characters of Chinese youth. Where did they get this selfishness? According to the theory of Marx, they should have been devoid of it. Communism triumphed in 1948-49, and the great cultural revolution began in 1967. Any youth who was 18 or 19 years old had been brought up under "socialism" imposed by the Chinese Communists. Now, if selfishness could be eliminated by this environment, they should not have had any in their characters. The very necessity to have a program to eliminate selfishness was a testimony to the fallaciousness of the original Marxist doctrine.

Of course it is possible to argue that the corruption and selfishness of Chinese youth was caused by the residual capitalist influences that remained after the communists had seized power. Even Lenin acknowledged that changing human nature was more difficult than staging a successful revolution. However, his trust was in the youth who would be raised in the new environment, and he was confident that one or two generations would be enough to produce fundamental and permanent change.

Plainly, the "Cultural Revolution" was a nail in the coffin of Marxism. Mao Tse-tung became the ideological mortician of Marx. Now the claim that one can perfect human nature in a generation or two with a controlled environment is largely discredited. This promise of communism is accordingly tarnished.

With the evidence showing that the two great promises of communism are false, the appeal of established communism to the young revolutionary intellectuals is diminishing. It is the exception now to meet young communist idealists with stars in their eyes. This accounts in very large measures for the rise of independent communist and revolutionary parties.

If the communist's dream of heaven on earth has been smashed, the reality of communist control in the world most assuredly has not been. Very plainly, no ideology whose adherents rule the lives of 1/3 of the world's population can be considered routed. Though the luster of the dream may have faded communism remains a fearsome force in the world today.

## THE PROGNOSIS

Prognosis is a medical term, meaning the prediction of the end result of the disease process. It is the responsibility of the physician to consider the prognosis before he prescribes treatment, because the nature of the treatment is determined not by the immediate symptoms alone, but by the prognosis also. Immediate pain may be agonizing, but treatment may be minor if the prognosis is good. On the other hand, pain may be minimal or nonexistent, yet a major surgical process is necessary because the prognosis, if surgery does not take place, is bad. This applies particularly in the case of cancer. The quality of the treatment is determined by the prognosis and not the symptoms alone.

What is the prognosis of communism? It should be considered from two points of view. Firstly, the statements of the communists. Their statements are quite clear. William P. Foster, Chairman of the American Communist Party for many years, wrote the book *The Twilight of World Capitalism.** The dedication reads: "To my great grandson, Joseph Manley Kolko, who will live in a communist United States."

With arrogant assurance, the communists have unhesitantly announced that they will conquer the U.S.A. It is not a matter of "if" but "when". The laws of history have ordained it. It is as certain that communism will prevail as that the sun will rise. This is a basic conviction of communism derived from its doctrines.

The claims of the communists could be ignored except for the record of achievement that backs their claim. This record is the second thing to be considered in assessing the prognosis. The facts are sobering. The WORLD MARXIST REVIEW of August, 1964, presented a table showing the growth in communist membership through the years. It is informative and disturbing. It should be born in mind that Lenin began the modern communist

*New York, International Publishers, 1949.

movement with about 25 supporters in 1903 and conquered Russia with about 40,000 supporters in 1917.

**Dynamics of Growth of the Communist Movement**

| Year | Number of Parties | Total | Membership in Non-socialist Countries |
|---|---|---|---|
| 1928 | 46 | 1,680,000 | 443,000 |
| 1935 | 61 | 3,141,000 | 785,000 |
| 1957 | 75 | 33 million | about 4.6 million |
| 1960 | 87 | 36 million | over 5.3 million |
| 1963 | 90 | 42.8 million | over 6 million |

Today the number of communists in the world is over 50 million. These communists monoplize power and control the assets of more than one billion of the world's population. The record of communist achievement outstrips by far the record of Hitler, Napoleon, or any conqueror of history?

It is sometimes said that since no movement has ever succeeded in conquering the world, no movement can ever succeed. That is like asserting in 1960 that since no human has ever set foot on the moon, no human can. The world is changing. Modern technology makes certain historic lessons obsolete. The instantaneousness of modern communications, the speed of modern transportation and the power of modern weaponry have opened possibilities for world conquest and control which did not previously exist.

If an individual who has a record of failure in all previous business undertakings announced to the Chamber of Commerce that he planned to build a factory in a certain city in the following year, the Chamber of Commerce is unlikely to pay much attention. If General Motors Company announced that it would build a factory to employ 5,000 people in that city, one can imagine the anticipation and excitement.

The record of past achievement by the International Communist Movement is such that their claim that they will conquer the world should be regarded with the utmost seriousness.

# IMPERIALISM 4

**A** s we have seen, the vision of communism is tarnished. The picture of a warless world inhabited by perfect people has lost its lustre. However there remains one doctrine that is a powerful recruiting force for communism. It is the Leninist doctrine of imperialism. The cry "Fight American Imperialism" rings around the world.

The term "American Imperialism" is a strange combination because, in the classical sense, America has no empire. The United States does not exercise political and administrative control over colonies.

The AFL-CIO has published a pamphlet, "Who is the Imperialist?" It contrasts the number of countries and people that have been given their political freedom by western powers since the second World War with the number of countries and people who have been denied their political freedom by the communist powers. From this comparison, it is obvious that the Soviet Union and the Peoples Republic of China are the imperialists and America and the western countries are the anti-imperialists.

However, this argument is based upon the old-fashioned definition of imperialism. It has little relevance to the concept of imperialism shared by the communists and radicals around the world. To them imperialism is defined in terms of economic power which leads to disguised political and administrative control.

As an introduction to the communist definition of imperialsm, I draw attention to a remarkable phenomenon that has been taking place within the United States in recent years. The primary targets of the America's radical bombers and arsonists have been the large banks with international branches. For instance, the Bank of America has had more than 50 branches bombed or set afire since the late 1960's.

Why is the Bank of America a primary target of the bombers and arsonists? The violent radicals consider that they are taking revenge on an institution which is a key agent of "American imperialism."

The doctrine of "imperialism" teaches that America is a thief who practices armed robbery with violence against other nations particularly the under-developed countries. The products of "imperialistic" thievery are then distributed to the American people, including the workers, so that American standard of living is higher than in other countries.

A leading exponent of this attitude has been the violent Weatherman organization. This group considers it self an armed urban guerrilla force at war with the United States. Members boast of their responsibility for many of the bombings. Before going underground, this group constituted the official leadership of Students for a Democratic Society (SDS). In the basic Weatherman document entitled "You Don't Need a Weatherman to Know Which Way the Winds Blows," the premise of America as an "imperialist" force in the world is bluntly expressed:

> We are within the heartland of a world-wide monster, a country so rich from its world-wide plunder that even the crumbs doled out to the enslaved masses within its borders provide for material existence very much above the conditions of the masses of people of the world. The US empire, as a world-wide system, channels

66

wealth, based upon the labor and resources of the rest of the world, into the United States. The relative affluence existing in the United States is directly dependent upon the labor and natural resources of the Vietnamese, the Angolans, the Bolivians and the rest of the peoples of the Third World. All of the United Airlines Astrojets, all of the Holday Inns, all of Hertz's automobiles, your television set, car and wordrobe already belong, to a large degree to the people of the rest of the world.*

This theory originated with Lenin, who in 1917 wrote the book "Imperialism, the Highest Stage of Capitalism." This book is probably the most influential book throughout the world today. It claims that the progress of capitalism creates monopoly in business and industry and the accumulation of capital. Ultimately, Lenin said, this capital falls into the hands of banks and becomes "finance capital."

Lenin stated:

We must give a definition of imperialism that will include the following five of its basic features: 1) the concentration of production and capital has developed to such a high stage that it has created monopolies which play a decisive role in economic life; 2) the merging of bank capital with industrial capital, and the creation, on the basis of this 'finance capital', of a financial oligarchy; 3) the export of capital as distinguished from the export of commodities acquires exceptional importance; 4) the formation of international monopolist capitalist combines which share the world among themselves, and 5) the territorial division of the whole world among the biggest capitalist powers is completed. Imperialism is capitalism in that stage of development in which the dominance of monopolies and finance capital has established itself; in which the export of capital has acquired pronounced importance; in which the division of the world among the international trusts has begun; in which the division of all territories of the globe among the biggest capitalist powers has been completed.†

The world has undergone many changes since Lenin wrote these lines in 1917. Most of the colonies have become independent

*Harold Jacobs, ed., *Weatherman* (Berkeley, Ramparts Press, 1970) p. 52.
†V.I. Lenin, *Imperialism, the Highest Stage of Capitalism* (Moscow, Foreign Languages Press, 1950) p. 143.

and the territories of the globe are no longer divided among the biggest capitalist powers.

The communists allege, however, that this freedom is more apparent than real. Political freedom, they say, is largely meaningless without economic freedom, and the economics of the ex-colonies are dominated by foreign capital. Economic domination without overt political power is called neo-colonialism. To the communists, then, it is neo-colonialism which is characteristic of imperialism today. An article entitled "Neo-Colonialism and its Socio-Economic Strategy" in POLITICAL AFFAIRS, theoretical journal of the Communist Party, U.S.A., states:

> It is in the garb of neocolonialism that imperialism is confronting the young independent states today, acting as the main stumbling block in the way of their economic and social progress. L.I. Brezhnev pointed out in his speech at the International Meeting of Communist and Workers' Parties in 1969 that 'today neocolonialism is no less dangerous than colonialism.' *

Discussing the role of banks, Lenin writes:

> As banking develops and becomes concentrated in a small number of establishments, the banks grow from humble middlemen into powerful monopolies having at their command almost the whole of the money capital of all the capitalists and small businessmen and also the larger part of the means of production and of the sources of raw materials of the given country and in a number of countries.†

Lenin argued that "finance capital" must be invested profitably. In order to secure maximun profit, it is exported to a foreign country. When capital goes to a foreign country, Lenin insisted it exploits the local population by paying low wages to the national workers and extracts the mineral or agricultural wealth which is transported back to the United States, where the raw material is processed and sold at a huge profit. Sometimes, he declared, the robbery is compounded because the underdeveloped countries

---

*K. Brutents, *Neo-Colonialism and its Socio-Economic Strategy* (Political Affairs, September 1971) p. 12
†Ibid, page 45.

often become markets for their own processed products which are sold back to them at inflated prices.

Following this doctrine of Lenin, the revolutionaries believe that America is the leading "imperialist" nation today. This is because American foreign investments are much greater than those of any other country. They claim that American foreign, diplomatic, and military policies are designed to protect American overseas investments and that this is the reason for the wide distribution of American military bases throughout the world.

The doctrine of imperialism is also used to explain the lack of revolutionary fervor which characterizes the working class in the industrialized countries. Some of the surplus profits of imperialism are used to bribe them, the communists claim, and thus the workers become beneficiaries of imperialist theft from the poor countries. This condition, consequently, makes them a working class aristocracy and dampens their revolutionary consciousness.

The Marxist-Leninists report that if any government threatens American investments, it is usually subverted from within or overthrown by military invasion. The favorite example given is American intervention in the Dominican Republic. The war in Vietnam is likewise treated as a simple manifestation of American imperialism. This is in spite of the fact that no one has yet been able to discover the investments which would justify such an expenditure of American blood and treasure.

This doctrine of imperialism is not confined to revolutionary circles within the United States. It is taught in most universities throught the world. The students are led to blame the United States for the poverty in their own countries. They assume that if American imperialism could be destroyed, prosperity would soon be the lot of all mankind.

## "IMPERIALISM" ANALYZED

Is this argument true? Certainly there are elements of truth in it. No error ever seduces a large number of people without an admixture of truth. Error devoid of truth is as unappetizing as an unbaited hook.

Lord Tennyson penned:

"That a lie which is half a truth is ever the blackest of lies,
That a lie which is all a lie may be met with and fought outright,
But a lie which is part a truth is a harder matter to fight."

(The Grandmother)

Selected facts combined with impeccable logic can produce absurd conclusions. To illustrate this, I present the argument that an increase in pregnancy reduces the population.

*Selected fact No. 1:* Pregnancy causes death. This is indisputable. Infant and maternal mortality are grim facts of life. Taking the figures for 1968 provided by the Department of Health, Education and Welfare, there were approximately 77,000 infant deaths and 1,000 maternal deaths, a total of 78,000 deaths due to pregnancy.

*Selected fact No. 2:* An increase in deaths reduces the population. This is unarguable.

*Conclusion*: An increase in pregnancy reduces the population.

The edifice of nonsense is constructed by selecting 2 percent of the truth and ignoring 98 percent. It ignores the 98 healthy babies in each 100 babies born. It concentrates on the subtractions and ignores the additions.

This edifice of nonsense known as "imperialism" is constructed by selecting one portion of reality and ignoring other parts. It ignores the benefits added by foreign investment to the country where the investment takes place.

The investment of capital in underdeveloped countries frequently confers great benefits upon the people in whose country the capital is invested. To illustrate this, I present the results of investment of American, British and Japanese capital in Australia. Although Australia is not exactly an underdeveloped country, it is still an alleged victim of "imperialism": Japanese as well as American.

Recently extensive deposits of minerals, including iron ore, have been discovered in Northwestern Australia. The area is desolate and isolated and there is scarcely a blade of grass or a drop of water within hundreds of miles. The climate, with searing high temperatures, is cruel to man or beast.

At great expense to the "imperialists", a railway is constructed to service the area. Wells are drilled to secure water and houses for workers and industrial buildings are constructed. With water from the wells available for irrigation, the land is tilled and lawns and trees planted. The necessary equipment is transported to the site and the operation commences. All this development has not cost Australians one cent.

The "imperialists" need labor. To persuade Australian workers to leave the cities, there must be substantial rewards. Wages must be much higher than those available in civilized areas. If an individual works for a year and saves his income, he can have quite a sum for investment.

The ore is transported to the coast, shipped overseas and used in manufacturing. A profit is made, part of which is paid to the "imperialist stockholders" in the form of dividends. A significant part is also paid to the Australian Government as taxes.

If we draw up a balance sheet of losses and gains, we find that Australia has lost a hill in the desert. But Australia has gained: 1) Skilled workmen; 2) High wages for workers with resulting benefits in nutrition, health, and housing for men, women, and children; 3) National income; 4) A garden in the desert. Surely Australia has gained much more than she lost in the process.

Australia has been the supposed victim of "American Imperialism" for many years. General Motors chose to invest some of its capital in Australia to build automobiles. They purchased land, built a factory, used Australian workers and raw materials and built an automobile called the Holden. This automobile was so suitable to Australian conditions and so competitive in price that it captured the major portion of the Australian automobile market. General Motors-Holden made the largest profit any firm had made in Australian history. It is true that a significant percentage of these profits were transferred to America to pay dividends to stockholders, and more than one Australian politician tried to make political capital from this by accusing the Americans of robbing the Australians. But these people ignored the contributions to Australia made by General Motors-Holden. These contributions included:

1. Better and cheaper automobiles.
2. The retention of capital in Australia that would have been spent to import automobiles.
3. Higher wages for thousands of Australians.
4. The technical training of thousands of Australians so that they became skilled workers.
5. Income from the export of Holden automobiles.
6. Taxation income.

To come closer to home, consider "American Imperialism" as it operates in Ciudad Juarez, Mexico, a rapidly growing Mexican city across the Rio Grande from El Paso, Texas.

The terrain is inhospitable desert. Nevertheless, the population is growing by leaps and bounds. On a recent visit to El Paso, I was informed that Juarez was the largest border city in the world; a claim which I have not checked.

What accounts for the phenomenal growth of Juarez? American firms have built factories there to take advantage of lower Mexican wages. The products of these factories are usually transported to the United States and sold at considerable profit.

What are the results in Mexico? Mexicans from a wide area have converged on Juarez hoping to secure employment in the factories. They come because income and conditions provided by factory employment are superior to those they previously endured. Many are successful and many are disappointed. Housing is inadequate and hygienic facilities are non-existent for some so that large shanty towns come into being. Some even live in holes in the ground.

Nevertheless, large numbers of Mexicans are living far better than before. Houses with running water and electric lights are being built, education and medical care are being provided, and the material quality of life is improved for many. The net result is advantageous for many Mexican citizens.

This is not to state that the situation cannot be improved. There are doubtless individual instances where investments work to the disadvantage of the local inhabitants. Such cases should be considered on their merits. Generally speaking, however, foreign capital investment improves material well-being for many. It is obviously wrong to assume that investment of foreign capital in an underdeveloped country is essentially evil. Foreign investment is like water and fire. Wisely controlled, they confer great benefits; uncontrolled they may be devastating.

## AMERICAN PROSPERITY AND FOREIGN INVESTMENTS

The claim that American prosperity is based on income secured from investment in underdeveloped countries is easily disproved by the facts. Here are some official statistics for 1969 as supplied by the Department of Commerce.

| | |
|---|---|
| Total U.S. assets and investments abroad | $146,134,000,000 |
| Total assets and investment of foreigners in the U.S.A. | 81,000,000,000 |
| Total income from U.S. foreign investments | 8,838,000,000 |
| Total payments by U.S. to foreign investors | 4,463,000,000 |
| Net income from U.S. foreign investments | 4,375,000,000 |
| Wages paid to U.S. employees in 1969 | 564,300,000,000 |

If every cent earned by foreign investment were paid in wages to American workers, it would pay less than 1 percent of the American wage bill. Consider the distribution of U.S. investment in foreign countries:

| | |
|---|---|
| Canada | 30 per cent |
| Europe | 30 per cent |
| Latin America | 18 per cent |
| Asia | 8 per cent |
| Africa | 5 per cent |
| Australia | 5 per cent |

Only 30 per cent of American foreign investment is in the underdeveloped countries of the Third World. This is probably one reason they remain underdeveloped. With little doubt, they could profit considerably by an increased investment.

A devastating critique of the Leninist doctrine of imperialism has been given by Greg Calvert, a former National Secretary of

SDS and a radical himself. In his book, *A Disrupted History,* Calvert wrote:

> We are living in the third stage of capitalist development, a stage which is called variously 'neocapitalism' or 'corporate capitalism'. After the stages of laissez faire and of monopolization, capitalism has entered a new era of development. Just as the era of laissez faire was characterized by competition and the building of the infra-structure of capitalist industrialization, and the era of monopoly capitalism was characterized by the consolidation of control by finance capital and the conquest of foreign markets through imperialism, so the third stage of development, neocapitalism, is characterized by the control of the economy by the giant corporations and the intensive expansion and development of investment, production, and the market within the advanced capitalist nations.

This New Left formulation runs counter to the classical position of the Old Left as derived from Lenin's work itself. Lenin did not foresee this development of neocapitalism. In fact, he argued that it was impossible. He stated:

'It goes without saying that if capitalism could develop agriculture, which today lags far behind industry everywhere, if it could raise the standard of living of the masses, who are everywhere still poverty stricken and underfed, in spite of the amazing advance in technological knowledge, there could be no talk of a superabundance of capital. This 'argument' the petit-bourgeois critics of capitalism advance on every occasion. But if capitalism did these things it would not be capitalism; for un-even development and wretched conditions of the masses are fundamental and inevitable conditions and premises of this mode of production. As long as capitalism remains what it is, surplus capital will never be utilized for the purpose of raising the standard of living of the masses in a given country, for this would mean a decline in profits for the capitalists, but for the purpose of increasing profits by exporting capital abroad to the backward countries.'

This analysis, advanced by Lenin in 1917, reveals precisely the inadequacy of his outlook and points the way toward an alternative understanding of the nature of our own era, the neocapitalist era, which began to take shape in the period following World War 1. In this new stage, capitalism has done precisely those things which Lenin argued it could not do--it has developed agriculture through the application of industrial technology (mechanization and agricultural science); it has raised the living standards of the masses within the capitalist countries (through the development of the internal consumer market); and it has even created additional, nonproductive outlets for investment in the development of waste production (military investment and variety of planned obsolescences).*

## THE EMOTIONAL FACTOR

Since the "imperialist" argument is so obviously fallacious, what is the explanation for its appeal to so many? It is not difficult to understand that those living outside the United States accept this argument because it provides a scapegoat on whom they can place the blame for the poverty and misery that surrounds them. The doctrine is especially valuable to demagogic politicians since it enables them to promise people an almost immediate deliverance from poverty. Prosperity, they allege, can be achieved by nationalizing American-owned industries and distributing the profits to the local people instead of to Americans. The argument is persuasive, but the promised prosperity proves elusive and never follows the expropriation.

Why does it appeal to educated American youth such as the Weatherman members? These people are the products of some of America's wealthiest homes and most prestigious universities. Most of them were first-rate students. However, their whole program is based upon this fallacious "imperialist" doctrine.

One bright young student named Steve Kelman wrote recently of how this doctrine of Imperialism was "taught" on the Harvard campus during 1969:

> A sophomore who gave a section on imperialism in the spring of 1969 happily confessed to me that the only non-Leninist view of the subject he had read was Joseph Schumpeter's brief and generalized essay 'Imperialism,' that he was ignorant of the fact that of American corporations' total assets of $1.3 trillion only $16 billion represents investment in the entire Third World and that in

*Greg Calvert and Carol Neiman, *A Disrupted History: The New Left and the New Capitalism* (New York, Random House, 1971) pp. 73-74 his view the definition of the term imperialism was any American investment abroad.*

Where passions are deeply stirred, reason is frequently the victim. Convictions tend to be in tune with the emotional vision. The Weatherman people are enraged and need an object on which to vent their rage.

In the book, *You Can Trust the Communists (to be Communists),* I listed the four factors that combine in the recruitment of a communist. They are: 1) Disenchantment with Capitalism, 2) Materialist Philosophy, 3) Intellectual Pride, and 4) Unfulfilled Religious Need.

The doctrine of "imperialism" disenchants people with capitalism and reinforces the resentment of those alienated from society. Materialist philosophy destroys faith in God, hope for the future, and meaning in the present. Intellectual pride convinces the individual that he is competent to direct the lives of others in their own interest. The need for religious fulfillment remains and a substitute is found in communion with a fellowship of like-minded peers in the worship of destruction.

The doctrine of imperialism thus plays a key role in the recruitment of communists and radicals generally. Loaded with half truths as it is, the doctrine of imperialism is the most powerful ideological weapon possessed today by the communists and associated radicals as they seek to gain recruits for their army of destruction.

*Steven Kelman, *Push Comes to Shove*, (Boston, Houghton-Mifflin, 1970) pp. 247-248.

# CHINESE COMMUNISM AND THE THOUGHT OF MAO TSE-TUNG

# 5

**N**o discussion of modern communism can ignore the role of the chairman of the Chinese Communist Party, Mao Tse-tung, and his "thought." About half the communists of the world are followers of Marxism-Leninism-Mao Tse-tung thought.

Mao has never been one to hide his beliefs. They are published in many languages and distributed in multiplied millions of copies. The Little Red Book of *Quotations from Chairman Mao Tse-tung* is familiar not only in China but wherever radicals gather throughout the world.

The world would have been saved much agony if statesmen had read the Mein Kampf of Adolph Hitler and had given serious attention to the statements therein. Similarly, serious study of and attention to The Thoughts of Mao Tse-tung may avert future tragedy.

In *The Communist Manifesto* Marx and Engels wrote, "We communists disdain to conceal our goals and aims." While this is not true in day-to-day activities it is usually the case in their pronouncements on fundamental theory. Mao Tse-tung is very frank in his statements.

The PEKING REVIEW is the report which is sent throughout the world to inform the supporters of the Chinese Communists of the official point of view on a given subject and to recruit new backers. Hence, the anti-communist reader of the PEKING RE-VIEW is eavesdropping on the lectures of the Peking Communists to their supporters.

The communists produce separate literature for their support-ers and for the general public. They classify literature for their supporters as Propaganda and that for the general public as Agita-tion. They define Propaganda as "that which conveys many ideas to a few people." It is designed to give the enlightened few an insight into the thought processes that underlie the communist programs. Propaganda requires concentration for comprehension. Agitation on the otherhand, is defined as "that which conveys one idea to many people." It tries to stimulate masses of people by one central idea. Its appeal is to the emotions.

The PEKING REVIEW is Chinese Communist "propaganda;" The CHINA PICTORIAL is "agitation." This latter magazine is designed to depict life in Communist China as "heaven on earth" and the color photography is appropriately glorious. Taken at face value, the conclusion that paradise exists in Red China is inescap-able.

As a matter of fact, the Chinese Communists are not the first totalitarian power to employ such propaganda techniques. The Soviet Communists have been doing it with the SOVIET PIC-TORIAL for years. And the Nazis also published beautiful pic-torial magazines to deceive the naive.

Nonetheless, from Chinese Communist propaganda, some idea of the official interpretation of what is taking place in Red China can be obtained. Attempts must always be made to read between the lines in official communist publications. One insignificant de-tail may provide a significant clue on internal developments. The presence of a picture of some communist leader may be informa-tive. Trying to figure out what is taking place behind the scenes in a communist country is like putting together an intricate jigsaw puzzle. The unifying design is communist theory.

Despite the problems, more information can be obtained from reading the literature published by the Chinese Communists themselves than from a visit to Red China. I am bewildered by the trust that people tend to put in the report of a visitor to Red China, whether that visitor is a ping pong player or a trained news reporter. In a closed society, where the people are afraid to talk to strangers, where the people are limited in the information they possess; where the rulers probably don't know fully what is taking place; even if the observer is honest and proficient, it is very difficult to do anything but relay information provided you by the host, the communist authorities. After the American ping pong team visited Communist China in 1971, some team members made reports on conditions in Red China over radio and television. One who was a supporter of Mao before he went there gave, naturally, a glowing report of conditions there. The tragedy is that some people considered the reports significant.

Let us take a hypothetical situation. Imagine that the American ping pong team visits South Africa to play a South African team. They fly to Johannesburg, where they are met at the airport by South Africa's smoothest diplomat. They are taken from the airport to one of South Africa's finest hotels where they enjoy a sumptuous meal. By a limousine they travel to a sports palace where they play the South African ping pong team. This is followed by a visit to the theater. The following day, in addition to a ping pong match, they visit a hospital where they watch a team of South African doctors perform a heart transplant.

Having spent a couple of days in Johannesburg in this manner, they fly to Capetown and Durban where similar schedules are provided. After having visited and seen South Africa, what report would they make on returning to America? The report could be, "There are no blacks in South Africa." It is possible that they would not have seen one black during their trip. From their observation, the major problem in South Africa did not exist.

We have heard reports from experienced newsmen that the majority of the Chinese people support the Chairman Mao Tse-tung. Unless one believes in multiple extrasensory perception there is no conceivable way to discover the real thoughts of the majority of the Chinese people. The sight of hundreds of thousands waving Mao's little red book testifies to the efficiency of communist regimentation but reveals little of the true thoughts of the people.

George Orwell depicted this divergence between public conduct and private thought in his prophetic book *"1984"*. He described Julia's obvious devotion to chastity at demonstrations of the "Junior Anti-sex League." This contrasted with her sexual conduct with Winston in the illusionary privacy of the woods.

Even with freedom of speech, identity of language and idiom, and unprecedented opportunities to express ideas, it remains extraordinarily difficult to know what a majority of people are thinking. The science of polling has developed in the effort to determine this. The opinion of a partisan is notoriously unreliable. Till the day of the election, a very intelligent friend of mine was certain that Barry Goldwater would be elected president in 1964. He had traveled all over the nation and the overwhelming majority of those to whom he spoke supported Goldwater.

Speaking at San Francisco State College, I stressed the limitations of the power of observation in discovering the thoughts of people in a foreign land.

One young lady said, "But our professors tell us that they can sense the attitude of the people."

I replied, "You travel through this neighborhood every day. You speak the language of the people. They are free to talk to you without fear. Please tell me, will the majority vote for Ronald Reagan or Pat Brown for governor?"

She said, "Now, I understand."

Despite her daily association with them, she did not have the faintest idea of what the majority thought on the dominant public issue of the day.

The question of whether the Chinese people do or do not support Mao Tse-tung and the communist regime is an open question. Nobody knows and there is no way of knowing. The techniques of control are adequate to regiment the actions of the people.

In such situations, the most reliable index of the acceptance or non-acceptance of the regime by the people is the refugee index. This index is the percentage of the people who are prepared to sacrifice their cultural heritage, their worldly possessions, their home, their friends, their family, and risk their lives to escape from the power of the regime.

Whenever there has been an opportunity to measure by this index, it has not favored the Chinese Communists. During the Korean War, the Chinese "volunteers" fought against the Koreans and the United Nations troops. A considerable number were taken captive. After the truce they were given the choice of returning to Red China and their families, or of accepting exile. A large majority chose to become exiles. That is a significant vote. Plainly, the fact that refugees from Red China swim to Hong Kong or Macao gives significant insight into the true thoughts of the people.

In these circumstances, the best method to find out what is taking place on the Chinese Mainland is to read the literature that the communists publish. From this literature it is clear that the "religion" of China is the "Thought of Mao Tse-tung." There are no hymns in the Christian hymnology which express greater adoration for Christ than the Chinese hymns to Mao Tse-tung.

The little Red Book entitled *Quotations from Mao Tse-tung* is the New Testament of the Communist Chinese. Over 400 million copies have been distributed in China. It is used evangelistically all around the world and has been the inspiration of many revolutionary movements.

One consequence of the Sino-Soviet conflict during the late 1950's and 60's was to release forces which inspired the creation of many independent violent revolutionary organizations throughout the world. These professed to be Marxist-Leninist-Maoist, or at least inspired by Chairman Mao. In the United States, one of these organizations was the Progressive Labor Party which was a Communist Party inspired by Mao and supporting the policies of the Chinese Communists. Members became very effective on the university campuses during the past decade. Recently, however, the Progressive Labor Party has repudiated the Chinese Communists because of Chinese Communist support for Pakistan in its short-lived war with India in December, 1971. Nonetheless, the organization still adheres to the revolutionary rules of Mao.

What sort of a man is Mao Tse-tung? Khrushchev knew him well. Concerning him, Khrushchev wrote:

"Mao Tse-tung has played politics with Asiatic cunning, following his own rules of cajolery, treachery, savage vengeance, and deceit. He deceived us for a number of years before we saw through his tricks. Talleyrand once said that a diplomat is given a tongue in order to conceal his thoughts. The same goes for a politician, and Mao Tse-tung has always been a master at concealing his true thoughts and intentions."*

The idea of Mao concealing his thoughts is hilarious. Mao Tse-tung has written voluminously and revealed his thoughts with great clarity. He has certainly not tried to disguise his infatuation with guns and war. A few specific quotations will show this:

"Every communist must grasp the truth, 'Political power grows out of the barrel of a gun.' "†

"WAR is the highest form of struggle for resolving contradictions, when they have developed to a certain stage, between classes, nations, states, or political groups."§

"All wars that are progressive are just, and all wars that impede progress are unjust . . . Not only do we communists not oppose just wars, we actively participate in them."**

"Revolutionary war is an antitoxin which not only eliminates the enemy's poison but also purges us of our own filth."††

One of Mao's most influential books is entitled *On Contradiction*. It is Mao's exposition and application of the communist philosophy of "Dialectical Materialism." The term "contradiction" is taken from the philosophy of dialectical materialism, and may be interpreted as "conflict."

Mao gives a very clear definition of materialism: "Man's knowledge of matter is a knowledge of the forms of motion of matter, because there is nothing in the world apart from matter in motion and the motion of matter must assume certain forms."§§

Matter in motion is the totality of being. It is from this basis that Mao Tse-tung and all communists operate. The motion of matter accounts for all human ideas, activity and society. The motion of

*Edward Crankshaw, Ed., *Khrushchev Remembers* (Boston, Little, Brown, 1971) pp. 461–462.
†Mao Tse-tung, *Quotations from Mao Tse-tung* (San Francisco, China Bks, 2d Ed. 1966) p. 61.
§*Ibid.*, p. 58.
**	*Ibid.*, p. 59.
††*Ibid.*, p. 60.
§§Mao Tse-tung, *On Contradiction* (San Francisco, China Bks, 4th Ed. 1964) p. 20.

matter is governed by certain laws. The basic law is that contradiction is universal in everything that exists.

"There is nothing that does not contain contradiction; without contradiction there would be no world."*

"Contradiction is universal, absolute, existing in all processes of the development of things and running through all processes from beginning to end."

The key to the thought and activity of Mao Tse-tung is the concept: conflict is life, and the absence of conflict is death.

Conflict is the breath of life. Some might suggest that Mao Tse-tung is projecting his own psychological characteristics into his philosophy. Since Mao loves a fight, he has developed a philosophy that makes fighting a creative act. I make no pretense of ability to disentangle the emotional and rational motives of Mao. Both his philosophy and life have majored in conflict.

Mao differentiates between the "universality" and "particularity" of conflict. He claims that every situation and process has its own individual contradiction and that this can only be perceived by a study of the particular case. Actually, Mao declares, a great event contains many contradictions which are interconnected. Since the intensity of contradictions varies with development, consistent study is imperative to determine the relative importance of each contradiction at a specific state. He writes:

> For example: At the time when capitalism of the era of free competition developed into imperialism, there was no change in the character of the two classes in fundamental contradiction, the proletariat and the bourgeoisie, or in the capitalist nature of such a society. However, the contradiction between these two classes became intensified, the contradiction between monopoly capital and non-monopoly capital emerged, the contradiction between metropolitan countries and colonies became intensified and the contradiction between capitalist countries, that is, the contradiction caused by the unevenness of their development, manifested itself in a particularly acute way, thus bringing about the special stage of capitalism, the stage of imperialism. The reason why Leninism is Marxism of the era of imperialism and of the proletarian revolution is that Lenin and Stalin have correctly explained these

---

*Ibid.,* p. 16

contradictions and correctly formulated the theory and tactics of the proletarian revolution for resolving them.*

When applied in practice, this gives the Communist Party great flexibility. They can select the contradiction on which to concentrate. They can change their attitudes to allies and enemies at will without renouncing the major contradiction. Flexible tactics work for the final resolution of the basic contradiction between the bourgeoisie and the proletariat and the outcome will be *proletarian victory throughout the world* or *communist dictatorship over the world.* This flexibility is expressed as follows:

> "From this it can be seen that if in any process a number of contradictions exist, only one of them is the principal contradiction, playing the leading and decisive role, while the rest occupy a secondary or subordinate position. Thus, in studying any process —if it is a complicated process in which more than two contradictions exist—we must devote our whole energy to discovering its principal contradiction. Once this principal contradiction is grasped, any problem can be solved readily.†

The relative strength and importance of the two forces in conflict vary from time to time and states:

> But, in any contradiction, whether principal or secondary, can we treat the two contradictory aspects as equal?
> "No we cannot. In any contradiction, at any time, the development of the contradictory aspects is uneven. Sometimes there seems to be a balance of forces, but that is only a temporary and relative state; the basic state is unevenness. Of the two contradictory aspects, one must be the principal and the other secondary. The principal aspect is the one which plays the leading role in the contradiction. The quality of the thing is mainly determined by the principal aspect of the contradiction that has taken the dominant position.
> "But this state is not fixed; the principal and the non-principal aspects of a contradiction transform themselves into each other and the quality of a thing changes accordingly. In a certain process

* *Ibid.,* pp. 26–27.
† *Ibid.,* p. 36.

or at a certain stage in the development of a contradiction, the principal aspect is A and the non-principal aspect is B; at another stage of development or in another process of development, the roles are reversed—a change determined by the extent of the increase and decrease, respectively, in the intensity of the struggle of the two aspects of the contradiction in the development of a thing.*

This development within a contradiction produces qualitative change:

The superseding of the old by the new is the universal, forever inviolable law of the world. A thing transforms itself into something else according to its nature and the conditions under which it finds itself and through different forms of leap; that is the process of the superseding of the old by the new. Everything contains a contradiction between its new aspect and its old aspect, which constitutes a series of intricate struggles. As a result of these struggles, the new aspect grows and rises to become the thing that dominates, while the old aspect dwindles and becomes the thing that gradually approaches extinction. And the moment the new aspect has won the dominant position over the old aspect, the quality of the old thing changes into the quality of the new thing. From this it can be seen that the quality of a thing is mainly determined by the principal aspect of the contradiction that has won the dominant position.†

He discusses the role of failure in communist programs in the light of this doctrine:

At certain times in the revolutionary struggle, difficulties outweigh advantages; at such times, difficulties constitute the principal aspect of the contradiction and advantages the secondary aspect. But through the efforts of revolutionaries, difficulties can be gradually overcome, an advantageous new situation is created, and the difficult situation yields place to the advantageous one. Such was the case after the failure of the revolution in China in 1927 and during the Long March of the Chinese Red Army. In the present Sino-Japanese War (1930–1940's), China is again in a difficult

*Ibid., pp. 36–37.
†Ibid., p. 37.

THE THREE FACES OF REVOLUTION

position; but we can change this state of affairs and bring about a fundamental change in the situation of both China and Japan.*

## WAR AND VIOLENCE

To Mao, war and violence are virtuous. He does not take the attitude that war is an unfortunate necessity to achieve an objective, but that war is good because of the effect it has on the participants who survive. He states this quite definitely in *Quotations of Mao Tse-Tung*, "Revolutionary war is an anti-toxin which not only eliminates the enemies poison, but which also purges us of our own filth."†

He teaches the doctrine of the therapeutic value of violence and war; that war is purifying. Obviously, he is looking at the cleansing power of war in a collective, not an individual sense. War cannot be good for the individual it kills. A Christian may believe this but not a materialist. He is looking at war from the viewpoint of the collective, from the viewpoint of the Party. This line of thought is not limited to Mao Tse-tung but goes back to Engels. Some communists try to be apologetic about their attitude to force and violence and claim that violence is forced on them by the reaction of the bourgeosie who violently defend their possessions. That is not the teaching of Mao Tse-tung, who teaches that war is good, because it is purifying. Engels makes the same point:

> That force, however, plays another role '(other than that of a diabolical power)' in history, a revolutionary role; that, in the words of Marx, it is the midwife of every old society which is pregnant with the new, that it is the instrument by the aid of which the social movement forces its way through and shatters the dead, fossilized political forms—of this there is not a word in Herr Duhring. It is only with sighs and groans that he admits the possibility that force will perhaps be necessary for the overthrow of the economic system of exploitation unfortunately, because all use of force, forsooth, demoralizes the person who uses it. And this in spite of the immense moral and spiritual impetus which has resulted from every victorious revolution! And this in Germany,

---

*Ibid., p. 39
†Mao Tse-tung, *op cit.*, p. 60.

where a violent collision—which indeed may be forced on the people—would at least have the advantage of wiping out the servility which has permeated the national consciousness as a result of the humiliation of the Thirty Years' War. And this person's mode of thought—lifeless, insipid and impotent—claims to impose itself on the most revolutionary party which history has known!*

Engels and Mao Tse-tung elevate the role of force from a necessary evil to a desirable good.

Another advocate of this doctrine who has been very influential in the modern revolutionary world is Frans Fanon of Algeria who wrote the book "The Wretched of the Earth." George Jackson, (a Black Panther and communist,) quoted Fanon: "Two men die with the stroke that slays the slave-master: the slave-master dies in a way that he can do no man any further harm; and then the slave mentality of the former victim dies."†

Violence is necessary because of the effect that it has on the character of the violent. Only through the successful use of violence can true revolutionary character be built.

These teachings of Mao Tse-tung, have contributed greatly to the formation of armed revolutionary groups throughout Southeast Asia, the Middle East and Africa, and to a lesser degree in North America and Europe.

Mao Tse-tung's attitude towards war is also reported by Nikita Khrushchev:

> I remember once in Peking, Mao and I were lying next to the swimming pool in our bathing trunks, discussing the problems of war and peace. Mao Tse-tung said to me, 'Comrade Khrushchev, what do you think? If we compare the military might of the capitalist world with that of the Socialist world, you'll see that we obviously have the advantage over our enemies. Think of how many divisions China, the USSR, and the other Socialist countries could raise.'
>
> I said, 'Comrade Mao Tse-tung, nowadays that sort of thinking is out of date. You can no longer calculate the alignment of forces on the basis of who has the most men . . . Now with the atomic bomb, the number of troops on each side makes practically no

*V.I. Lenin, The State and Revolution *op. cit.*, pp. 34–35.
†*The Black Panther,* August 28, 1971 p. 13.

difference to the alignment of real power and the outcome of a war. The more troops on a side, the more bomb fodder.'

Mao replied by trying to assure me that the atomic bomb itself was a paper tiger! 'Listen, Comrade Khrushchev,' he said. 'All you have to do is provoke the Americans into military action, and I'll give you as many divisions as you need to crush them—a hundred, two hundred, one thousand divisions.'*

## COMMUNIST RULE OVER CHINA

Mao Tse-tung has ruled China in accordance with the principle that conflict is life. The creation of conflict has been the rule since the seizure of power. This has resulted in the sacrifice of at least 34 million human lives. This is reported in the 1971 U.S. Senate document entitled "The Human Cost of Communism in China"† The report says:

> Since 1949 China has been subjected to a pattern of wave after wave of mass campaigns breaking upon the countryside and only gradually receding. These campaigns, sometimes overlapping, have followed each other in such a way as to allow few moments of calm. Mao has indeed been a proponent of permanent revolution. Each of these campaigns has claimed millions of victims; all have been infused with the Maoist belief in the desirability of struggle and the necessity for violence; some have resulted in large-scale purges or the elimination of whole groupings within the society.

The report lists some of these campaigns:

> There was the Agrarian Reform of 1949–50 which brought about the execution of several million landlords.
>
> Then came the campaign against counterrevolutionaries of 1951–52 during the first twelve months of which it was estimated that one and one-half million were executed.
>
> The 3-anti and 5-anti campaigns of 1951–53 which purged the business, finance and industrial circles with executions and a wave of suicides. All of these were linked to bandit suppression campaigns from 1949 to 1956.

*Khrushchev, *op. cit*, pp. 467, 470.
†op. cit., pp. 10, 13.

The second decade of communist power in China began with that most grandiose campaign "The Great Leap Forward" of 1958–60:

> This mobilized tens of millions of the Chinese to smelt iron in primitive and ineffective backyard furnaces (a testament of the Chairman's ignorance of the modern scientific world) and sought to push the Chinese peasants into communal-type militarized living, replete with, in some cases, separation of sexes and families, communal dining halls, and abandonment of all personal and family items. The human cost of this grandiose Maoist scheme in terms of wasted energy and resources, suffering, and death can probably never be reckoned.

## THE GREAT CULTURAL REVOLUTION

The most recent violent campaign organized by Mao was the Great Cultural Revolution. The loss of life was appalling. The U.S. Senate report stated: "There have been the struggles waged in the wake of the Cultural Revolution, such as that in Kwangsi in the summer of 1968 where an estimated 50,000 were killed in the city of Wuchow alone."

Why was the Great Cultural Revolution organized in China? I followed the reports of the different stages of the Cultural Revolution through the pages of the PEKING REVIEW while they were happening and tried to make sense of the reports. The impression was that insanity was in control in China. It is only in retrospect that we can understand the real motivation and purposes that lay behind it.

The official reasons given in the PEKING REVIEW were two-fold: 1) to purge the youth of China of their own filth (based on Mao Tse-tung's statement "Revolutionary war is an anti-toxin which purges us of our own filth). And 2) to purge the Communist Party of its accumulated filth.

The Great Cultural Revolution was directed to the purification of Chinese youth in general and the purging and purification of the Chinese Communist Party in particular. In retrospect it has also become clear that it was a conflict for control and power within the Communist Party. It was also designed to give military experience to Chinese youth.

The climax of the Great Cultural Revolution was the dethronement and downfall of Liu Shao-chi who had been the co-theorist and co-leader of Chinese Communism with Mao Tse-tung for thirty years. Liu was President of the Peoples Republic of China and his books had almost equal status with the books of Mao Tse-tung. A generation of communists was reared on his book *How to be a Good Communist.* In the pages of the PEKING REVIEW, one could observe the tidal wave of abuse rise, and finally overwhelm him. During the early stages of the campaign, he was never named. He was always referred to as the No. 1 person within the party who is following the capitalist road. Only after many months of increasing attacks did he become "the renegade, traitor and scab, Liu Shao-chi" the title now bestowed on him.

Liu's book *How to be a Good Communist* was also attacked because it concentrated on self-discipline and not on the Dictatorship of the Proletariat. The book takes the existence of the Dictatorship for granted and concentrates on instructing communists on how they must sacrifice self-interest for the Party.

I remember reading one story published in the PEKING REVIEW before the Great Cultural Revolution. A soldier in war was struck above the heart by a bullet but was unhurt because it lodged in the book *How to be a Good Communist* which the soldier carried in his tunic. How the mighty are fallen!

One charge against Liu was that he advocated "economism." This referred to promoting material rather than moral incentives for the Chinese workers. The paradox is that, while they attacked Liu, they applauded Stalin who shamelessly utilized material incentives in the Soviet Union.

A more sophisticated argument against Liu Shao-chi was that he stated that the principal contradiction in China was between the advanced social relations, socialism, and the primitive mode of production. For this reason the emphasis should be on industrialization and modern technology. This ran counter to the teachings of Mao that politics must be in command, and that the consciousness of the people was more important than technology.

## PURGING THE PARTY

One publicly announced reason for the Great Cultural Revolution was to purge the Communist Party. The officials of the Communist Party are called cadre or cadres. As the years pass, their idealism and zeal tends to fade and they become domineering and selfish. They bureaucratize and form an elite class with privileges. To avoid this, Mao maintains the party must be purged periodically so that it can be renewed and revived.

Stalin confronted the problem of how to keep the Communist Party of the Soviet Union on its toes. His solution was "selective liquidation." No party membr could feel secure since possible expulsion and liquidation hung over him like the sword of Damocles. Obviously, life in the Party was a competition for physical survival.

Mao, on the other hand, followed the ideas of Leon Trotsky. In 1924, Trotsky had complained that the Communist Party of the Soviet Union was becoming bureaucratic. He said that the students constituted the purest revolutionary elements, and he suggested that the students be mobilized and given the task of purging and purifying the Communist Party. The plan of Trotsky was not implemented in Russia, but Mao Tse-tung applied it in China 43 years later.

Mao closed the schools and urged the youth of China to dare to make revolution. He urged them to attack the strongholds of the Communist Party and its leading personalities with the only one sacrosanct individual being Mao himself. The slogan was, "Dare to struggle, dare to win." Thus, China was subjected to the ordeal of government by lynch mob.

## YOUTH PURIFICATION

The purging of the Party was not the sole purpose of the Great Cultural Revolution. It was designed to purge Chinese youth of their accumulated filth. For they were growing up without conflict and becoming selfish. They must, Mao believed, pass through the furnace of danger, privation and imminent death in order to become worthy heirs fit for their revolutionary task. Conflict was encouraged. Youthful mobs, waving the little Red book of Mao Tse-tung fought with other youthful mobs waving the same book and they sometimes fought with soldiers. Both sides, of course, professed to be the genuine followers of Mao.

It may be asked, which side did Mao prefer? The answer is that he simply did not care. Rather, it was the provision of conflict for the young which enthused him. For those who survived the conflict would be purged and purified and worthy of the title "Maoist."

Fortunately, there were a few witnesses to report the raging conflict. One of these was a British Engineer, George Watt, who went, in 1966, to Lanchow, a walled city in Western China, to supervize the construction of a textile factory which his firm, Vickers-Zinner, was building there. He saw and he suffered, but he did not understand. He was arrested and convicted by a peoples court of being a British spy. He describes some of his experiences:

> On the afternoon of December 19, 1966 I was in a small Russian-built plane somewhere over Central China and about 40 minutes' flight from my final destination, the old walled city of Lanchow.
>
> At Lanchow Airport I was met by my interpreter, Mr. Gin, who embraced me as if I were an old friend. He and his companions bowed and smiled.
>
> After dinner that first evening Mr. Gin briefed me on what I could and could not do while I was in Lanchow. It took two hours in all. I cannot recall everything he said but the main points were:
>
> I was not allowed to hold the hand of a Chinese girl or to be familiar with her. Even a friendly smile at a waitress could be misconstrued.
>
> I was not to take photographs of anything or anybody without permission. I was not to enter Chinese homes and I was not to leave the hotel without an interpreter.
>
> There was no place outside the hotel where Europeans could eat. I could go shopping only on Saturday afternoons. The hotel doors would be locked at 10 every night.

## MURDER OF CHILDREN

Towards the end of my first week in Lanchow I was taking a Sunday stroll with a British colleague, accompanied of course by Mr. Gin, along the road which led from the hotel to the city.

About a quarter of a mile from the hotel, near the bank of the Yellow River we saw a group of about a dozen Red Guards ahead of us. They were shouting, blowing whistles, and were obviously highly excited. One of them was carrying a bundle.

Suddenly he threw the bundle to the ground and they all gathered round, red books containing the thoughts of Mao raised above heads, shouting: 'Wa, wa, wa.'

Then they walked on still cheering.

The bundle was the nude body of a boy of about three years old. He was dead and had been badly burnt.

It was my first taste of the savagery which could be so suddenly unleashed in this frightening country. I felt physically sick.

Months later I was to learn that this was a fairly common form of action against 'enemies of the people.' A wife, husband, or child would be killed or badly maltreated to intimidate the offender's family.

That evening a political commissar arrived at the hotel to warn us not to mention what we had seen on the bank of the Yellow River and 'not to spread alarming rumours.'

## FATE OF CHINESE WHO ENTERTAIN FOREIGNERS

Soon I was to experience fear myself. Two senior Chinese engineers had invited all the Europeans at the Friendship Hotel—there were about 30 of us, British and German, with one or two wives and a few children—to dinner at the hotel.

It was a much better meal than we usually had there and the wine flowed. One of our hosts, who could speak English, made a speech saying the dinner was to welcome us to China.

It was a couple of days later that Mr. Gin suggested that I might like to visit the curio and antique shop in the city. It is situated in a corner of a wide open space called Anti-Revisionist Square. When we approached the shop, the square was filled with a howling mob.

Then I saw my host of two nights before. He was strung up by the neck to a lamp-post and he was dead.

I turned to Mr. Gin in horror. 'Why, why?' was all I could say.

Solemnly he told me: 'He has been punished for a number of crimes. He has taken the capitalist road and has lorded it over his comrades by *wasting public funds on high living and needlessly entertaining foreigners.*'

And all the time, as he spoke, Mr. Gin watched my face with hardly a blink of his eyes. He was trying to gauge my reaction to this ghastly scene.

I felt guilty, confused, and partly to blame for that poor man's death. I was sure I had been brought to that scene to test my reactions."

## CIVIL WAR

There had been fighting somewhere to the east of the city. We Europeans had heard rumours about it, but had deliberately avoided asking any questions.

Work at the site had been stopped and we had been told to stay in the hotel for a few days. It was sticky weather, with the temperatures soaring into the 90s.

One afternoon, a few of us had strolled into the hotel courtyard to get some fresh air. Hearing the rumble of heavy traffic on the road outside, we looked through the gates and saw a parade of grey, open lorries packed with Red Guards carrying home-made spears.

There must have been 50 vehicles. They came trundling by about 20 feet apart at about five miles an hour. And across the radiator of each truck was lashed a human being. Some trucks had two people. All had been spreadeagled diagonally and tied down with wire or rope.

Other captives in groups of two, three or four, had been strapped to the backs or roofs of each driving cab.

They were young and old, women as well as men. Some had been wounded. Many were in a state of complete collapse."

We were in the middle of a vicious battle for power between Mao Tse-tung and his one-time friend, President Liu Shao-Chi.

Tens of thousands of workers from various parts of China had been drafted in to work on the vast complex of plants outside the city. . . . Food was becoming short.

The food shortage was so severe that the peasants hid much of their produce in mountain caves instead of giving it to the State. The explosion came when some site workers, discovering these food caches killed six or seven peasants.

In the next few days I watched with mesmerised fascination the preparations for a civil war. One day at the site I found the workers cutting up narrow piping into six-foot lengths to use as spear shafts.

This was piping that had already been fitted and installed. I almost went berserk. 'Are you crazy?' I yelled. 'These are the arteries of this site . . . if you cut them out you kill this site.'

I was ignored. They carried on fashioning the pipe lengths into crude spears by lashing screwdrivers, chisels, and other sharp tools to the ends.

On approaching the hotel that evening, I saw hundreds of people making large blocks out of mud, stone, and concrete. They used them to block up the ground floor windows and doors of their homes and shops. Men were hauling up baskets of stones to the roofs to lay out on the parapets for action. Rope ladders dangling from upper-story windows showed how they were entering and leaving their fortress homes.

"Later that night we heard the noise of hammering metal. In the back courtyard of the hotel was an anvil and a portable charcoal forge. Around them were the hotel waiters and cooks—and they too were making spears. Broom handles and lengths of bamboo were being used for shafts and the heads were being fashioned from the tops of nearby railings. Some simply had kitchen knives and forks lashed to the end.

This do-it-yourself weapon-making went on for two or three days until one morning we were awakened at about four o'clock by the most terrifying screaming.

From our bedroom windows we saw about a dozen fires on the outskirts of the city. We could only look and wonder.

This was quite obviously a fight between the city folk and the workers from the plants. But the thing that really astounded me was the fact that both sides were backed up by troops. Soldiers from the city were firing on those who were normally stationed out at the sites. And the 'site' soldiers were firing back.

The battle swayed along the road outside the hotel for two or three days. Dead and injured lay all over the place. During a lull, I made a dash for the shop at the entrance to the hotel to get some sweets and fruit for the children and some beer for ourselves.

The old man who ran it was dead. The inside had been wrecked and the old man, a spear driven right through his stomach, was suspended in the space of the counter flap by the ends of the spear being placed on each side of the counter.

He had once owned that shop and, when the communist revolution took over, had been allowed to remain as manager.

THE THREE FACES OF REVOLUTION

> I had to get my family out of this mad, mad country. They could not take this sort of thing much longer, and I could not stand watching their misery.*

The fighting as observed by George Watt was part of a massive civil war that was raging throughout China. The full military dimensions of the Great Cultural Revolution have only become known as reports have slowly filtered out. Some of these reports are from Red Guards who participated in the fighting and escaped to Quemoy or Hong Kong when the People's Army was restoring order in 1968. From such reports it is apparent that massive armies, numbering tens of millions, fought with each other, often with primitive homemade weapons, but sometimes with light machine guns, heavy machine guns, mortars, and 60-mm artillery, and that the casualties were very heavy, possibly in the millions.

The communist authorities told us that the Great Cultural Revolution was a fight, but this statement was interpreted as a symbolic reference to doctrinal and psychlogical conflict. CHINA PICTORIAL (Vol. 2, 1967) contains the double-page headline, "Chairman Mao Reviews Eleven Million Mighty Cultural Revolutionary *Fighting Forces*" above the picture of Mao Tse-tung and Lin Piao. The words "fighting forces" were meant quite literally.

Details of the fighting on the Island of Amoy are described by one of the Red Guard leaders, Chen Yung-sheng, who escaped by swimming to Quemoy when the People's Revolutionary Army was restoring order in 1968. This book contains his answers to questions concerning events on the mainland during the Great Cultural Revolution asked by Japanese scholars, industrialists, businessmen and newsmen during a visit he made to Japan from January 22–26, 1969.

Some of the details of the fighting revealed by Chen are:

> On March 7, 1967, under the sponsorship of several Red Guard leaders from the Amoy University, including Su Hui-ming, Wu Kuo-yao, Shen Kuo-wei and Wu Mo-sui, all the Red Guard organizations in Amoy and its suburban areas which shared the same

*George Watt, *The Sun* (Sydney, Australia), Jan. 4–8, 11, 1971

political view were merged together to form a new organization—the 'Promote Alliance Faction'. It had about 200,000 members. Three weeks before that (on February 16), our rival organization —the 'Revolutionary Alliance Faction'—was established in the same way. Its leaders, including Lin Chin-ming and Wu Lien-kuang, were also students of the Amoy University. . . . In the wake of the annexations, armed clashes began to take place between the two groups and gradually became violent.

On July 31 of the same year, because one of our members, a girl student in the Amoy University, was arrested by the 'Revolutionary Alliance Faction' and taken to its headquarters at the foot of the Wulao Mountain in suburban Amoy for torture, our leader Wu Kuo-yao led several thousand persons to surround its headquarters. But, before we could rescue her, we were counter-surrounded by members of the 'Revolutionary Alliance Faction,' of course, we refused to surrender. Soon afterwards, our reinforcement totalling about 70,000 persons, including students, factory workers and shop workers, arrived and re-surrounded the other side. Thus they surrounded us and we surrounded them. It was difficult to say who surrounded whom. Nearly all the Red Guards in Amoy were mobilized. The battlefield was extended to the Wulao Mountain. The clash lasted three days, resulting in our victory. The leader of the other side, Lin Chin-ming, was killed in the conflict. After the battle, all the remnants of the 'Revolutionary Alliance Faction' in Amoy fled to the countryside. . . . After its withdrawal to the countryside, the 'Revolutionary Alliance Faction' was not only not reconciled to its defeat but, on the contrary, had always wanted to 'liberate' the whole Amoy island. Therefore, on the morning of August 19, they launched a large-scale counter-attack against us. The weapons they used included light machineguns, heavy machineguns, mortars and 60-mm artillery.

"Question: How many Red Guards were killed in the armed clashes in Amoy?

"Answer: Because some corpses were collected or destroyed by the other side, it was impossible to count the actual number of bodies. I can give you an example to show how heavy the casualties were. After a battle at the end of December, 1967, we collected the corpses on the battlefield and placed them in the classrooms of the Mingli Elementary School in Amoy. There were so many corpses that every classroom was jam packed. The Mingli Elementary School was on Shengping Road and was the best equipped elementary school in Amoy. . . . The fact that all the classrooms of such a big school were filled with corpses shows how high the number of deaths was."

The role of the communist leadership in encouraging these battles was revealed by this statement:

"On August 21, Chen Po-ta, head of the Central Cultural Revolution Group in Peiping, expressed his attitude toward this armed clash. He said: 'The Promote Alliance Faction is a rebel faction and the Revolutionary Alliance Faction is a conservative faction.' I did not know what his motive was in saying this, but one thing I did know: He encouraged us to continue the armed fightings and tried to use us to defeat the 'Revolutionary Alliance Faction.' "

If we consider such battles raging over the entire communist mainland, spread over a period of two years, we gain some idea of the magnitude of the slaughter. Were the survivors purified?

## THE SINO-SOVIET CONFLICT

Long ago Mao Tse-tung decided that the leaders of the Soviet Union had forsaken socialism and the pathway to communism. He is convinced that they have returned to capitalism and become "imperialist." The term he uses to describe the Soviet regime is "Social Imperialism."

The use of the term "imperialist" has ominous overtones as it signifies an expansionist and aggressive nature which threatens all neighbor nations. The use of the term implies that China is in danger of military aggression from the Soviet Union.

The Chinese Communist view of the Soviet Union is stated by Chiao Kuan-hua, leader of the Communist Chinese delegation to the United Nations in a speech to the U.N. General Assembly, November 26, 1971. He states:

The Soviet representative tried hard to deny that the Soviet Union is a superpower and that, like the United States, the Soviet Union attempts to monopolize nuclear weapons and push its policies of nuclear blackmail and nuclear threats against other countries. Such an attempt is utterly futile. Everyone knows that it is precisely the Soviet Union and the United States, which possess large quantities of nuclear weapons, that have up to now obstinately refused to undertake the obligation not to be the first to use nuclear weapons, and they have continued to maintain large numbers of armed forces and military bases on foreign soil, including nuclear armed forces and nuclear bases. The Partial Nuclear Test Ban Treaty and Treaty on Non-Proliferation of Nuclear Weapons jointly devised by the United States and the Soviet Union are something entirely imposed on others; they are aimed at monopolizing nuclear weapons and controlling other countries. We can never agree to them. The Soviet leadership has carried out aggression, subversion, control and interference against other countries. This is clearly known to the representatives of many countries present here. China had her own experience in this respect, and here I will not speak at length about the relevant history. Countless facts have shown that what the Soviet leadership is practising is certainly not socialism but, as Lenin put it, socialism in words, imperialism in deeds, that is, social-imperialism.

It appears that not only is there a contradiction between the Soviet Union and Communist China but that it has become, in Mao's view the most intense contradiction. His attitude to contradictions is expressed: "Among the numerous big and small contradictions determined or influenced by the basic contradiction, some become intensified, some are temporarily or partially resolved or mitigated, and some emerge anew; consequently the process reveals itself as consisting of different stages. If people do not pay attention to the stages in the process of development of a thing, they cannot deal properly with its contradictions."*

Mao has always tried to discern the most intense contradiction at each stage so that he can concentrate against it even if it means making concessions to opponents with whom the contradiction is temporarily or partially mitigated. He explains this by discussing the history of the relationship of the Chinese Communist Party to Chiang Kai-shek and the Kuomintang. He states:

As to the Communist Party, no matter in which period, it always sides with the great masses of people to oppose imperialism and feudalism; in the present period of the Anti-Japanese War, because

*Mao Tse-tung, On Contradiction, op. cit., pp. 26–27

> the Kuomintang shows itself in favor of resisting Japan, the Communist Party has adopted a mild policy toward it and toward the domestic feudal forces. Because of these conditions, an alliance of the two parties is brought about at one time, and a struggle at another; and even during the period of the alliance between the two parties, there also exists a complicated state of affairs in which alliance and struggle take place at the same time.*

The conviction that the conflict with the Soviet Union is the most intense contradiction at present accounts for the change in attitude of the leaders of the Chinese Communist Party towards President Nixon and the United States as revealed by the invitation to President Nixon to visit China and the present "detente". Mao's conviction that socialism must replace capitalism has not changed. This will be achieved when the socialist "gun" is sufficiently powerful. In practice this means the Chinese Communist gun as they recognize few other regimes as "socialist." It takes time to develop the massive military might, and strategic mobility is required. Given time, the thermonuclear capacity and logistic mobility can be achieved. The purity of purpose of the Chinese masses can be maintained by a massive indoctrination in the Thoughts of Mao Tse-tung even in the event of Mao's death.

The danger is that the Soviet Union might decide to destroy China's thermonuclear factories by a pre-emptive strike during the present period of vulnerability.. In an attempt to discourage this overtures towards the other imperialist, the United States, have been made.

Some communist revolutionaries have interpreted Mao's concessions as a betrayal of the revolution. Others, such as the Black Panthers, understand and commend:

> For some 50 years, Mao Tse-tung has worked diligently and unremittingly for the Chinese revolution; theorizing about its many stages and eventually carrying them through to completion, with the period of socialist construction still in progress. It's been said that in the 30's and late 20's (the lean years of the Chinese revolution), Chairman Mao was right when most others were wrong, invariably advancing along the correct path, depending

*Ibid., p. 30

upon the specific historical conditions in China at a particular period in time. After half a century of struggle, a man like Chairman Mao does not abrogate his principles overnight.

In 1945, Mao Tse-tung went to Chungking, sat, talked, and toasted with Chiang Kai-shek. Did Chairman Mao betray the revolution when he did this? Certainly not. He simply realized logically that the People's Liberation Army was not yet strong enough to defeat Chiang. So he sat and talked and stalled for time. Four years later he talked with a gun and seized the time. Chairman Mao knew exactly what to do and when to do it. He moved with the ebb and flow of the struggle. He won; Chiang lost. The reality of China at that time proved Chairman Mao correct. In view of the changing world situation, the Communist Party of China must keep pace with the reality of the situation, or face the possibility of becoming obsolete and anachronistic.*

In the mind of Mao, the same fate will inevitably befall the U.S.A. as that which befell the China of Chiang Kai-shek.

*The Black Panther, April 15, 1972.

# THE BLACK PANTHER PARTY     6

The power of the Thought of Mao Tse-tung is shown by the emergence of the Black Panther Party within the United States.

This party claims to be communist: the leaders take pride in this classification. They resent with justification, that many refuse to take their claim to be communists seriously and continue to regard them as racist gangsters. The Black Panther Party claims to be the Marxist-Leninist vanguard of the forces of revolution within the U.S.A.

Huey Newton, Founder, Minister of Defense, and Supreme Commander of the Black Panther Party, stated at Boston College November 18, 1970: "The Black Panther Party is a Marxist-Leninist Party, because we follow the dialectical method and we integrate theory with practice."* Marxist-Leninist is, of course, a synonym for communist.

*The Black Panther, January 23, 1971.

*103*

The dominant doctrinal influence on the Black Panthers is the "Thought of Mao Tse-tung," and, their major textbook is the little red book *Quotations from Chairman Mao Tse-tung.*

The Black Panther Party was formed by Huey Newton and Bobby Seale in Oakland, California, in 1966. Seale tells the story of how they secured their first funds with the help of Mao's little red book.

The Red Book became such a key thing with the Cultural Revolution that was going on in China, and Huey says, 'You know what? I know how we can make some money to buy some guns.' I said, 'How?' 'We can sell these Red Books. I know that many black brothers on the block wouldn't even buy a Red Book, but at the same time I do know that many of those leftist radicals at "Cal" will buy the Red Book.' Huey went on to talk about the 26,000 person community at "Cal", and how maybe a third or maybe a quarter of them were radicals or liberals who'd be interested in the Red Book since it was being publicized so heavily.

The next thing you know, Huey asked me, 'How much money do you have?' And I said, 'Well, I have about 45 dollars or 50 dollars on me.' He said, 'Well, let's go buy a batch of Red Books and go up to "Cal" and sell them. I bet we can get a dollar apiece for them.' I said, 'Right on, brother.'

You know what we did? We went over to the China Book Store in San Francisco and we bought up two batches of the Red Books, 30 in a package, and got back over there and we sold them at "Cal" campus some Red Books. We sold them Red Books inside of an hour. That shocked us. At a dollar apiece. So we took all that money and we went back to the bookstore and bought all the Red Books the man had left in the store. I think we had three or four more packages. We bought out all the Red Books. Paying 30 cents for them. We told them, 'We are the Black Panther Party,' and could an organization get a discount, and the next thing I know, we had enough money to buy two shotguns.

We got up to Cal the next day at ten A.M., right around the time the student traffic gets heavy in front of Sather Gate. Huey would be saying with his sales pitch, 'Power comes out of the barrel of a gun. Quotations from Chairman Mao Tse-tung. Get your Red Book.' I would say, 'All you free speechers up here who lost Mario Savio, read the Red Book and do it like the Red Guards did it. We made our party over $170.

And if you ever had a 'Freedom Now' feeling, you would have sure got it if you saw how we took off to buy some shotguns.

So we sold them Red Books and made the money. We used that money to buy guns. Me and Huey and the brothers in the core organization used the Red Books and spread it throughout the organization. Because Huey made it a point that the principles and the revolutionary principles concisely cited in the Red Book should be applied whenever they can be applied . . . So, from there we righteously used the Red Book. Because we talked about it, and Huey had us practicing the principles. And from Fanon, and from Malcolm X—his autobiography and other material on him. Huey integrated all these principles of the brother revolutionaries. We taught from all these materials, and every time we ran into something with Che Guevara too.

"He knew the Red Book sideways, backward and forward. You got brothers in the Party that got to know the Red Book cattycorner . . . 'The Red Book and what else? The gun! The Red Book and what else? The gun!' That's what Huey would say.*

The Black Panthers have studied the little red book, and Huey Newton has understood and applied its lessons. He constantly uses the terminology of Mao and applies it creatively. This is illustrated by his reaction to the quarrel that developed with Eldridge Cleaver.

To illustrate: as the Black Panther Party grew Newton and Seale were joined as leaders by Eldridge Cleaver who became the Minister of Information. For a time this triumvirate got along well and the Party prospered. In February, 1971, a bitter quarrel erupted between Newton and Cleaver, resulting in the equivalent of gang warfare with casualties.

Discussing this conflict, Newton explained that he welcomed all contradictions, because it was only through resolution of contradiction that "qualitative transformation" was attained. To those unfamiliar with dialectical terminology this is nonsense. But to Communists, it was a perceptive and significant statement, and Newton used the conflict with Eldridge Cleaver brilliantly, indeed. Huey Newton is one of the most effective Marxist-Leninists of this era. The qualitative transformation caused by his conflict with Cleaver was that the Black Panther Party changed its public

*Ramparts, October 26, 1968, pp. 30, 32.

emphasis from killing police to helping the black community. The slogan "off the pig" was replaced by "serve the people." Newton had applied the lesson taught by Mao.

Newton's Black Panther Party has expertly applied the Leninist formula, "Find out what people want; promise it to them, and go to work to get it for them so that you can come to power over them."

Though the Panthers are orthodox communists in some ways they also remain a revolutionary group with a specialized interest: the American Black Community. The Black Panthers revealed their program for appealing to this segment of the population in a 1966 platform called: "What we want—what we believe." It was designed to fit the desires of the black community.

1. We want freedom. We want power to determine the destiny of our Black Community. We believe that black people will not be free until we are able to determine our destiny.

2. We want full employment for our people. We believe that the federal government is responsible and obligated to give every man employment or a guaranteed income. We believe that if the White American businessmen will not give full employment then the means of production should be taken from the businessmen and placed in the community so that the people of the community can organize and employ all of its people and give a high standard of living.

3. We want an end to the robbery by the CAPITALIST of our Black Community. We believe that this racist government has robbed us and now we are demanding the overdue debt of forty acres and two mules. Forty acres and two mules was promised 100 years ago as restitution for slave labor and mass murder of black people. We will accept the payment in currency which will be distributed to our many communities. The Germans are now aiding the Jews in Israel for the genocide of the Jewish people. The Germans murdered six million Jews. The American racist has taken part in the slaughter of over fifty million black people; therefore we feel that this is a modest demand that we make.

4. We want decent housing fit for shelter of human beings. We believe that if the white landlords will not give decent housing to our black community, then the housing and the land should be made into cooperatives so that our community, with government aid, can build and make decent housing for its people.

5. We want education for our people that exposes the true nature of this decadent American society. We want education that teaches us our true history and our role in the present-day society.

We believe in an educational system that will give to our people a knowledge of self. If a man does not have knowledge of himself and his position in society and the world, then he has little chance to relate to anything else.

6. We want all black men to be exempt from military service.

We believe that Black people should not be forced to fight in the military service to defend a racist government that does not protect us. We will not fight and kill other people of color in the world who, like black people, are being victimized by the white racist government of America. We will protect ourselves from the force and violence of the racist police and the racist military, by whatever means necessary.

7. We want an immediate end to POLICE BRUTALITY and MURDER of black people.

We believe we can end police brutality in our community by organizing black self-defense groups that are dedicated to defending our black community from racist police oppression and brutality. The Second Amendment to the Constitution of the United States gives a right to bear arms. We therefore believe that all black people should arm themselves for self-defense.

8. We want freedom for all black men held in federal, state, county and city prisons and jails.

9. We want all black people when brought to trial to be tried in court by a jury of their peer group or people from their black communities, as defined by the Constitution of the United States.

We believe that the courts should follow the United States Constitution so that black people will receive fair trials. The 14th Amendment of the U.S. Constitution gives a man a right to be tried by his peer group. A peer is a person from a similar economic, social, religious, geographical, environmental, historical and racial background. To do this the court will be forced to select a jury from the black community from which the black defendant came. We have been, and are being tried by all-white juries that have no understanding of the "average reasoning man" of the black community.

10. We want land, bread, housing, education, clothing, justice and peace. And as our major political objective, a United Nations-supervised plebiscite to be held throughout the colony in which only black colonial subjects will be allowed to participate, for the

purpose of determining the will of black people as to their national destiny.

This was not their final program. Newton is quite frank on this score for he classifies it as only a survival program which allows the Black Panther Party to survive and work for the revolution.

The Black Panther Party following standard Communist organizational models, is operated in accordance with Communist "Democratic Centralism." In the words of one Panther leader:

> Party members should know that our unity is based upon the principles of democratic centralism. It is dialectical in appearance and in essence. It is the pillar upon which rests our ability to survive, function and develop as a dynamic force, regardless of internal contradictions or external attacks. Democratic centralism applies to every member of the organization—community workers, Panthers, officers and members of the central committee. All must adhere to this principle.*

The Black Panther Party is an unorthodox communist group in some aspects. For instance, the Black Panther Party admits only blacks to membership. Nevertheless, the Black Panthers are not racists because this decision is not based on racial superiorty. It is merely tactical since they believe this membership provision enhances the groups appeal to militant blacks. Nevertheless, the Panthers racial "exclusiveness" flies in the face of other more traditional, communist groups which attempt to make the Party appeal as broad as possible.

The decision of the Black Panthers to utilize the force of nationalism has also been the cause of considerable dissension in communist ranks. The Progressive Labor Party in particular has objected to it. The leaders of P.L. claim that social class is dominant and all nationalism is reactionary—a view which led them to reject the claim of the Black Panthers to constitute the revolutionary vanguard.

The Black Panther Party claims that it is communist; it acknowledges and applies the philosophy of Dialectical Materialism; it is organized in accordance with Democratic Centralism; it prac-

*Randy Williams, The Black Panther, March 8, 1971.

tices Proletarian Internationalism and is busily working to promote violent revolution in the United States. These facts justify its claim to be a communist party. Nevertheless, when judged by classical Marxist-Leninist doctrines, it is heretical on one fundamental point.

The basic Marxist idea has always been that the working class or proletariat is the primary revolutionary force. The Black Panthers do not accept this for they believe that the "Lumpen Proletariat" has now assumed the primary revolutionary role.

Communist doctrines identify the lumpen proletariat as consisting of "The dregs" of the working class, made up of the unemployed, unemployable and criminal elements. This group is considered unfit for revolutionary discipline by the orthodox Marxist-Leninist. The Black Panthers claim that the unemployed, outcasts and criminals will make the revolution. Newton even used the doctrines of dialectical materialism to reach this conclusion in a speech reported in *The Black Panther* newspaper:

In 1917, an event occurred in the Soviet Union that was called a revolution. In 1917, the Soviet Union was basically an agricultural society, that of a very large peasantry. There was a set of social conditions existing there at that time that were responsible for the development of a small industrial base. The people who worked in this industrial base, they called them proletarians. Lenin, using Marx's theory, saw the trends because he was not a historical materialist, he was a dialectical materialist, and, therefore, he was very interested in the ever changing status of things. He saw that while the proletarians were a minority at that time, in 1917, they had the potentiality to carry out a revolution because their class was on the upsurge and the peasantry was on the decline. The proletarians were destined to be a popular force. They also carried the necessary properties to carry out a revolution that resembled a socialist revolution.

In this country, the Black Panther Party, taking careful note of the dialectical method, taking careful note of the social trends and the ever changing nature of things, sees that while the lumpen proletarians are the minority and the proletarians, the majority, we also see that technology is developing at such a rapid rate that we'll start with automation, go to cybernation, and then go from there probably into technocracy. . . . If the ruling circle remains in power, the proletarian worker, the proletarian working class, will definitely be on the decline, because they will be unemployables and, therefore, swell the ranks of the Lumpens, who are unemployables. Unemployables because the ruling circle does not need them any more. So every worker is in jeopardy because of the rule of the ruling circle. And this is why we say that the lumpen proletarians carry the potentiality for revolution and, in the near future, will be the popular class, the majority.*

In another portion of the very same speech, Newton noted that the Black Panther Party had changed drastically from its beginning days in 1966 when the organization was "black nationalist" in orientation. Now, Newton said, the Panthers are "revolutionary intercommunalists".

Nationality, as a concept, was viewed as no longer meaningful. People were either living in "liberated communities" (mainland China, or North Vietnam, for instance) or they were living under capitalist rule. Huey Newton made clear that the objective of the Black Panthers in the 1970's would be to work for the "liberation" of its communities in the United States.

There was a very practical conclusion to this theoretical discussion. At the time Newton made this speech, Eldridge Cleaver was still a Black Panther in good standing. He was anxious to return from Algeria to work for revolution in the U.S. To do this, Cleaver needed a sanctuary where he could be safe from American police. "Liberated communities" would mean the existence of sanctuaries in the ghetto where the Black Panthers would be the de facto government.

The Black Panthers had been working to this end for some time and had adopted the slogan "community control of the police". If the city or state police were not allowed in a black community, the Black Panthers were confident they could become the de facto government.

This plan was advocated at a conference for a United Front against Fascism which the Black Panthers conducted in California, July 18–20, 1969. At this conference, Attorney William Kunstler made a speech applauding the killing of white police by black mobs and informed the blacks that they had a political right

*Huey Newton, The Black Panther, January, 23, 1971.

to shoot any white policeman who set foot in the black areas. If white policemen faced death, they would cease to enter the ghettos and these would become sanctuaries for black revolutionaries.

A colleague of mine attended the conference and recorded Kunstler's speech. This is the complete text of that speech delivered on July 19, 1969, in Oakland, California.

Tonight I was asked to talk about the right to self-defense from a legal point of view. Because I am not wholly a lawyer in a nonpolitical sense, I want to talk about it from two points of view: legal and political. The law is simple. The law is that every man has the right in every state to defend his home, his life, person, and the lives and persons of those he loves or has a duty to protect from any molestation by any person, whether he is wearing a uniform or not. That's the law, the simple law. It is in existence in the State of California, the State of New York, and all the states in between and out to Hawaii, and up to Alaska.

Now from the political point of view the black communities around the United States have learned, and hopefully many more will learn, that this is a political weapon as well as a legal weapon. It does no good to hear a lawyer tell you, you have the right to self-defense if you do not understand politically what self-defense is.

One community in the United States learned this lesson well, and I think to talk about it is to talk about Oakland, Harlem, Bedford-Stuyvesant, Watts, and so on. That community is Plainfield, New Jersey. You will remember during the Newark rebellion in Plainfield, New Jersey, some 40 Garand M1 rifles were found missing from the Armory. (Applause) The governor of New Jersey, Richard Hughes, ordered the police to search every home in the central ward of Plainfield, the black ghetto of Plainfield, to find those missing Garand rifles. Three hundred police—state police, city police—broke into every black home in the central ward to try to find those guns. I am happy to say that not a single gun was found. (Applause) What happened after that was, with the exception of one more episode which I will tell you about in a moment, the police structure in Plainfield has not molested the black community. There has not been a white policeman in the central ward of Plainfield since July of 1967. (Applause)

Now the other episode in Plainfield which made it certain that this would be so, occurred some weeks after the theft of the guns.

One white policeman by the name of John Gleason moved into the central ward of Plainfield on a Saturday afternoon. He marched down a street leading under a railroad underpass and then he shot a black man by the name of Bobby Lee Williams through the stomach. Bobby Lee Williams fell to the ground at this intersection near the railroad underpass. Gleason began to retreat out of the ghetto. He was followed by a crowd of black men and women, and a block and a half past the intersection he was stomped to death. (prolonged applause) In my opinion he deserved that death. (Applause)

Now these are words which I might never have said several years ago until I lived a little longer and spent a little more time watching what happens in the black ghettos of the metropolitan areas of this country. Gleason signed his death warrant when he shot Bobby Lee Williams, an unarmed man, through the stomach. *The crowd, justifiably, without the necessity of a trial, and in the most dramatic way possible, stomped him to death* (emphasis added). The reason was one that comes back from 400 years—from the power structures that have preyed upon the ghettos the way vultures prey on meat. This is a sad story of the control of the black community. The right to self-defense legally is tied up intimately with the right of self-protection of the black ghetto. Without that self-protection, the black ghetto is at the mercy of whatever power structure happens to sit in the city halls throughout this country. The policeman, with the modern armory which he possesses, with his immunity, essentially to prosecution for whatever he does, can only be stopped in one way: if he knows that he might fall like Gleason if he violates the rights of black men, women, and children in the ghetto areas of the United States. (Applause)

There is only one way to let him know that, and that is to be in a position to retaliate if the community is invaded.

You have a perfect right legally to possess certain weapons. I won't go into the nature of each one—you know it as well as I do, but in most states a weapon that cannot be hidden on the person, with the exception of certain automatic rifles, can be legally maintained by you. That goes for semi-automatic carbines, ordinary rifles, of whatever caliber. If the power structure knows that you are determined to use that piece if your community is invaded, if people you love or respect or who are merely your sisters and brothers are being unjustly persecuted, victimized and destroyed by police, you have the right to use whatever force is necessary to prevent that depredation of human rights.

It is hard for lawyers sometimes, like myself, who come out of the middle class, who have come out of an environment which is one in which language such as I am using tonight was not what we learned. But life teaches many lessons, as most of you know, and after you have lived awhile and after you have seen what happens in ghetto after ghetto, then you begin to understand sometimes that fear of retaliation is possible, until we reach the millennium, the only fear that prevents those who prey on the oppressed from going too far. It won't stop them entirely, that would be asking too much, but it will slow them down, and in Plainfield it did stop them. It cost a grievous bullet wound in Bobby Lee Williams' stomach; it cost the conviction for murder of a man and a woman who were convicted for the murder of John Gleason and whose appeals are pending. Bobby Lee Williams, because he refused to testify for the state at those trials, has just been indicted for an attempt to murder John Gleason, although it is hard to realize how you an attempt to murder somebody when you are lying on the ground with a 38-caliber bullet in your guts, which is exactly what the position of Bobby Lee Williams was. That case goes to trial this September.

I would just like to add a few words before I quit, on this subject of self-defense. The Black Panther Party, as you all know, is named the Black Panther Party for Self-Defense; one of the cardinal principles which I have learned to regard as one of the most important, because it is most important, is to secure your community. Sometimes it is difficult to march ahead when you have a fear-ridden community that winces every time a siren goes down the street. Sometimes it is difficult to operate as human beings when every knock on the door might bring the pig inside. Often it is almost impossible to live knowing that you are almost an outlaw in the old English sense where every man could take your life without penalty or fear. It is difficult to live that way, and yet as most of you know much better than I, that is the way life in the ghetto runs in this day and age, in America 1969. If you have the power to defend yourself by weapons that are legal, then you have the power to start to rid the ghetto of the overriding fear of invasion that paralyzes so much action. You have the power to put an end to one of the chief drawbacks of all black communities—the control of the black community by the white policeman.

Now I say to you, and I'm speaking both as a lawyer and as a human being, that what I am advocating here is perfectly legal; it is perfectly in the American tradition; it is in the tradition of all men who respect themselves and their families and their friends are

# THE THREE FACES OF REVOLUTION

those who share their common scene in society; that you must stand ready until a better age arrives to protect yourself, your community, your friends, your lives, your property, and the very things that give life meaning. You must be able to stand as a man and a woman, and if you have to, it is better where it is necessary to retaliate, than to bend the head or bare the back for one more minute. One more minute of back bending, one more minute of scraping to the voice of white authority, is one minute too much. You cannot afford to spend that minute. You must stand up to defend yourself. And if you are ready, I hope that you won't have to. But don't shrink if you have to. It is almost worse to be ready and able to defend yourself, and to freeze on the trigger when the time comes, because then you will have told the power structure that they need not fear you, and you open up the whole sad trail of misery and depredation that has characterized life on this continent for so many years. Power to the people.

After this conference, the Black Panthers organized fronts which they called National Committees to Combat Fascism (NCCF). The objective of these committees was to secure community control of the police. At this point, some of the white supporters of the Panthers parted company with them. These white radicals claimed community control of the police should be advocated for black communities only. The Black Panthers however, thought such obvious partisanship would weaken their case so they insisted that advocacy be universal.

Berkeley was chosen as the city in which they would attempt to establish a black sanctuary by legal means. The National Committee to Combat Fascism secured 15,000 signatures to place on the April 6, 1971, ballot a proposal to establish community control of the police. This proposal called for the abolition of the Berkeley police force and the division of Berkeley into three areas: 1) the black area; 2) the university area; and 3) the white area. Each area would then select its police from the residents of the area. The population of Berkeley was 113,000, with about 30,000 blacks.

The Panthers were confident that if the vote was favorable, they would control the police in the black area. A sanctuary would then exist because police from neighboring areas would have no jurisdiction in the black area.

However, the proposal was defeated by 33,712 votes to 16,142,

*114*

with the black community voting against it overwhelmingly. The claim of the Black Panthers to represent the Black Community was proved fallacious.

In Algiers, Cleaver was ruling dictatorially; he operated a state within a state. His power was unrestrained. For instance, when Timothy Leary, the drug cultist, escaped from a California prison, he took refuge with Cleaver in Algiers. He and Cleaver disagreed concerning the use of drugs so Cleaver placed him under arrest. There was no indictment, no trial, no due process. Cleaver delivered the verdict and his henchmen carried it out.

The conflict between Huey Newton and Eldridge Cleaver erupted with the unexpected violence of an earthquake. Shortly before the break, most of the leading Panthers in America were either in prison or out on bail. Huey Newton was out on bail awaiting a second trial for the alleged killing of an Oakland policeman. Bobby Seale was on trial for the murder of an informer in the Panther ranks in Connecticut, and twenty-one Panthers were on trial in New York for conspiracy to commit violence. Some of the imprisoned Panthers wrote a letter to the Weatherman people which was critical of party leadership, and they were expelled from the party. Two Panthers out on bail, Michael Cetawayo Tabor and Richard Daruba Moore, absconded with Newton's secretary, Connie Matthews Dabor. Newton contended that these actions jeopardized all Panther prisoners, the lives of Bobby Seale and himself, and placed a burden on all Panthers on trial. He classified them as counter-revolutionary renegades and expelled them from the party. Cleaver, however, protested. Shortly thereafter, a public quarrel between Newton and Cleaver took place on radio and television. The vials of wrath were thereby opened and each expelled the supporters of the other from the party. Execution squads were organized by each side to make the expulsions permanent.

Newton attempted a Marxist analysis of the conflict. He did not merely criticize Cleaver, he criticized the Black Panther Party and redirected its program. In an article entitled, "On the Defection of Eldridge Cleaver from the Black Panther Party and the Defection of the Black Panther Party from the Black Community," he stated:

As dialectical materialists we recognize that contradictions can lead to development. The internal struggle of opposites based upon their unity causes matter to have motion as a part of the process of development. We recognize that nothing in nature stands outside of dialectics, even the Black Panther Party. But we welcome these contradictions, because they clarify and advance our struggle. We had a contradiction with our former Minister of Information, Eldridge Cleaver. But we understand this as necessary to our growth. Out of this contradiction has come new growth and a new return to the original vision of the party.

The original vision of the Party was to develop a lifeline to the people, by serving their needs and defending them against their oppressors who come to the community in many forms . . . We knew that this strategy would raise the consciousness of the people and also give us their support. Then, if we were driven underground by the oppressors, the people would support us and defend us.

For a time the Black Panther Party lost its vision and defected from the community. With the defection of Eldridge Cleaver, however, we can move again to a full scale development of our original vision and come out of the twilight zone which the Party has been in during the recent past.

The only reason that the Party is still in existence at this time, and the only reason that we have been able to survive the repression of the Party and murders of some of our most advanced comrades is because of the Ten-Point Program—our survival program.

When we formed the Party, we did so because we wanted to put theory and practice together, in a systematic manner. We did this through our basic Ten-Point Program.

We realized at a very early point in our development, that revolution is a process . . . This process moves in a dialectical manner and we understand the struggle of the opposites based upon their unity.

A lot of so-called revolutionaries simply do not understand the statement by Chairman Mao that 'Political power grows out of the barrel of a gun.' They thought Chairman Mao said political power *is* the gun, but the emphasis is on grows. The culmination of political power is the ownership and control of the land and the institutions thereon, so that you can then get rid of the gun. That is why Chairman Mao makes the statement that, 'We are advocates of the abolition of war, we do not want war; but war can only be abolished through war, and in order to get rid of the gun, it is necessary to take up the gun.'

Under the influence of Eldridge Cleaver the Party gave the community no alternative for dealing with us, except by picking up the gun. This move was reactionary simply because the community was not at that point. Instead of being a cultural cult group, we became, by that act, a revolutionary cult group.

This structure can only exist with the support of the people and it can only get its support through serving them. This is why we have the service to the people program - the most important thing in the Party. We will serve their needs, so that they can survive through this oppression. Then when they are ready to pick up the gun, serious business will happen. Eldridge Cleaver influenced us to isolate ourselves from the Black community. We had all sorts of profanity in our paper and every other word which dropped from our lips was profane.

The correct handling of a revolution is not to offer the people an 'either-or' ultimatum. We must instead gain the support of the people through serving their needs. Then when the police or any other agency of repression tries to destroy the program, the people will move to a higher level of consciousness and action.

So the Black Panther Party has reached a contradiction with Eldridge Cleaver and he has defected from the Party, because we would not order everyone into the streets tomorrow to make a revolution . . . This contradiction and conflict may seem unfortunate to some, but it is part of the dialectical process. The resolution of this contradiction has freed us from incorrect analyses and emphases.

We are now free to move toward the building of a community structure which will become a true voice of the people, promoting their interests in many ways. We can continue to push our basic survival program. We can continue to serve the people as advocates of their true interests. We can truly become a political revolutionary vehicle which will lead the people to a higher level of consciousness, so that they will know what they must really do in their quest for freedom, and they will have the courage to adopt any means necessary to seize the time and obtain that freedom.*

After the fight with Cleaver, the program of the B.P.P. underwent a dramatic change. The party seemed to become much less militant. There was less emphasis on guns and killing police and more on free breakfasts, free shoes and free health clinics.

*The Black Panther Intercommunal News Service, April 17, 1971.

## EXTORTION

The Black Panthers are so convinced of their role as representatives of the people that they consider it their natural right to tax the black community. They demand that successful black businessmen donate to them on a weekly basis. When a black businessman refuses to give, they picket and harass his place of business. They do not see this as extortion and even publicize their actions in the BLACK PANTHER:

> For over a month and a half (since July 31), brothers and sisters from the Black Panther Party and the Black community have picketed Bill's Liquor Store #2 in protest of Bill Boyette's and Cal-Pac Tavern and Liquor Owners' Association's refusal to make regular weekly donations to the Black Panther Party sponsored People's Community Survival Programs.
>
> The boycott of his store has been initiated for primarily two reasons: One, because our people's needs as a whole, for survival under the oppressive American system of government—the need to eat, to have decent clothing and shoes, quality medical care, etc., —are so great that the programs the Black Panther Party has initiated to alleviate those needs require more help; and that help has to come from our own, our own who are able. Secondly, by contributing even the requested small weekly, minimal amounts, the Black Businessman, who depends upon the Black community for the survival of his business, could return some of his profits to those who deserve and need it - his community, his neighbors - and could advance tremendously the need for unity in the Black community.
>
> However, Bill Boyette still refuses to donate. Momentarily (last week) in a meeting with Huey P. Newton, Servant of the People, he admitted his mistakes and the Boycott of his store was ended. On Tuesday, September 13, members of the Black community who were beginning to shop at Bill Boyette's store again, because they thought he had returned to the Black community, were dismayed to find that Boyette had betrayed his family once more. Leaflets were being distributed in his store which denounced the Black Panther Party, the People's Survival Programs, and the Servant of the People, Huey P. Newton. The community immediately resumed and continued support of the boycott.
>
> Albert McKee, president of the Fidelis Realty Companies of

Oakland, along with other Black Businessmen in the Bay Area have formed an 'Ad Hoc Committee to Preserve Black Business'. The committee was formed not to defend the Black community, nor to fight the corporate monopolies that victimize and control black businesses as well as the rest of the community but to preserve Black businesses from the People's control. We find this a sad commentary on the awareness and concern for unity in the community among these Black Businessmen. Bill Boyette, Albert McKee and the rest of those Black Businessmen should have formed an Ad Hoc Committee to preserve the Black Community. Rather than help to build the machinery which could become the liberating force for our oppressed community, they have chosen to be tools of the monopoly capitalist who would continue to divide and oppress our people. These Black Businessmen need not defend themselves from the Black Panther Party nor the Black Community, for our fight is not with them.

This Ad Hoc Committee has absurdly charged that the Black Panther party is demanding that only money be donated to the People's Community Survival Programs. This is not the case, for the Black Panther Party has always been willing to accept the actual commodities needed to maintain the People's Survival Programs, in lieu of cash or monetary donations. *The contradiction has arisen out of the unwillingness of Bill Boyette, Cal-Pac and now this Ad Hoc Committee to donate either money or commodities, on a regular, weekly basis* (emphasis added).

They are still attempting to shrewdly divert the issue. The issue is not the people's request for these small, minimal donations regularly, but their continued and persistent refusal to support, through their contributions, the Attica Defense Fund, the George Jackson People's Free Health Clinic, the Angela Davis Free Food Program, the David Hilliard People's Shoe Factory and the rest of our Community Survival Programs. They are aware that in order for these programs to be maintained and effectively serve the people, such donations are necessary. And they also know that they have only been asked to donate according to their capabilities - a reasonable request. On Friday, September 17, Albert McKee, representing Bill Boyette and the Ad Hoc Committee, held a press conference at Bill's liquor store pledging continued support to Bill Boyette, but not the People's Survival Programs.

In spite of the refusal of some Black Businesses to donate, there are others who would serve the interests of the people and who are continuing to do so. And, on Saturday, Septembr 18, the Black

Panther Party was able to distribute free women's summer shoes and free food to the people. A Free Food and Free Shoe Rally and press conference was held at the site of Bill's Liquor Store #2. A statement of our continued intent to serve the people and their needs was ready by Deputy Minister of Information of the Black Panther Party, Elbert Howard.

Bill Boyette glowered from behind his cash register and made malicious statements about the Black Panther Party to the press. He had to make them to the press, for the people were busy trying on their new shoes from the David Hilliard People's Free Shoe Factory and receiving much needed groceries from the Angela Davis People's Free Food Program.

Boyette made that statement that 'a leopard can't change his spots . . .' and 'the Black Panther Party is trying to change their image . . . they were carrying guns and rifles last year . . . they're just trying to look nice, but we know what they're like.' Yes, we are doing the same thing that we did last year and the year before that.*

Since the party had de-emphasized violence and enshrined service, it has appeared less militant. In actuality it has followed the teachings of Lenin by endeavoring to forge links with the masses. The objective has not changed. The more support the Black Panther Party can recruit in the black and white community, the greater its menace to the future freedom of both black and white.

## PRISONERS

The Black Panther program to recruit, teach, and train convicts has achieved remarkable success. This has contributed to a crisis in the prisons.

The Black Panthers were deeply involved in the violence at Attica and San Quentin in 1971.

One of those recruited in prison was George Jackson who became a writer and revolutionary leader while behind bars. Jackson became a martyr to the Black Panthers and the revolutionary left when he was shot and killed in a prison escape try in 1971. Three

*The Black Panther, Sept. 25, 1971.

white prison guards and two white prisoners caught up in the Jackson escape effort also died.

The "Black Panther" published an interview with Jackson not long before his death which discusses revolutionary activity in prison:

> Interviewer: In the past 6 months, a profound change has occurred in the prison population, in terms of the consciousness of the inmates, whereas before they had been easily divided by racism, which was instigated by the prison authorities. At that time they were beginning to see the prison authorities as their enemies and inmates of all races as their natural allies. Can you tell us how that consciousness developed, how extensive it is; and what forms it took?

> George: Well to begin with, of course, the recent influx of the political teachers, the political animals, from the Black Panther Party - I think they were first instrumental in the changes from conservatism that prisoners in the prison population and people, in general, here in fascist America live in. At one time the prison population, the prisoner class could have been considered one of the most conservative classes in the country . . . We'll give credit first to the Party, and to the system for placing political teachers at our disposal here. Secondly, the support that our movement has gotten from partisans from the street, from the outside. The average convict considers himself the doomed man right from the beginning. And that ray of hope, or sense of community created by the recent expressions of solidarity from the street, that (ray) found effect on the revolutionary consciousness inside the joint. It's always been my contention that if we could raise the hard-left military and political cadre in fascist America, that cadre would come from either the prisons or the dissident elements within the armed forces.

> Question: What forms did this new consciousness take?

> George: To clear that up first, I'll have to go into a little background. Some years ago, the rise of the Black revolutionary . . . created situations here in the joint that caused polarization between all Blacks and all Whites regardless of status. And by status I mean convict-cop, convict-pig. In other words, I'm saying that the prisoner code broke down as a result of the White convicts being threatened by the political thrust and the open antipathy demonstrated by Blacks against Whites in general. At the time I guess I

was part of it, too. At the time we made no efforts to distinguish between the White convict and the White guard. Because the White convicts identified openly and clearly and without reservations with right-wing ideas, and racism. So when we'd strike, we'd strike with both barrels: one at the convict, and one at the pig. And some of it is our fault. Of course, revolution is a process. We're going through a process. And well, that's the background.

The new consciousness stems from the fact that like I said, the political teacher, the Black Panther 'concentration camped', as a result of the political thrust on the street, brought new ideas. You know revolutionary, scientific socialism, and anti-racism. And we attempted to make them understand that we're all equally uniformly repressed by the administration.

Question: How wide-spread was this throughout the California penal system, when you had some success?

George: The Black vanguard within the Black political machine, within the joint is state-wide; is state-wide.

Question: How extensive is the cooperation, the consciousness to cooperate among Black, White and Chicano prisoners; to what extent has that been successful?

George: It varies from joint to joint. In Soledad, we were doing well, because the joint is set-up differently - security wise. And it was easier to disseminate our line. And the pigs in that area seemed to be generally, let's call them, provincial. The typical, rustic, provincial mentality. And they weren't able to cope with the situation. Here in San Quentin, it's different. These pigs are drawn from the metropolitan area around here in the Bay Area. And they're clearly very, very highly politicized to the right. There's an infrastructure.

Question: What do you see as the future in the prisons? What's the relationship between the prison movement and the outside movement?

George: I'll reiterate that I feel that the building of revolutionary consciousness of the prisoner class is paramount in the over-all development of a hard left revolutionary cadre. Of course the revolution has to be carried by the masses. But we need a cadre; we need a bodyguard; a political worker needs a bodyguard. We see ourselves as performing that function. The terms of existence here in the joint conditions the brothers for that type of work. Although I have become more political recently, from listening to Comrade Newton, and from reading the Party paper, I've gained a clearer understanding of the tie-in between political and military activities. *I still see my function as military* (emphasis added).

I feel that any movement on our part, political, will have to be accompanied by a latent threat. And all the projects for survival that Comrade Newton has started and developed, I think that they're going to have to be defended. And that defense is going to depend upon cadre, cadre violence, secret sort of stuff, that we can't go into here too extensively.

Question: More concretely, people on the outside are asking what kinds of things can they do, that will really be effective, to support the movement in the prisons.

George: That, of course, depends upon their level of commitment, and their consciousness . . . We have some hopefully, who will be a little more aggressive, and will do the things that must be done here and there. And I speak of violence here . . . Later on we'll search each other out and build a People's Army. Build a People's Army from these small decentralized groups.

I feel that the military thing will grow as we give the people these projects . . . The ideal or the simple, foolish notion that violence won't work in America is ridiculous. When we have the tools - a shotgun is the deadliest weapon in the world for close, city fighting; and a child can use one. All you do is point the thing; and if the thing you want to shoot is moving, you just follow through with your swing. But we have to study these things. And it's a process; it's going to take time.*

Huey Newton delivered the eulogy at Jackson's funeral. His threats were chilling:

> Some people say that we can't get rid of this kind of physical conflict with more of it. Well I would take issue with it . . . We will tear his legs off, we'll tear his head off and we'll take the example from George Jackson. In the name of love and in the name of freedom, with love as our guide, we'll slit every throat that threatens the people and our children. We'll do it in the name of peace, if this is what we have to do; because as soon as it's over, then we can have the kind of world where violence will no longer exist.
>
> We know that all of us will die someday. But we know that death has two kinds of characters, the reactionary kind and the revolutionary kind. One death is significant and the other is not. *George*

*The Black Panther, August 28, 1971, pp. 6–8.

*certainly died in a significant way, and his death will be very heavy; while the ones that fell, the ones that fell that day in San Quentin, their deaths will be lighter than a feather* (emphasis added) because it's insignificant; and even those who support them now will not support them in the future, because we're determined to change their minds. We'll change their minds or else in the people's name we'll have to wipe them out thoroughly, wholly, absolutely and completely.*

## THE BLACK PANTHERS AND MAO TSE-TUNG

This statement by Huey Newton illustrates that the Black Panther Party is a Marxist- Leninist (communist) party scientifically exploiting social forces and aiming to destroy the United States government by force and violence. The communists use social forces; they do not create them. One social force they are using effectively is the discontent of the prison population. Conditions in prisons are appalling. The communists are using the prisoners to help them to advance their program for the destruction of society. Of course, the majority of the prisoners are not aware of this.

The doctrines of the Black Panther Party are derived primarily from the teachings of Mao Tse-tung. Huey Newton is steeped in the thoughts of Mao Tse-tung. He uses the terminology of Mao Tse-tung even though the meaning is obscure to the uninitiated.

Who would know what the terms "light" and "heavy" mean in relation to death?

However, Mao Tse-tung writes:

All men must die, but death can vary in its significance. The Ancient Chinese writer Szuma Chien said, 'Though death befalls all men alike, it may be weightier than Mount Tai or lighter than a feather.' To die for the people is weightier than Mount Tai, but to work for the fascists and die for the exploiters and oppressors is lighter than a feather.†

This passage from Mao Tse-tung accounts not only for the words used by Huey Newton, but it may also explain why so much

*The Black Panther Supplement, September 4, 1971, pp. g and h.
†Mao Tse-tung, On Contradiction, op cit., p. 174.

attention has been given to the death of Jackson, while the deaths of the white guards and prisoners have been ignored.

The Black Panthers are now operating a dual party in line with the teachings of Lenin. The Party functions both legally and illegally. Lenin taught that if a party can function openly and legally, it must be associated with an illegal party and that the legal party must be under the control of the illegal branch.

The programs devised to link the party with the black masses is paying dividends. These programs provide free food and clothing distribution and free medical care. The Black Panther newspaper announced that the Party was distributing 10,000 free full bags of groceries, with a dozen large grade AA eggs in every bag, on June 24, 1972 in the civic auditorium of Oakland, California. In addition, 2,500 pairs of brand new women's shoes would be given away and 10,000 sickle cell anemia tests would be carried out. All this would be associated with a voter registration drive. This rally would also launch the political campaign of Bobby Seale for Mayor of Oakland.

The Black Panther Party succeeded in having four members elected to the Berkeley Community Development Council Board of Directors in elections held on May 24, 1972. The function of the BCDC board of directors is to dispense federal poverty funds on behalf of the poor. Since the Black Panther Party operates in accordance with the principles of Democratic Centralism and the members are under discipline and must carry out all the orders of the Party, this gives the Party control of federal funds.

On March 29, 1972, the Black Panther Party published a revised party platform. It is very similar to the original platform published in 1966. The major difference is that it does not call directly for a United Nations supervised plebiscite with only blacks voting to secure land, bread, housing, education, clothing, justice and peace, but implies a separate state by quoting directly from the American Declaration of Independence. Point No. 10 in this platform is:

WE WANT LAND, BREAD, HOUSING, EDUCATION, CLOTHING, JUSTICE, PEACE AND PEOPLE'S COMMU- NITY CONTROL OF MODERN TECHNOLOGY.

# THE THREE FACES OF REVOLUTION

When, in the course of human events, it becomes necessary for one people to dissolve the political bonds which have connected them with another, and to assume, among the powers of the earth, the separate and equal station to which the laws of nature and nature's God entitle them, a decent respect to the opinions of mankind requires that they should declare the causes which impel them to the separation.

We hold these truths to be self-evident, that all men are created equal; that they are endowed by their Creator with certain unalienable rights; that among these are life, liberty and the pursuit of happiness. That, to secure these rights, governments are instituted among men, deriving their just powers from consent of the governed; that, whenever any form of government becomes destructive of these ends, it is the right of the people to alter or to abolish it, and to institute a new government, laying its foundation on such principles, and organizing its powers in such form, as to them shall seem most likely to effect their safety and happiness. Prudence, indeed, will dictate that governments long established should not be changed for light and transient causes; and, accordingly, all experience hath shown that mankind are more disposed to suffer while evils are sufferable, than to right themselves by abolishing the forms to which they are accustomed. But, when a long train of abuses and usurpations, pursuing invariably the same object, evinces a design to reduce them under absolute despotism, it is their right, it is their duty, to throw off such government, and to provide new guards for their future security.*

The Panthers have not renounced the revolution; they are preparing for it with Leninist insight and devotion.

*Christian Anti-Communism Crusade Newsletter, June 15, 1972, p. 3.

# PART II:
# ANARCHISM

# ANARCHISM                                    7

**C**ommunism continues to exercise a powerful influence in the world revolutionary movement, but its dominant position in some western countries is being challenged by the revival of anarchism which has been the phenomenon of the past decade. At radical gatherings today the black flag of anarchy flies alongside the red flag of communism.

The situation on the campuses has certainly changed from that which existed when I had my first debate with a communist in 1940. It was at the University of Queensland, located in Brisbane, the capital city of the state of Queensland, Australia. My opponent was Max Julius, one of the leading university intellectuals and a member of the Central Committee of the Australian Communist Party. At that time, the entire radical movement at the university was either communist or sympathetic to communism, and the entire revolutionary movement was committed to the support of the Soviet Union. A non-communist revolutionary was unthinkable. In my university career, which was quite extensive, I did not meet one anarchist.

In 1970, I returned to deliver a lecture at the University of Queensland. The University of Queensland is probably the most radical university of Australia judged by the violent demonstrations that have taken place there. What a transformation had occurred! A great table filled with literature occupied a prominent place near the center of the campus, and a crowd of radicals milled around it.

But the amazing thing was the difference in the literature. The table was filled with a variety of revolutionary literature, but none was authored by communists loyal to the Soviet Union. The books on communism were written by Bukharin, not Lenin or Stalin. In fact, most of those around the table wore badges bearing the one word, "Anarchy." Unbelievably, in the universities of the western world today, there are probably more followers of Mikhail Bakunin, the anarchist, than there are of Karl Marx, the communist.

A serious study of the present revolutionary movement must, therefore, include a study of the doctrines of anarchism and the role of anarchists in the current revolutionary scene.

It is difficult to define political anarchism because, unlike communism, it is not a centrally directed movement with a central committee and with clear-cut doctrines. There are about as many forms of anarchism as there are anarchists, and an individual anarchist is apt to protest that the anarchism under discussion is not true anarchy.

Speaking at the University of Redlands, California, I stated that, historically, the anarchists practiced individual terrorism including bombing, arson, and assassination. I also stated that the anarchists controlled the unions which were active participants in the Spanish Civil War.

A protesting student said: "You contradicted yourself. You said the anarchists were terrorists; that they planted bombs and assassinated other people. No anarchist can force his will on any other person, and therefore anybody who uses bombs is not an anarchist. You said that the anarchists controlled the unions in the Spanish Civil War. Those who control others cannot be anarchists by definition because anarchy is the doctrine of total personal liberty."

I replied:

Let me put it this way. Throughout history people who called themselves anarchists have been terrorists. People who called themselves anarchists controlled the unions that were active in the Spanish Civil War. This discussion is not an exercise in semantics. It is not a discussion of the root meaning of the word anarchy. It directs attention to the doctrines and actions of those people who have called themselves anarchists and who call themselves anarchists at this present juncture in our history.

The University College Dictionary defines anarchy as a "state of society without government or law."

The communists have their own definition of anarchism, and it is distinctly hostile. The "Dictionary of Philosophy" published by the Soviet Union, 1967, defines anarchism as follows:*

A petty-bourgeois socio-political trend that is hostile to all authority, including the dictatorship of the proletariat, and counterposes the interests of petty private ownership to the progress of society based on large-scale production. Anarchy has its philosophical foundations in individualism, subjectivism, and voluntarism. The emergence of anarchism is connected with the names of Schmidt, Proudhon, and Bakunin, whose utopian theories were criticised in the writings of Marx and Engels . . .

Pierre Proudhon (1809–1865) of France is often called the father of modern anarchy. His most famous thesis, Property is Theft, was expounded in his book "What is Property" published in 1840.

Mikhail Bakunin (1814–1876), a Russian aristocrat, who advocated anarchistic terror, was a charismatic personality. Born a prince and of huge stature, he was intoxicated with violent revolution. He was attracted to violence as the moth to the candle. His climactic moment was during the violence of the French commune when he stood on the ramparts and proclaimed the dominance of anarchy in the French commune.

Bakunin was both a supporter and an opponent of Marx. At

*M. Rosenthal and P. Yudin (eds.) *Dictionary of Philosophy* (Moscow, Progress Publishers, 1967) p. 19.

times he called himself a Marxist, and he even translated Marx's "Das Capital" into Russian. But he also fought Marx bitterly. The First International disintegrated, in fact, because of the conflict between Marx and Bakunin.

Marx and Bakunin differed in three areas.
1. The necessity for a post-revolutionary State.
2. The historic instrument of revolution.
3. The role of individual terror.

(1) Both Marx and Bakunin agreed that the State is an instrument of violence whereby the dominant economic class (in capitalism, the bourgeoisie) imposes by force its will upon the subject economic class. They agreed that the capitalist state must be destroyed by force. However, Marx proposed a "Workers State" to follow revolution, while Bakunin demanded the absence of any State machinery whatever.

(2) Marx insisted it would be the Proletariat which would lead the revolution to destroy the Capitalist State while Bakunin favored the "Lumpen Proletariat" (the unemployables and criminals) for the revolution in Southern Europe. He tended to emphasize subjective consciousness rather than economic class.

(3) Marx favored mass violence carried out by the working class masses, but Bakunin advocated individual terror to stimulate the masses.

Despite the antipathy of anarchism to organization, Bakunin organized a secret society of terrorists to implement destruction. One of Bakunin's associates in this society was the terrorist Nechayev and together they produced the infamous and blood-curdling document known as "The Revolutionary Catechism":*

## THE REVOLUTIONARY CATECHISM
The Duties of the Revolutionary toward Himself

1. The revolutionary is a doomed man. He has no personal interest, no business affairs, no emotions, no attachments, no property and no name. Everything in him is wholly absorbed in the single thought and the single passion for revolution.

*Robert Payne, *The Life & Death of Lenin,* (New York, Simon & Schuster, 1964), pp. 23–34.

2. The revolutionary knows that in the very depths of his being, not only in words but also in deeds, he has broken all the bonds which tie him to the social order and the civilized world with all its laws, moralities and customs and with all its generally accepted conventions. He is their implacable enemy, and if he continues to live with them it is only in order to destroy them more speedily.

3. The revolutionary despises all doctrines and refuses to accept the mundane sciences, leaving them for future generations. He knows only one science: the science of destruction. For this reason, but only for this reason, he will study mechanics, physics, chemistry, and perhaps medicine. But all day and all night he studies the vital science of human beings, their characteristics and circumstances, and all the phenomena of the present social order. The object is perpetually the same: the surest and quickest way of destroying the whole filthy order.

4. The revolutionary despises public opinion. He despises and hates the existing social morality in all its manifestations. For him, morality is everything which contributes to the triumph of the revolution. Immoral and criminal is everything that stands in its way.

5. The revolutionary is a dedicated man, merciless toward the State and toward the educated classes; and he can expect no mercy from them. Between him and them there exists, declared or concealed, a relentless and irreconcilable war to the death. He must accustom himself to torture.

6. Tyrannical toward himself, he must be tyrannical toward others. All the gentle and enervating sentiments of kinship, love, friendship, gratitude and even honor must be suppressed in him and give place to the cold and single-minded passion for revolution. For him there exists only one pleasure, one consolation, one reward, one satisfaction—the success of the revolution. Night and day he must have but one thought, one aim—merciless destruction. Striving cold-bloodedly and indefatigably toward this end, he must be prepared to destroy himself and to destroy with his own hands everything that stands in the path of the revolution.

7. The nature of the true revolutionary excludes all sentimentality, romanticism, infatuation and exaltation. All private

hatred and revenge must also be excluded. Revolutionary passion, practiced at every moment of the day until it becomes a habit, is to be employed with cold calculation. At all times and in all places the revolutionary must obey, not his personal impulses, but only those which serve the cause of the revolution.

## THE RELATIONS OF THE REVOLUTIONARY TOWARD HIS COMRADES

8. The revolutionary can have no friendship or attachment except for those who have proved by their actions that they, like him, are dedicated to revolution. The degree of friendship, devotion and obligation toward such a comrade is determined solely by the degree of his usefulness to the cause of total revolutionary destruction.

9. It is superfluous to speak of solidarity among revolutionaries. The whole strength of revolutionary work lies in this. Comrades who possess the same revolutionary passion and understanding should, as much as possible, deliberate all important matters together and come to unanimous conclusions. When the plan is finally decided upon, then the revolutionary must rely solely on himself. In carrying out acts of destruction each one should act alone, never running to another for advice and assistance except when these are necessary for the furtherance of the plan.

10. All revolutionaries should have under them second-or third-degree revolutionaries—i.e. comrades who are not completely initiated. These should be regarded as part of the common revolutionary capital placed at his disposal. This capital should, of course, be spent as economically as possible in order to derive from it the greatest possible profit. The revolutionary should regard himself as capital consecrated to the triumph of the revolution; however, he may not personally and alone dispose of that capital without the unanimous consent of the fully initiated comrades.

11. When a comrade is in danger and the question arises whether he should be saved or not saved, the decision must

not be arrived at on the basis of sentiment, but solely in the interests of the revolutionary cause. Therefore it is necessary to weigh carefully the usefulness of the comrade against the expenditure of revolutionary forces necessary to save him, and the decision must be made accordingly.

## THE RELATIONS OF THE REVOLUTIONARY TOWARD SOCIETY

12. The new member, having given proof of his loyalty not by words but by deeds can be received into the society only by the unanimous agreement of all the members.
13. The revolutionary enters the world of the state, of the privileged classes, of the so-called civilization, and he lives in this world only for the purpose of bringing about its speedy and total destruction. He is not a revolutionary if he has any sympathy for this world. He should not hesitate to destroy any position, any place, or any man in this world. He must hate everyone and everything in it with an equal hatred. All the worse for him if he has any relations with parents, friends or lovers; he is no longer a revolutionary if he is swayed by these relationships.
14. Aiming at implacable revolution, the revolutionary may and frequently must live within society while pretending to be completely different from what he really is, for he must penetrate everywhere, into all the higher and middle classes, into the houses of commerce, the churches and the palaces of the aristocracy, and into the worlds of the bureaucracy and literature and the military, and also into the Third Division and the Winter Palace of the Tsar.
15. This filthy social order can be split up into several categories. The first category comprises those who must be condemned to death without delay. Comrades should compile a list of those to be condemned according to the relative gravity of their crimes; and the executions should be carried out according to the prepared order.
16. When a list of those who are condemned is made and the order of execution is prepared, no private sense of outrage

should be considered, nor is it necessary to pay attention to the hatred provoked by these people among the comrades or the people. Hatred and the sense of outrage may even be useful in so far as they incite the masses to revolt. It is necessary to be guided only by the relative usefulness of these executions for the sake of the revolution. Above all, those who are especially inimical to the revolutionary organization must be destroyed; their violent and sudden deaths will produce the utmost panic in the government, depriving it of its will to action by removing the cleverest and most energetic supporters.

17.   The second group comprises those who will be spared for the time bieng in order that, by a series of monstrous acts, they may drive the people into inevitable revolt.

18.   The third category consists of a great many brutes in high positions distinguished neither by their cleverness nor their energy, while enjoying riches, influence, power and high positions by virtue of their rank. These must be exploited in every possible way; they must be implicated and embroiled in our affairs, their dirty secrets must be ferreted out, and they must be transformed into slaves. Their power, influence and connections, their wealth and their energy will form an inexhaustible treasure and a precious help in all our undertakings.

19.   The fourth category comprises ambitious officeholders and liberals of various shades of opinion. The revolutionary must pretend to collaborate with them, blindly following them, while at the same time prying out their secrets until they are completely in his power. They must be so compromised that there is no way out for them, and then they can be used to create disorder in the state.

20.   The fifth category consists of those doctrinaires, conspirators and revolutionists who cut a great figure on paper or in their cliques. They must be constantly driven on to make compromising declarations: as a result the majority of them will be destroyed, while a minority will become genuine revolutionaries.

21.   The sixth category is especially important: women. They can be divided into three main groups. First, those frivolous,

thoughtless and vapid women, whom we shall use as we use the third and fourth category of men. Second, women who are ardent, capable and devoted, but who do not belong to us because they have not yet achieved a passionless and austere revolutionary understanding; these must be used like the men of the fifth category. Finally, there are the women who are completely on our side—i.e., those who are wholly dedicated and who have accepted our program in its entirety. We should regard these women as the most valuable of our treasures; without their help we would never succeed.

## THE ATTITUDE OF THE SOCIETY TOWARD THE PEOPLE

22. The Society has no aim other than the complete liberation and happiness of the masses—i.e., of the people who live by manual labor. Convinced that their emancipation and achievement of this happiness can only come about as a result of an all-destroying popular revolt, the Society will use all its resources and energy toward increasing and intensifying the evils and miseries of the people until at last their patience is exhausted and they are driven to a general uprising.

23. By a revolution the Society does not mean an orderly revolt according to the classic western model—a revolt which always stops short of attacking the rights of property and the traditional social systems of so-called civilization and morality. Until now such a revolution has always limited itself to the overthrow of one political form in order to replace it by another, thereby attempting to bring about a so-called revolutionary state. The only form of revolution beneficial to the people is one which destroys the entire state to the roots and exterminates all the state traditions, institutions and classes in Russia.

24. With this end in view, the Society therefore refuses to impose any new organization from above. Any future organization will doubtless work its way through the movement and life of the people; but this is a matter for future genera-

tions to decide. Our task is terrible, total, universal and merciless destruction.

25. Therefore, in drawing closer to the people, we must above all make common cause with those elements of the masses which, since the foundation of the state of Muscovy, have never ceased to protest, not only in words but in deeds, against everything directly or indirectly connected with the state: against the nobility, the bureaucracy, the traders, and the parasitic kulaks. We must unite with the adventurous tribes of brigands, who are the only genuine revolutionaries of Russia.

26. To weld the people into one single unconquerable and all-destructive force—this is our aim, our conspiracy and our task.

## NIHILISTS

In Russia, in the second half of the nineteenth century, the revolutionary anarchists were often called nihilists. This was to indicate that they accepted nothing in the established system of ethics, morality and culture. Their attitude was total rejection, and their program—total destruction.

The anarchists preceded the Marxists, for Proudhon preached his ideas while Marx was still an adolescent. Later Marx criticized Proudhon caustically.

The anarchists were active in Russia in the late nineteenth century and they concentrated on terror by bomb and gun. Actually, the Bolsheviks rose in Russia in conflict with the anarchists. Attacking the anarchists, Lenin said: "The anarchists have two laws. Law No. 1, there shall be no laws; and Law No. 2., Law no. 1 is not binding."

In his famous textbook, "Left-wing Communism, An Infantile Disorder," Lenin wrote:*

Bolshevism grew up, took shape, and became steeled in long years of struggle against petty-bourgeois revolutionism, which

*V.I. Lenin, *Left-wing Communism, An Infantile Disorder* (Moscow, Foreign Languages Publishing House, 1940) pp. 26–28.

smacks of, or borrows something from, anarchism, and which falls short, in anything essential, of the conditions and requirements of a consistently proletarian class struggle. For Marxists, it is well established theoretically—and the experience of all European revolutions and revolutionary movements has fully confirmed it—that the small owner, the small master (a social type that is represented in many European countries on a very wide, a mass scale), who under capitalism always suffers oppression and, very often, an incredibly acute and rapid deterioration in his conditions, and ruin, easily goes to revolutionary extremes, but is incapable of perseverance, organization, discipline and steadfastness. The petty bourgeois 'driven to frenzy' by the horrors of capitalism is a social phenomenon which, like anarchism, is characteristic of all capitalist countries. The instability of such revolutionism, its barrenness, its liability to become swiftly transformed into submission, apathy, fantasy, and even a 'frenzied' infatuation with one or another bourgeois 'fad'—all this is a matter of common knowledge. But a theoretical, abstract recognition of these truths does not at all free revolutionary parties from old mistakes, which always crop up at unexpected moments, in a somewhat new form, in hitherto unknown vestments or surroundings, in a peculiar—more or less peculiar—situation.

Anarchism was not infrequently a sort of punishment for the opportunist sins of the working-class movement. The two monstrosities were mutually complementary.

What did Lenin mean by opportunism? He referred to activity which concentrated upon taking advantage of opportunities to improve economic and social conditions under capitalism instead of concentrating upon the destruction of capitalism.

Bolshevism, Lenin said, believed in trying to improve conditions in order to enlist the masses in a movement to destroy capitalism, but opportunism considered programs of economic betterment sufficient in themselves. When the efforts to secure lasting improvement failed, the reaction tended to be blind rage and anarchistic violence.

## VIOLENCE

Lenin emphasizes the difference in the types of violence advocated by the communists and anarchists. This difference is important:

> At its inception in 1903, Bolshevism took over the tradition of ruthless struggle against petty-bourgeois, semianarchist (or dilet-tante-anarchist) revolutionism, the tradition which has always existed in revolutionary Social-Democracy.
> This party considered itself to be particularly 'revolutionary,' or 'Left', because of its recognition of individual terror, assassination —a thing which we Marxists emphatically rejected. Of course, we rejected individual terror only on grounds of expediency, whereas people who were capable of condemning 'on principle' the terror of the Great French Revolution, or in general, the terror employed by a victorious revolutionary party which is besieged by the bourgeoisie of the whole world, were ridiculed and laughed to scorn already by Plekhanov, in 1900–1903, when he was a Marxist and a revolutionary.*

Lenin claims that violence, like all else, must be used scientifically. The role of the communists was to lead the masses, to think for the masses, to agitate the masses. Close contact with the masses was essential to do this effectively. Consequently, any act which separated communists from the masses was wrong. After terroristic violence, it was necessary to flee and remain in hiding and, thus, contact with the masses was broken. It was impossible to organize the masses in this situation. For this reason, Lenin concluded, individual violence was wrong. The communists should stimulate; the masses should act.

Lenin advocated mass violence because in such circumstances, the communists were both hidden and protected by the masses so they could continue their active leadership. When the mob burned the Bank of America in Isla Vista, near Santa Barbara, California, that was typical Leninist violence. However, when an individual or small group planted a bomb at night in the Bank of America in Irvine, California, that was anarchist violence.

It should be noted that Lenin's rejection of individual terror was

*Ibid.*, p. 28–29.

not moral but pragmatic. A similar argument concerning the nature of true revolutionary violence is raging today, and those who refuse to learn the lessons of history are condemned to repeat them.

## ANARCHISM IN AMERICA

Anarchism has a long and ignoble history in America. An anarchist assassinated President William McKinley, and anarchists have carried out numerous terrorist acts.

One of America's best-known anarchists was Emma Goldman (1870–1940) who in her lectures, attempted to expound the virtues of anarchism. She found it easier to be specific when indicating the things anarchism opposed than when describing how society would operate if anarchism prevailed. She stated that anarchists are against five things; 1) All government; 2) All laws; 3) All private ownership of property; 4) All religion; and 5) All forms of the family.

Are these five institutions to which anarchism is so hostile really necessary? Most people would agree that they are. Because of the nature of man, these institutions are necessary so that man can live in reasonable peace and contentment.

The regime of anarchism is possible only if human nature is essentially good. Only if we assume that uninhibited human conduct, free from all external authority, will invariably promote universal well-being, does anarchism become a viable option for society.

For anarchism to work, it is insufficient that conduct be good most of the time. It must be good all the time. If human impulses are 99 percent beneficient and only 1 percent aggressive, the conduct resulting from unrestrained impulses loosed during that moment of aggression can produce irretrievable havoc. Human life is fragile and it can be terminated by one impulsive blow. Needless to say, a life of penitence cannot resurrect the dead.

Human nature is complex but most serious observers have reached the conclusion that it contains substantial aggressive elements. The poet laments, "man's inhumanity to man
Makes countless thousands mourn." (Robert Burns)

The prophet Jeremiah cries, "The heart is deceitful above all things and desperately wicked. (Jer. 17:9)

St. Paul protests, "When I would do good, evil is present with me."

The English political scientist, Thomas Hobbes, stated that in the state of nature, the prevailing condition is one of "war of each against all" with the consequence that "life is dull, brutish and short."

From an entirely different vantage point, Sigmund Freud reached the conclusion that because the psyche possesses a death instinct, human nature is incurably aggressive.

## GOVERNMENT

Because of the nature of man, laws are necessary to define the limits of permissable behavior and government is needed to make and to enforce the laws. Government should provide protection against internal and external enemies and provide for the administration of justice. Laws are also necessary to restrain government from arbitrary action against citizens and to enable citizens to predict the consequences of their actions.

Anarchist Emma Goldman scorns the customary conclusions concerning human nature. She writes,

> But what about human nature? Can it be changed? And if not, will it endure under Anarchism?
>
> Poor human nature, what horrible crimes have been committed in thy name? Every fool, from king to policeman, from the flat-headed parson to the visionless dabbler in science, presumes to speak authoritatively of human nature. The greater the mental charlatan, the more definite his insistence on the wickedness and weaknesses of human nature. Yet, how can any one speak of it today, with every soul in a prison, with every heart fettered, wounded, and maimed? John Burroughs has stated that experimental study of animals in captivity is absolutely useless. Their character, their habits, their appetites undergo a complete transformation when torn from their soil in field and forest. With human nature caged in a narrow space, whipped daily into submission, how can we speak of its potentialities?*

*Emma Goldman, *Anarchism* (New York, Dover Publications, 1969) pp. 61–62.

This reply is irrelevant as it provides no evidence concerning the conduct of "animal" man in his "natural" state. Anarchism is based on blind faith.

During a 1969 debate at the University of Texas, Greg Calvert, former national secretary of SDS, introduced himself as an "anarchist" of sorts. His cure for the ills of mankind was the totally permissive upbringing of all children. Would Calvert and the anarchists deny the existence of mental illness? Would they claim that all psychosis is environmentally induced? What about brain damage at birth? What about genetic inheritance? If the possibility of non-environmental psychosis is admitted, some authority is necessary to restrain the possible homicidal impulses.

Of course, the environment is important and influences character and conduct, but man is a genetic as well as an environmental being. Some, including the author, believe he is also a spiritual being.

Plainly, if there exists the possibility of aggressive conduct, some mechanism of protection is essential. If this protection were the sole responsibility of each individual, communal life would be impossible. The need to be safe from others would dominate all thoughts and acts and the only ultimate security would be isolation. Not only would communities disappear but in time man as such would also disappear.

## LAWS

Laws are necessary to solve the universal dilemma that the exercise of freedom by one may prevent the exercise of freedom by another, or by many. A favorite expression of the neo-anarchists is, "do your own thing." Disputing with one anarchist at Long Beach State College several years ago, I accused: "You will not allow me to do my own thing. My thing is to breathe pure air, uncontaminated by carcinogenic toxins. You will not allow me to do this." He was smoking and I was being forced to breathe the smoke of his cigarette. Such illustrations could be multiplied ad nauseam. Actions by individuals obiously interfere with the freedom of others. How can a just distribution of freedom be secured?

Every law restricts a freedom, but it also restricts destruction of feedom. A good law results in a net increase in freedom. A red light at a crossing near a school may deny temporary freedom of movement to a motorist but grant children the freedom to live. A law to limit driving to the right side of the road denies freedom to drive on the left side but hopefully enables more people to reach their destinations sooner and in safety. Thus, it increases the freedom of movement.

Freedom of speech is a cherished American freedom. Some regard this freedom as absolute, but this cannot be so since speech by one individual may deny freedom of speech to another. As a result some "speaking" should be prohibited by law.

During question time following a speech at Penn State University, a young man arose and contended that freedom of speech was absolute. I replied that I could inform him of a way he could be lawfully imprisoned as a result of speaking. I suggested that if he visited the local airport and falsely announced he had placed a bomb in the luggage of a plane about to depart, he would soon be in custody. He replied, "It is putting the bomb in the luggage, not saying you have done it that causes arrest." I pointed out that no bomb had been placed in the luggage. No overt act had been committed. Speech and speech alone had taken place.

Comprehension struck him like a physical blow. He stopped speaking in the middle of a sentence; his mouth fell open; he sat down abruptly.

Consider the consequences of such speech. The authorities would search the luggage in a futile quest for the bomb. The departure of the plane is delayed. If I were departing on that plane to deliver a speech, I would be delayed and conceivably unable to speak. His "freedom of speech" would have prevented my "freedom of speech."

Law is essential to resolve this dilemma. The alternative to goverment by law is government by arbitrary authority. No one can rationally calculate the consequences of his actions. This produces hesitancy and confusion, and minimizes freedom.

Anarchists can only function when they are a small minority and when they enjoy the protection of a strong police force. Without this protection they are liable to exterminate each other. The experience of Yippie leader Abbie Hoffman in Chicago before the Democratic National Convention in 1968 is a case illustration. Abbie went to Chicago to organize the demonstrations at the

convention, and one of his major objectives was to bait and humili-
ate the police.

After Abbie checked into an apartment in Chicago, he was
informed that a man with a gun was waiting for him to leave the
apartment, and this man had announced his intention of shooting
the Yippie leader. What does a good anarchist do in these circumstances? Abbie called the police.

## PRIVATE PROPERTY

Love of private property is almost universal. It motivates men and
has contributed to the construction of the material base of civilization. Recognizing this, the communists often propose agrarian
reform designed to give private property to peasants.

Generally love of property has been regarded as cultural or
derived from the social environment. However, recent anthropo-
logical studies suggest it may be more deeply based within human
nature. To be sure the anarchists have a formidable opponent in
property.

## RELIGION

The meaning and purpose of life is the primary question that
perplexes thinking man. Is there true value in the recurrent cycle
of birth, life and death? Is life continuous? The thoughtful being
cannot escape seeking answers to these questions. Answers are
essential to happiness and tranquility. Unanswered, these questions often provoke senseless rage.

The religions of the world are formalized attempts to answer
these questions and to provide man with a measure of hope. To
those gripped with destructive rage, religion is a natural enemy in
that it may persuade people to "rather bear those ills we have than
fly to others that we know not of," to quote Shakespeare's Hamlet.

It is easy to understand why anarchism is the avowed enemy of
all religion.

## THE FAMILY

The family is a very durable institution. Man is not a solitary being. "And the Lord said, It is not good that man should be alone" (Genesis 2:18). The monogamous, partriarchal family has contributed substantially to the liberation of women for it has lightened the labor of child-bearing and eased the burden of child-rearing. The family has developed tenderness, sympathy, and un-selfishness. Recent prison literature from communist Russia testifies to its unbelievable durability. Solzhenitsyn's book *The First Circle* tells the story of the lives of cultured and intelligent men in the debasing environment of Soviet prisons. The common emotional factor that united peasant and scientist, communist and anticommunist was concern for the well-being of their wives and chidlren and eagerness to see them.

Care for those he loves and for whom he is responsible gives an individual an interest in the maintenance of an environment of economic stability and physical security. It dampens destructive fervor. No wonder anarchists regard the family as an enemy.

Absolute individual liberty is only possible for an individual in utter isolation, and in those circumstances it is apt to reduce itself to the liberty to die. The problem of society is more difficult. It is how to maximize individual liberty when each action of each individual may infringe the liberties of others.

Nevertheless, it is not difficult to understand the appeal of anarchism. The longing for liberty is innate and most people will accept considerable insecurity as the price of liberty. If this were not so, life in a well-conducted prison would be welcome to many because it provided regular and adequate food, substantial shelter, protective clothing and free medical and dental services. However, most people are willing to exchange these advantages for the freedom to live in what is often called the "rat race" of society.

Everyone is born an anarchist. "Doing your own thing" characterizes life in the cradle. Physical and psychological maturity is developed as the ability to control impulses willingly in the interest of others is attained. Maturity involves the ability to postpone pleasure.

Even so, the urge to abandon restraints and "do what comes naturally" remains with us. Anarchism is essentially regression and need not be learned. An individual may experience instantaneous conversion to anarchism simply by abandoning restraint and indulging impulse. This is one big difference between anarchism and communism. To become a communist is an arduous and difficult process. It involves choice, commitment, self-discipline and study. Anarchism on the other hand involves unlearned activity in essentials. Of course, the techniques of destruction, such as making bombs, require study and self-discipline.

## THE RELATION OF THE ANARCHISTS TO THE COMMUNISTS

The anarchist-communist relationship is one of love-hate. They are allies in destruction and enemies in most other things. When not fighting the capitalist enemy, they are likely to fight each other. This has been true throughout history and is true today.

The anarchists are the allies of the communists during the revolution and the victims of the communists after the revolution. This has been the case in the past and history is almost certain to be repeated should communism triumph.

The first to be exterminated by the Bolsheviks after they had seized power in Russia were the anarchists. Daniel Cohn-Bendit, the revolutionary student leader of France describes the fate of one group of anarchists:*

> The Makhnovchina, better perhaps than any other movement, shows that the Russian Revolution could have become a great liberating force. It was inspired by Makhno, a young Ukranian anarchist, and has been almost totally ignored by bourgeois historians no less than by Stalinist and Trotskyist apologists and for good reason. It shows the Bolsheviks stifling workers and peasants with lies and calumnies, and then crushing them in a bloody massacre.
>
> Geographically, the Makhno movement covered a region inhabited by seven million people and measuring some 150 miles in diameter. Its centre was the small Ukrainian town of Gulye Polye with 30,000 inhabitants.

*Daniel and Gabriel Cohn-Bendit, *Obsolete Communism, the Left-Wing Alternative* (London, Deutsch, 1968) p. 220.

> The movement flourished from 1918 until the summer of 1921, when it was finally crushed by the Red Army."

Anarchism is essentially a transitory phenomenon. They are efficient destroyers but cannot build. If they are successful in their efforts to destroy all authority, they create the most unendurable condition known to man, total anarchy.

Obviously, life is unendurable when each individual must protect his life against all others. Each contact with another would become a dangerous confrontation and produce great inner tension. If each individual could kill at will with impunity, no society could exist. For these reasons, people will always choose authoritarianism and coercion as the alternative to anarchy. In reality, the anarchists are only the shock troops of the totalitarians and the servants of communism.

Meanwhile, anarchism retains its appeal for the young. It is a delightful fad in which to indulge for a time provided you are young and healthy, and there exists a permissive society to provide essential food, clothing, and shelter—along with the physical security of a good police force!

Indulgence of the bodily appetites has always been one of the characteristics of the anarchists, but the development of a doctrine that society can be destroyed by such indulgence is the achievement of modern revolutionaries whom I have called the Sensualists—and whose best known spokesman is Herbert Marcuse.

# PART III:
# SENSUALISM

# THE SENSUALISTS 8

"The first part of the Yippie program, you know, is kill your parents, because until you're prepared to kill your parents you're not really prepared to change the country, because our parents are our first oppressors."

These words were spoken by Jerry Rubin, Yippie leader, to a gathering at Kent State University two weeks before that campus erupted in violence on May 4, 1970.

Jerry Rubin is one of the leading practitioners of Sensual Revolution. He summarizes his program with the words, "We've combined youth, music, sex, drugs, and rebellion with reason—and that's a combination hard to beat."

Rubin began his revolutionary career as a member of the Progressive Labor Party during the time when that party supported the Chinese Communists. But he found traditional communist doctrines limited in their appeal to youth. However, he realized that many young people could be attracted and recruited by doctrines that promoted unlimited self-indulgence, so he included drug usage and sexual license in his revolutionary program. He directed his appeal to the natural rebelliousness of youth and its desire for experimentation, expanded experience and excitement. Rubin believed that once recruited, drugged and debauched, these youth could be used for the destruction of society.

Rubin wrote the book, *Do It!* which is described by its publishers, Simon and Schuster, in these words:

> This book will become a Molotov cocktail in your very hands. Jerry Rubin has written the Communist Manifesto of our era. *Do It!* is a Declaration of War between the generations—calling on kids to leave their homes, burn down their schools and create a new society upon the ashes of the old.

Rubin dedicates the book to Nancy, dope, color TV, and violent revolution.

Another leading sensual revolutionist is Abbie Hoffman. His books include *Revolution for The Hell of It* and *Steal This Book.* One of his specialties is encouraging girls in their early teens to run away from home, panhandle on the streets and join the shock troops of the revolution. He plays the role of a modern Fagan as he teaches children the techniques of theft. His attitude to the family is shown by the following extraction from "Revolution for the Hell of It.":*

> About eight months ago I was picking my way through the garbage-strewn streets between Avenues B and C when a mite of a girl bumped into me. She must have been about thirteen or so and was off to St. Marks Place to practice her trade. She was a panhandler. She was barefoot, her dungarees were at least three sizes too big, and her long yellow hair was tangled in the silver beads she had around her neck. We struck up a conversation. She was from Ohio; she had been down here three weeks and found the going tough. After about fifteen minutes of listening to problems like 'finding a decent crash pad . . . the number of times you get burned down here . . . my parents got me on a permanent paranoid trip' and the like, I suggested, 'Why don't you go home?' She got very indignant. Assuming a pose even Bonnie Parker would have dug,

*Abbie Hoffman, *Revolution for the Hell of It,* (New York, Dial Press, 1968).

she pointed her finger in my face and spat out, 'WHY DON'T YOU!'

I went to school on that. It was the last time I ever considered it an alternative for anyone. Runaways are the backbone of the youth revolution. We are all runaways, age is irrelevant. A fifteen-year old kid who takes off from middle-class American life is an escaped slave crossing the Mason-Dixon line. They are hunted down by professional bounty hunters, fidgety relatives and the law, because it is against the law to leave home (translate: bondage) until you have finished your servitude. Many a stool has been known for turning in a known runaway when the reward became big enough.

Rubin and Hoffman formed the anti-organization, the Youth International Party (Yippies). This alleged party has no constitution and no officers. It is a technique to produce mobs for demonstrations for various purposes. In their roles as Yippie leaders, Rubin and Hoffman were indicted and convicted for conspiracy to entice people to cross state lines to create a riot at the 1968 Democratic National Convention in Chicago.

Theory usually anticipates practice and the yippies are basically only carrying out the ideas of the leading theoretician of the Sensual Revolution, philosopher Herbert Marcuse.

After a lifetime of academic eminence but popular obscurity, Marcuse suddenly emerged toward the end of the past decade as the most influential theorist of the New Left. Revolutionaries appeared throughout Europe and America quoting the teachings of Herbert Marcuse. These included Rudy Dutsche of Germany and Daniel Cohn-Bendit of France. Rioting Italian students chanted, "Marx, Mao, and Marcuse." When the revolutionary students seized the buildings at Columbia University in 1968 the leaders paid tribute to Marcuse. It was paradoxical that a group with the slogan, "Trust no man over thirty," should pay tribute to a man over 70 years old. During the past few years, his luster in the New Left has dimmed, but his ideas remain powerful.

Herbert Marcuse was born in Berlin, Germany, in 1898. He was educated at the Universities of Berlin and Freiburg where he received his Ph.D. He has taught at Harvard University, Columbia University, Brandeis University and the University of

California at San Diego, where he served as a Professor of Philosophy and directed the graduate studies of Angela Davis, among others.

His published books include: *Reason and Revolution* (1941), *Eros and Civilization* (1955), *Soviet Marxism* (1961), *Repressive Tolerance* (1965) *Negations* (1965), *One Dimensional Man* (1968), *An Essay on Liberation* (1969) and *Five Lectures* (1970).

The following anecdote reveals something of the character and message of Marcuse. After attending his classes at the University of California at San Diego, a woman accused Marcuse of demoralizing the youth by advocating sexual license. Marcuse replied: "Madam, you don't understand. You misrepresent me. That is not what I teach at all. What I teach is much worse. I'm teaching the political consequences of the sexual revolution."

The books of Marcuse are not light reading. They are written for the serious and informed student. They abound with technical terminology and esoteric quotations. However, once his code has been broken, his message is comprehensible.

Marcuse claims to be a critical philosopher whose purpose is to structure the world, not merely to describe it. For this reason, it is sometimes difficult to distinguish the border between the philosopher's description of what is and what is desired. In general it may be assumed that favorable description implies prescription.

The thoughts of Marcuse fit into four distinct categories. It is almost as though there are four separate Marcuses. They are: 1) The Marxist; 2) The Freudian; 3) The Marxist-Leninist; and 4) The Absurd.

## THE MARXIST

Marcuse proudly proclaims that he is a Marxist. He emphasizes the alleged qualities of the Young Marx whose humanism was more overt than the better-known, older Marx. He claims the young Marx was primarily concerned with the alienation of the individual from the product of his work, his society and himself. He was more concerned with the individual and less with classes and economic forces.

Whether this is true or not, Marcuse has convinced many people that it is. He has popularized the concept of Marxist alienation.

As a Marxist, he lacks the revolutionary optimism of Marx. Marx was convinced that capitalism was producing its own grave-diggers and maintained that the consciousness of the proletariat must be a revolutionary consciousness. In his view, the working class would overthrow capitalism.

History has convinced Marcuse that this is not the case in modern industrial societies. This presents him with the problem: 1) Capitalist society is increasingly evil and must be overthrown; but 2) there is no revolutionary class strong enough to overthrow it.

He expresses the anguish this causes him in a speech delivered on December 4, 1968, at the twentieth anniversary program of THE GUARDIAN a leading radical newsweekly:

"Let me start by pointing out the two contradictions with which our movement—and I say our—is faced. On the one hand, we all feel, we experience, we have it in our bones, that this society is getting increasingly repressive, destructive, of the human and natural capabilities to be free, to determine one's own life, to shape one's own life without exploiting others.

"We have to admit that a large part, if not the majority, of this population does not really feel, is not aware, is not politically conscious of this need for change."*

He analyzes this problem as follows:

Radical change without a mass base seems to be unimaginable. But the obtaining of a mass base—at least in this country—and in the foreseeable future—seems to be equally unimaginable. What are we going to do with this contradiction?

The answer seems to be very easy. We have to try to get this support. We have to try to get this mass base. But here we meet the limits of democratic persuasion with which we are confronted today. Why the limits? Because a large, perhaps a decisive, part of the majority, namely the working class, is to a great extent integrated into the system; and on a rather solid material basis, and not only superficially.†

*Massimo Teodori, ed., *The New Left-A Documentary History* (New York, Bobbs, Merrill, 1969) p. 469.
†*Ibid.*, p. 470.

The grievous situation calls for a re-examination of classical Marxist concepts. He discusses what this re-examination must include:

> First, the notion of the seizure of power. Here, the old model wouldn't do any more. That for example, in a country like the United States, under the leadership of a centralized and authoritarian party, large masses concentrate on Washington, occupy the Pentagon and set up a new government, seems to be a slightly too unrealistic and utopian picture.
>
> We will see that what we have to envisage is some kind of diffuse and dispersed disintegration of the system, in which interest, emphasis and activity is shifted to local and regional area.
>
> The second concept that should be re-examined is the role of the working class. And here I would like to say a few words to one of the most defamed notions today, namely the concept of the new working class. I know what can be said against it, and what has been said against it. It seems to me that the concept of the new working class simply comprehends and anticipates tendencies that are going on before our own eyes in the material process of production in capitalism, namely that more highly qualified salaried employees, technicians, specialists, and so on, occupy a decisive position in the material process of production.*

He emphasizes local action:

> What we can envisage is not, as I said, this large centralized and coordinated movement, but local and regional political action against specific grievances—riots, ghetto rebellions and so on, that is to say, certain mass movements which in large part are lacking political consciousness and which will depend more than before on political guidance and direction by militant leading minorities.†

His prescription for action is:

> The Left must find the adequate means of breaking the conformist and corrupted universe of political language and political behavior. The Left must try to arouse the consciousness and conscience of the others, and breaking out of the language and behav-

* *Ibid.*, p. 471.
† *Ibid.*

ior pattern of the corrupt political universe, a pattern which is imposed on all political activity, is an almost super-human task and requires an almost superhuman imagination, namely the effort to find a language and to organize actions which are not part and parcel of the familiar political behavior, and which can perhaps communicate that what is here at work are human beings with different needs and different goals which are not yet and I hope never will be co-opted.

Such behavior would and must appear as foolish, childish and irrational, but that may very well be the token that here is the attempt, and the at least temporarily successful attempt, to go beyond, to break out of the repressive universe of the established political behavior.*

He does not advocate unity:

> I want to add one thing here that may almost appear as heretic —no primitive unification of strategy. The left is split! The left has always been split! Only the right, which has no ideas to fight for, is united!
>
> Now the strength of the New Left may well reside in precisely these small contesting and competing groups, active at many points at the same time, a kind of political guerrilla force in peace or so-called peace, but, and this is, I think, the most important point, small groups, concentrated on the level of local activities.†

He is intransigent towards the Liberals:

> I would suggest not an alliance even with the Devil, as Lenin said, because the Devil today has become much too strong. He will eat us up. No alliance with liberals who have taken over the job of the un-American committee.§

Marcuse sees no hope of true socialism emerging in the Soviet Union. He blames this primarily on the United States and Western Europe as the infant Soviet State needed to arm itself to defeat the capitalist invaders and this corrupted its own vision. Its vision was destroyed by the necessity for peaceful coexistence with capitalist

---

*Ibid.*, pp. 471–472.
†*Ibid.*
§*Ibid.*

powers. He remains hopeful, however, about the possibilities in Cuba and China. He writes:

> Show us, where is this kind of socialism? We will say, it is perhaps, it is probably going to be built up in Cuba. It is perhaps being built up in China. It is certainly fighting in Vietnam (against) the supermonster. But they will look around and say, 'No, this isn't socialism. Socialism, as we see it, socialism is what we have in the Soviet Union. Socialism is the invasion of Czechoslovakia.' Socialism, in other words, is a crime.*

Marcuse laments the change in the consciousness of the working class that has been brought by the consumer society. This change is not superficial but has reached the instinctual level. The workers obtain deep satisfaction from their automobiles, television sets, homes, refrigerators, boats and other consumer items provided by capitalist society. Marcuse feels that this society completely controls their lives because it administers leisure time as well as working time. It provides the entertainment particularly through control of TV and Radio and it controls all sources of information. The administered society, Marcuse maintains, gives no room for revolutionary consciousness to grow. He laments this tragedy:

> The so-called consumer economy and the politics of corporate capitalism have created a second nature of man which ties him libidinally and aggressively to the commodity form. The need for possessing, consuming, handling, and constantly renewing the gadgets, devices, instruments, engines, offered to and imposed upon the people, for using these wares even at the danger of one's own destruction, has become a 'biological' need in the sense just defined. The second nature of man thus militates against any change that would disrupt and perhaps even abolish this dependence of man on a market ever more densely filled with merchandise —abolish his existence as a consumer consuming himself in buying and selling. The needs generated by this system are thus eminently stabilizing, conservative needs: the counterrevolution anchored in the instinctual structure.†

---

* *Ibid.*, pp. 469–470.
†Herbert Marcuse, *An Essay on Liberation*, (Boston, Beacon Press, 1969) p. 11.

The slogan of communism is "from each according to his ability, to each according to his need." However capitalism has changed the nature and therefore the needs of man, Marcuse declares. It has built false needs into the consciousness which should not be fulfilled, so he insists that it is necessary to change the nature of man first and change his environment later. This thinking contradicts the teaching of Marx that environment creates human nature.

Overall, Marcuse is ambivalent concerning the working class so he does retain elements of orthodox Marxism. He writes:

> By virtue of its basic position in the production process, by virtue of its numerical weight and the weight of exploitation, the working class is still the historical agent of revolution; by virtue of its sharing the stabilizing needs of the system, it has become a conservative, even counterrevolutionary force. Objectively, 'in-itself,' labor still is the potentially revolutionary class; subjectively, 'for-itself,' it is not.
>
> In the advanced capitalist countries, the radicalization of the working classes is counteracted by a socially engineered arrest of consciousness, and by the development and satisfaction of needs which perpetuate the servitude of the exploited. A vested interest in the existing system is thus fostered in the instinctual structure of the exploited, and the rupture with the continuum of repression —a necessary precondition of liberation—does not occur. It follows that the radical change which is to transform the existing society into a free society must reach into a dimension of the human existence hardly considered in Marxian theory—the 'biological' dimension in which the vital, imperative needs and satisfactions of man assert themselves. Inasmuch as these needs and satisfactions reproduce a life in servitude, liberation presupposes changes in this biological dimension, that is to say, different instinctual needs, different reactions of the body as well as the mind.
>
> We would have to conclude that liberation would mean subversion against the will and against the prevailing interest of the great majority of the people. In this false indentification of social and individual needs, in this deep-rooted, 'organic' adaptation of the people to a terrible but profitably functioning society, lie the limits of democratic persuasion and evolution.*

*Ibid., pp. 16–17.

He reached a conclusion alien to Marx. The revolution will have to be imposed by a minority against the will of the majority.

If the working class will not make the revolution, who will? Marcuse turns to two groups: 1) Those who reject capitalist society instinctively and intellectually, and 2) those who do not reap the material benefits provided by the society.

The first group contains radical professors and students. The second contains the national minorities such as Blacks, Mexican-Americans, Puerto Ricans, American Indians, the criminals and prison inmates, and the insane. These categories, Marcuse is convinced, contain the infantry of the revolution.

Concerning the blacks, he writes:

> The ghetto population of the United States constitutes such a (revolutionary) force. Confined to small areas of living and dying, it can be more easily organized and directed. Moreover, located in the core cities of the country, the ghettos form natural geographical centers from which the struggle can be mounted against targets of vital economic and political importance.*

He justifies racial revolt with reference to the Leninist doctrine of imperialism:

> The racial conflict still separates the ghettos from the allies outside. While it is true that the white man is guilty, it is equally true that white men are rebels and radicals. However, the fact is that monopolistic imperialism validates the racist thesis: it subjects ever more non-white populations to the brutal power of its bombs, poisons, and money; thus making even the exploited white population in the metropoles partners and beneficiaries of the global crime. Class conflicts are being superseded or blotted out by race conflicts: color lines become economic and political realities—a development rooted in the dynamic of late imperialism and its struggle for new methods of internal and external colonization.
>
> The fact is that, at present in the United States, the black population appears as the 'most natural' force of rebellion.†

*Ibid., p. 57.
†Ibid., pp. 57–58.

He is also ambivalent about the students:

Revolutionary in its theory, in its instincts, and in its ultimate goals, the student movement is not a revolutionary force,
perhaps not even an avant garde so long as there are no masses
capable and willing to follow, but it is the ferment of hope in
the over powering and stifling capitalist metropoles: it testifies
to the truth of the alternative—the real need, and the real possibility of a free society.*

Nonetheless, as a Marxist, he is pessimistic. He concludes:

But the struggle for the solution has outgrown the traditional
forms. The totalitarian tendencies of the one-dimensional society
render the traditional ways and means of protest ineffective—
perhaps even dangerous because they preserve the illusion of popular sovereignty. This illusion contains some truth: 'the people,'
previously the ferment of social change, have 'moved up' to become
the ferment of social cohesion. Here rather than in the redistribu-
tion of wealth and equalization of classes is the new stratification
characteristic of advanced industrial society.
However, underneath the conservative popular base is the sub-
stratum of the outcasts and outsiders, the exploited and persecuted
of other races and other colors, the unemployed and the unemployable. They exist outside the democratic process; their life is the
most immediate and the most real need for ending intolerable
conditions and institutions. Thus their opposition is revolutionary
even if their consciousness is not. Their opposition hits the system
from without and is therefore not deflected by the system; it is an
elementary force which violates the rules of the game and, in doing
so, reveals it as a rigged game. When they get together and go out
into the streets, without arms, without protections, in order to ask
for the most primitive civil rights, they know that they face dogs,
stones, and bombs, jail, concentration camps, even death. Their
force is behind every political demonstration for the victims of law
and order. The fact that they start refusing to play the game may
be the fact which marks the beginning of the end of a period.
Nothing indicates that it will be a good end. The economic and
technical capabilities of the established societies are sufficiently
vast to allow for adjustments and concessions to the underdog, and

* *Ibid.*, p. 60.

their armed forces sufficiently trained and equipped to take care of emergency situations . . . The facile historical parallel with the barbarians threatening the empire of civilization prejudges the issue; the second period of barbarism may well be the continued empire of civilization itself. But the chance is that, in this period, the historial extremes may meet again: the most advanced consciousness of humanity, and its most exploited force. It is nothing but a chance. The critical theory of society possesses no concepts which could bridge the gap between the present and its future; holding no promise and showing no success, it remains negative. Thus it wants to remain loyal to those who, without hope, have given and give their life to the Great Refusal.*

## THE FREUDIAN

So, although a patron of Marxism, Marcuse finds no effective revolutionary force in the teachings of Marx applicable to modern day conditions. In his quest to find such a force, he turns to Freud. The choice seems strange since the teachings of Marx and Freud concerning human nature are irreconcilable. Marx taught that human nature is formed by the experiences of this life, whereas Freud insisted that the human psyche is formed from the experiences of countless evolutionary generations. Freud taught that these experiences are stored in the genetic inheritance, and the experiences of this life have minimal influence on instinctual nature. If Freud is right, the Marxist program to regenerate human nature is nonsense.

In fact, both Freud and the communists have recognized the irreconcilability of Marx and Freud. For many years the communists have prohibited publication of the teachings of Freud.

Concerning communism, Freud writes:

> The communists believe that they have found the path to deliverance from our evils. According to them, man is wholly good and is well-disposed to his neighbor; but the institution of private property has corrupted his nature. The ownership of private wealth gives the individual power, and with it the temptation to ill-treat

*Herbert Marcuse, *One Dimensional Man* (Boston, Beacon Press, 1964) pp. 256–257.

his neighbour; while the man who is excluded from possession is bound to rebel in hostility against his oppressor. If private property were abolished, all wealth held in common, and everyone allowed to share in the enjoyment of it, ill-will and hostility would disappear among men. Since everyone's needs would be satisfied, no one would have any reason to regard another as his enemy; all would willingly undertake the work that was necessary. I have no concern with any economic criticisms of the communist system; I cannot enquire into whether the abolition of private property is expedient or advantageous. But I am able to recognize that the psychological premises on which the system is based are an untenable illusion. In abolishing private property we deprive the human love of aggression of one of its instruments, certainly a strong one, though certainly not the strongest; but we have in no way altered the differences in power and influence which are misused by aggressiveness, nor have we altered anything in its nature. Aggressiveness was not created by property. It reigned almost without limit in primitive times, when property was still very scanty, and it already shows itself in the nursery almost before property has given up its primal, anal form . . . If we do away with personal rights over material wealth, there still remains prerogative in the field of sexual relationships, which is bound to become the source of the strongest dislike and the most violent hostility among men who in other respects are on an equal footing. If we were to remove this factor, too, by allowing complete freedom of sexual life and thus abolishing the family, the germ-cell of civilization, we cannot, it is true, easily foresee what new paths the development of civilization could take; but one thing we can expect, and that is that this indestructible feature of human nature will follow it there.*

Freud conceived no utopias. He was convinced that human aggressiveness would express itself in any society. Freud was aware of the dangers lurking in all societies. For civilization to survive, he was sure that it must be protected against unrestrained aggression.

As a Marxist, Marcuse is convinced society must be destroyed. From the teachings of Freud, he perceives how this may be achieved. The weapon he selects is sexual license.

Marcuse's most influential book is *Eros and Civilization,* subti-

*Sigmund Freud, *Civilization and Its Discontent* (New York, Norton, 1962) pp. 59–61.

163

tled "A Philosophic Inquiry into Freud." This book was first published in 1955, but he published a political preface to it in 1966. In this preface he states:

> It was the thesis of Eros and Civilization, more fully developed in my One-Dimensional Man, that man could avoid the fate of a Welfare-Through-Warfare State only by achieving a new starting point where he could reconstruct the productive apparatus without that 'innerworldly asceticism' which provided the mental basis for domination and exploration. This image of man was the determinate negation of Nietzche's superman: man intelligent enough and healthy enough to dispense with all heros and heroic virtues, man without the impulse to live dangerously, to meet the challenge; man with the good conscience to make life an end-in-itself, to live in joy in life without fear. 'Polymorphous sexuality' was the term which I used to indicate that the new direction of progress would depend completely on the opportunity to activate repressed or arrested organic, biological needs: to make the human body an instrument of pleasure rather than labor.*

Society cannot be destroyed by a workers' rebellion, Marcuse wrote, but it can be de-energized so that it collapses in the face of external pressure from the "International Proletariat" of the Third World. The key to this is to "resexualize" the human body; to transform it into an instrument of pleasure rather than labor.

From the teachings of Freud, the rationale becomes clear.

Freud said that the human psyche consisted of three parts, the ID, the Ego, and the Superego. The ID is the area of the instincts and is the source of most human conduct and of human energy. The Ego is the section of consciousness, reason, and judgment. It is a recent evolutionary addition and does not contribute as much as is generally believed to human conduct. The Superego is the conscience, the repository of guilt and it harmonizes the conflicts between the ID and Ego.

Human energy, Freud taught, comes from the Id. It is derived from the two basic instincts: The Sex Instinct or Eros, and the Death Instinct or Thanatos. The sex instinct gives rise to the life forces while the death instinct generates aggression and cruelty.

*Marcuse, Eros & Civilization (Boston, Beacon Press, 1955) pp. XIV–XV.

Civilization requires energy; unpleasant work must be done. This energy, Freud declared, is sublimated sexual energy. Energy for work is secured by limiting sexual activity to monogenic, reproductive, patriarchal sex. All other forms of sexual activity are forbidden. Some are classified as perversions. The energy that could have been spent in sexual license is sublimated and becomes the life-giving energy of society.

Freud stressed that sexual license would deenergise and destroy civilization. Because he wished to preserve civilization, he counseled sexual restraint.

Marcuse acknowledges the accuracy of Freud's analysis, and it provides Marcuse with what is a method to destroy society. The method is: open up all channels of sexual indulgence; permit all perversions. Sexual energy will be spent and there will be none available for "civilized societal relations."

The result is described in Marcuse's *Eros and Civilization:*

> No longer used as a full-time instrument of labor, the body would be resexualized. The regression involved in this spread of the libido would first manifest itself in a reactivation of all erotogenic zones and, consequently, in a resurgence of pregenital polymorphous sexuality and in a decline of genital supremacy. The body in its entirety would become an object of cathexis, a thing to be enjoyed—an instrument of pleasure. This change in the value and scope of libidinal relations would lead to a disintegration of the institutions in which the private interpersonal relations have been organized, particularly the monogamic and patriarchal family.*

Marcuse emphasizes that sexuality will be enlarged. The body will be "resexualized." Genital primacy will be abolished as more areas of the body are eroticized, and all human contact becomes sexual.

Marcuse appears to find this prospect alluring. But the end result could scarcely be considered human. The individual would spend his days in a state of masturbatory, thumb-sucking euphoria —without family, without society, without passion and without goal.

It is hard to take the vision of "resexualized" man seriously.

*Ibid.,* p. 201.

However the destructive consequences of sexual license are apparent. This change in life style must have political consequences.

It has been said that genius is the application of a simple idea. Marcuse has applied a very simple idea, "skilled labor is not necessary for destructive purposes." A moron equipped with a hammer can do untold damage in an electronics laboratory.

The present phase of the revolution, Marcuse believes, is destructive. The welfare through warfare state must be dismantled. Why try to recruit skilled labor for this stage? The communists go to great pains to recruit and train skilled and disciplined individuals. Such people are needed to impose the dictatorship of the proletariat but not for the present destructive phase, so recruit on the basis of self-indulgence rather than self-discipline. A hundred can be recruited for self-indulgence for every one who will respond to the call for self-discipline. This leads to a new moral code. If you have an urge; indulge it. If you have an appetite, satiate it. Indulgence is good, control is evil. Marcuse has mobilized the appetites of the body for the destructive phase of the Marxist revolution.

I make no claim to the expertise needed to decide how much of the Freudian argument is right, and how much is wrong. However, it is an observable phenomenon that sexual over-indulgence depletes energy. The primary impression gained from observing a large group of so-called hippies is that they lack exuberance and energetic expression.

I have occasionally taken a visitor to observe the hippies who used to abound on the Sunset Strip in Los Angeles. Whereas a group of normal teenagers is noisy and active, the hippies are strangely silent and slow in their movements. There was a minimum of laughter and conversation, and little horse-play. Most just stood around as if on display. The picture is one of lack of vitality and boredom.

It is significant that Marcuse wishes to rob most youth of all heroes and heroic virtues while he exalts the revolutionary virtues of Fidel and Che. The strategy is clear. Inspire the revolutionaries to heroic acts! Weaken the supporters of the status quo. Youth needs heroes to inspire them.

Marcuse writes: "The actual may considerably deviate from the ideal, the fact remains that, for a whole generation, 'freedom,' 'socialism,' and 'liberation' are inseparable from Fidel and Che and the guerrillas—not because their revolutionary struggle could furnish the model for the struggle in the metropoles, but because they have recaptured the truth of these ideas, in the day-to-day fight of men and women for a life as human beings: for a new life."*

Herbert Marcuse has no monopoly on this prescription to destroy society. Timothy Leary, guru of the drug cult, has a similar philosophy. With him, drugs are primary and sex secondary. His slogan is, "drop out, tune in, turn on." If enough young people could be persuaded to drop out of society in this fashion, society would not continue to function. However, at least till recently, Leary thought that dropping out of society was enough. Drugs would produce an expanded consciousness. No direct political action was necessary.

Norman O. Brown, author of *Love's Body* exalts sex but neglects politics. He thinks sex is enough in itself. At this point he and Marcuse part company. Marcuse believes sexual activity must lead to active political protest. The hippies follow the philosophy of Leary and Brown; the Yippies that of Marcuse. The Yippies are the politicized hippies.

## THE MARXIST-LENINIST

Marcuse pays little attention to the structure of the society that would follow a successful revolution. However, he does discuss the subject briefly towards the end of his book, *An Essay on Liberation,* and it is clear that his vision is a Leninist one.

Concerning the organization of the post-revolutionary state, Marcuse writes:

> What kind of life? We are still confronted with the demand to state the 'concrete alternative.' The demand is meaningless if it asks for a blueprint of the specific institutions and relationships which would be those of the new society; they cannot be determined a priori; they will develop, in trial and error, as the new society develops . . . However, the question cannot be brushed aside by

*Marcuse, *An Essay on Liberation,* op. cit., p. 86.

saying that what matters today is the destruction of the old, of the powers that be, making way for the emergence of the new . . . The system of corporate capitalism has the right to insist that those who work for its replacement justify their action.*

Then Marcuse commits himself. In a discussion of the role of anarchy during and after the revolution, he reveals his concept of the basic structure of post-revolutionary society.

> To be sure, within the repressive society, and against its ubiquitous apparatus, spontaneity by itself cannot possibly be a radical and revolutionary force. It can become such a force only as the result of enlightenment, education, political practice—in this sense indeed, as a result of organization. The anarchic element is an essential factor in the struggle against domination: preserved but disciplined in the preparatory political action, it will be freed and "aufgehoben" in the goals of the struggle. Released for the construction of the initial revolutionary institutions, the anti-repressive sensibility, allergic to domination, would militate against the prolongation of the 'First Phase,' that is, the authoritarian bureaucratic development of the productive forces.†

It is difficult to escape the conclusion that "the authoritarian bureaucratic development of the productive forces" is a synonym for the "dictatorship of the proletariat." This is particularly true as he uses the Marxist-Leninist "First Phase" in quotes.

The role he assigns to the anarchists is the role allotted them by the communists. They contribute during the revolutionary process but have no place in post-revolutionary society. The term "aufgehoben" is a German word expressing the dialectic concept of fulfillment and negation. The anarchists fulfill their purpose during the revolutionary process. With the consummation of the revolution they are negated. To clarify all doubts, I wish Marcuse would specify the authority which would appoint the bureaucrats in the post-revolutionary society.

Marcuse expresses views in tune with Leninism on the subjects of tolerance and violence.

In "Repressive Tolerance" he writes:

*Ibid.
†Ibid., page 89.

Liberating tolerance, then, would mean intolerance against movements from the Right and toleration of movements from the Left. As to the scope of this tolerance and intolerance . . . it would extend to the stage of action as well as of discussion and propaganda, of deed as well as of word.*

He advocates action to forcibly prevent free speech. Apparently he would favor "Thought Police"—the ultimate in authoritarianism.

When Marcuse discusses violence, he shows his viewpoint is very similar to that of Lenin.

Several years ago, I heard Marcuse speak at a psychoanalytic symposium. He began in this fashion: "I agree with the previous speaker that in our society, violence cannot be eliminated entirely, so we must reduct it to a minimum. The main practitioners of violence are the government and the police so all our actions should be concentrated against them."

He regards governmental activity as primary violence, therefore revolutionary violence is merely counterviolence. It is permissible and benevolent. He writes:

Even in the advanced centers of civilization, violence actually prevails: it is practiced by the police, in the prisons and mental institutions, in the fight against racial minorities; it is carried, by the defenders of metropolitan freedom, into the backward countries. This violence indeed breeds violence. But to refrain from violence in the face of vastly superior violence is one thing, to renounce a priori violence against violence, on ethical or psychological grounds (because it may antagonize sympathizers) is another. Non-violence is normally not only preached to but exacted from the weak—it is necessity rather than a virtue, and normally it does not seriously harm the case of the strong.†

He goes further and claims that revolutionary violence is progressive—a Leninist idea if such there be:

*Herbert Marcuse, *A Critique of Pure Tolerance* (Boston, Beacon Press, 1968), pp. 110–111.
†*Ibid.*, p. 102.

The historical calculus of progress (which is actually the calculus of the prospective reduction of cruelty, misery, suppression) seems to involve the calculated choice between two forms of political violence: that on the part of the legally constituted powers (by their legitimate action, or by their tacit consent, or by their inability to prevent violence), and that on the part of potentially subversive movements.*

His ideas on Law and Order are precise: "Law and order are always and everywhere the law and order which protect the established hierarchy."†

This is nonsense. The law-abiding citizen craves security for his person and his property. This is true, independent of color or economic status. The poorest inhabitant of the ghetto needs good police protection against thieves, extortionists and murderers. Any government which cannot provide security, loses legitimacy.

## THE ABSURD

In *Psychology Today* magazine Marcuse was interviewed by two men called Keen and Raza:§

Keen: "One of your friends told me of luring you to Montana for a lecture with the promise that he would show you wild mountain sheep. I take it that somewhere in your vision of utopia, there must be a wild place."

Marcuse: "Yes, but not too wild, we don't want animals who eat each other and eat humans, we must not ignore the fact that nature is by no means gentle. It is just as cruel as the human reality. That is why I insist that the liberation of man involves the liberation and reconciliation of nature."

Raza: "The wolf also shall dwell with the lamb and the leopard also shall lie down with the kid, and the calf and the young lion and the fattling together."

Marcuse: "My allergy against the scriptures is not such that I must say a priori that every single thing in the scriptures is reactionary and repressive."

*Ibid.*, p. 107.
†*Ibid,* page 116.
§*Psychology Today,* Feb. 9, 1971, p. 62.

Marcuse proposes to stop the cycle of life without stopping life. He demands animals stop killing other animals but, naturally, he suggests no program to accomplish this.

What would happen if fish ceased eating shrimp and birds did not eat insects?

If some ordinary person made a statement like this, he would be held in contempt. High academic stature seems to confer the right to indulge in stupidity without suffering the consequences. If the pacification of man must wait on the pacification of nature, the wait will be long. Incredibly, Marcuse claims to reject God but deifies his own imagination.

Will the real Herbert Marcuse please stand up?

The personal prestige of Herbert Marcuse has diminished considerably during recent years. This is doubtless due, at least in part, to his advancing years and the associated decline in activity. However, the influence of his ideas continues, and contributes to the disintegration of the family and society in America as well as around the world. Typical is the experience of anguished parents trying to persuade their 17-year old son to return to high school. He dropped out in his junior year to live with an older girl in self-indulgent idleness on the fringe of a college community. He self-righteously proclaims, "I'm a revolutionary," as he quotes Herbert Marcuse.

# A PERSONAL INTERLUDE     9

The sensuous revolutionaries claim that they must present in their personal lives the qualities that will characterize the new society they wish to create. Herbert Marcuse spoke along these lines to an audience celebrating the 20th anniversary of the radical weekly, *The Guardian.*

"Because our goals, our values, our own and new morality, our OWN morality, must be visible already in our actions. The new human beings who we want to help to create—we must already strive to be these human beings right here and now."

What are the qualities of this new morality? These would surely include honesty, intelligence, tolerance, courage and compassion.

With the hope that it may cast light on the degree to which such qualities are demonstrated by one leading spokesman of the new morality, I present the documented story of my "confrontation" with Marcuse in the spring of 1970. I will restrict personal comments to a minimum and allow the facts to speak.

On January 2, 1970, I received a letter from the extension Department of the University of California at San Diego inviting me to participate in a proposed debate with Professor Marcuse. The debate was to be part of a course entitled "Conservative and Traditional Views on Contemporary Issues". I accepted the invitation.

On March 13, 1970, THE TRITON TIMES, the student newspaper of the San Diego campus published the following letter by Herbert Marcuse:

"I strongly protest against the university sponsorship of Dr. Fred Schwarz in the course 139X of the Extension Division.

"Dr. Schwarz is the chief of the so-called "Christian Anti-Communism Crusade." The publication, "Danger on the Right" by Arnold Forster and Benjamin R. Epstein (1964), sponsored by the Anti-Defamation League of B'nai Brith, devotes a whole chapter to Dr. Schwarz, to which I refer for documentation. It presents him as a hate-monger and rabble-rouser of apparently hysterical stature. The same chapter also reports on the way his Crusade is financed.

"It is of course not only legitimate but also desirable that the university offer a course on conservative or rightist thought (in the case of Dr. Schwarz a euphemism and misnomer), but I find it intolerable that the university stoops to the official sponsorship of hate propaganda. I quote from "Danger on the Right":

> In the course of his activities he delivers several hundred talks a year mostly to middle-class, middle-aged audiences. The tenor of such 'education' talks is illustrated by two of recent vintage. At one, he stated as an undisputed fact that the Communist take-over of the United States is set for 1973, a date which almost all America-savers have agreed on, and proceeded to terrifying details of what his listeners faced when the Reds seized power. He grew dramatic, stepped close to the edge of the platform as if to bring the Reds nearer, and told them that a basic aim of the enemy is 'to liquidate the bourgeoisie'.
>
> 'If you own shares of common stock, it means you! Now, fifteen million Americans own common stock! If the Reds win, it means the gallows!'
>
> At another meeting, Schwarz's Reds were evidently short of rope and had to rely on revolvers. After working his listeners to the edges of their seats with horrendous tales, with the pauses and

the studied emphasis of the trained performer, the Doctor said 'When they come for you . . . on a dark night, in a dank cellar, and they take a wide bore revolver with a soft nose bullet, and they place it at the nape of your neck . . .'

At Phoenix, Arizona, Schwarz said: 'The hour of their (the Communists) final conquest draws near. I think my prediction of world conquest for the Communists for 1973 was too conservative. They are running ahead of schedule. There are one billion people in Communist laboratories today being organized and exploited for world conquest. This is six times the population of the United States . . . Their Godless doctrine of communism is being taught children at a ratio of 5 to 1 over doctrines taught in any school anywhere . . . If Communism takes the world, it will be unrestrained. People will be animals, to be disposed of. Imagine them coming for you.'

At San Francisco he told an audience: 'I believe he (Khrushchev) has chosen San Francisco as headquarters of the World Communist Dictatorship. The Mark Hopkins Hotel will make splendid offices for him . . . the people of San Francisco—those they don't dump in the Bay—can be put in the Nevada desert, which is quite handy.'

"The stuff indeed speaks for itself.

"I was told that Dr. Schwarz intends to attack me, and I was asked whether I would appear at his lecture. I like to be attacked if my critics have read and, preferably, understood my books. This does not seem to be the case of Dr. Schwarz, as shown by his "exegesis" of what he thinks is my philosophy, or that of Marx and Freud. I therefore declined the invitation.

"I was also told that the university acted "under pressure" in organizing the course. Under pressure by whom? Is the university no longer free or capable of setting up its own courses? If it was indeed "under pressure" that Dr. Schwarz was given the privilege to speak at the lead-off section, it seems that the university, in that deal, agreed to provide the largest possible forum for the sort of propaganda marketed by Dr. Schwarz.

"In order to avoid any possible misinterpretation, I repeat: I think the university must offer a course on conservative and rightist thought, but I find the selection of some of their self-styled protagonists unworthy of an academic institution.

"I consider the appearance of Dr. Schwarz in a university course an insult to the intelligence of any serious audience, a mockery of genuine education and a mockery of conservative thought."

My published reply in the TRITON TIMES (March 18, 1970) was as follows:

Dr. Marcuse appears to hold his colleagues and the students at the University of California at San Diego in low esteem. He would protect them from the danger of hearing me lecture. He does not think they are capable of recognizing "a hate-monger and rabble-rouser of apparently hysterical stature" and making their own judgment. In his letter to Dr. Martin N. Chamberlain—Director, University Extention, UCSD, published in your edition of March 13, he strongly protests that I am to deliver one lecture entitled "A Rebuttal to the Left" in the series "Conservative and Traditional Views on Contemporary Issues."

If everything Dr. Marcuse says about me in his letter were true (and much of it is false), it would still indicate that I represent a significant influence meriting study. The fact that the book "Danger on the Right" by Arnold Forster and Benjamin Epstein, which is sponsored by the Anti-Defamation League of B'nai Brith, devotes a whole chapter to me, indicates this. In passing, I mention that this chapter contains 32 provable errors of fact.

I have read the available books of Herbert Marcuse. These include: Reason and Revolution, Negations, Soviet Marxism, Eros and Civilization, One Dimensional Man, and an Essay on Liberation. I have also read several essays and articles written by Dr. Marcuse. I do not claim to have understood all that he has written. I sincerely doubt if Herbert Marcuse has done this. I do claim that I have understood sufficient to justify comment and criticism. The extent of my understanding I leave to the verdict of those who hear the lecture.

I intend to discuss the message of Herbert Marcuse on the basis of the books he has written himself and not on those of his enemies. For example, I do not intend to take the writings of the Progressive Labor Party, which are critical of Herbert Marcuse, as the basis for an attack on him. I would consider this unworthy of a scholar.

Herbert Marcuse deserves credit for his consistency. He has advocated intolerance towards movements which he considers to be from the right. In his essay, Repressive Tolerance, included in the book, A Critique of Pure Tolerance, he states:

'Liberating tolerance, then, would mean intolerance against movements from the Right, and toleration of movements from the Left . . . it would extend to the stage of action as well as of discussion and propaganda, of deed as well as of word.'

I hope Herbert Marcuse will not be completely consistent and that he does not intend to engage in action as well as discussion and propaganda to prevent my presenting the scheduled lecture.

The letter of Herbert Marcuse provoked considerable interest and stimulated discussion in the editorial pages of many newspapers. This all served to promote interest in the program scheduled for April 2, 1970.

Harold Keen, News Director of a San Diego TV station, invited me to appear for an interview on his "Encounter" program. I accepted and Harold Keen conducted the TV interview on March 18, 1970.

During the session, Keen said, "Herbert Marcuse has accused you of being a hate-monger and a rabble-rouser of apparently hysterical stature. Are you a hate-monger?"

I replied, "I certainly do seem to arouse some people. I appear to have aroused Herbert Marcuse. Whether that makes me a rabble-rouser is a matter of opinion. As for being a hate-monger, I am too happy to hate. God and life have been good to me. You cannot hate while you are happy."

Keen gave Herbert Marcuse a chance to air his position on TV on April 1. The verbatim transcript of the interview follows. I have inserted quotations from the writings of Marcuse which conflict with the statements he made to Harold Keen:

INTRODUCTION BY HAROLD KEEN: Tomorrow is an important milestone at the University of California at San Diego (UCSD): the ten-week course on Conservative and Traditional Views begins with Dr. Fred Schwarz, controversial head of the Christian Anti-Communism Crusade as the first speaker. Recently we interviewed Dr. Schwarz. Tonight "Encounter" presents equally controversial Dr. Herbert Marcuse, UCSD's internationally known Marxist Philosophy Professor who has protested Dr. Schwarz's appearance tomorrow.

KEEN: Dr. Marcuse, in protesting Dr. Fred Schwarz's appearance on the campus Thursday, isn't this a denial of his right of freedom of speech such as you yourself enjoy at UCSD?

MARCUSE: It is not at all a denial of freedom of speech. I never protested Dr. Schwarz's appearance on campus. I would never have protested his speaking at the free speech area on the plaza of Revelle college or for that matter at any other location. I protested exclusively against the University sponsorship of his appearance in an accredited course. It seems to me there's an essential difference between freedom of speech and academic freedom, and I do not believe that the principles of academic freedom can apply to Dr. Schwarz.

KEEN: Why not?

MARCUSE: Because the principles of academic freedom presuppose certain qualifications. In the broadest sense, a knowledge of the facts and the ability or willingness to analyze these facts as objectively as possible. I think I can show that this is not the case, at least I have no evidence whatsoever that Dr. Schwarz has these qualifications.

KEEN: Well, you claim then that he doesn't have the academic qualifications that earn the right to lecture at UCSD for credit although you would be willing to allow him to speak generally to the student body.

MARCUSE: I certainly would.

KEEN: Now on what grounds do you claim he doesn't have these academic qualifications?

MARCUSE: Well, let me give you only, and I think it is fair, examples from his recent interview with you. He, Dr. Schwarz, says that I reportedly was a member of the Spartacus League in 1917.

KEEN: Which he described as a fanatical young group of communists in Germany similar to the today's Weatherman section of the Students for a Democratic Society?

MARCUSE: I never was a member of the Spartacus League. Maybe I should apologize for it. I was a member at that time of the rather conservative Social Democratic Party which was violently anticommunist. The Spartacus League has absolutely nothing to do with the Weatherman faction of SDS. It was an organization rooted in the German working class and it certainly was against any individual terror.

[I apologize to Dr. Marcuse for having stated that he was a Sparticist. The source of my information was a pamphlet entitled

178

"Marcuse", published by the Australian Communist Party. In the introduction, it states categorically, "In 1918 he was a sparticist."]

> KEEN: Now what else in his interview with me do you challenge?
>
> MARCUSE: Well, for example, he says that I envisage after the revolution, and I quote, I think literally, "an authoritarian bureaucratic organization of the productive forces." The fact is that I have consistently criticized the Stalinist construction of socialism and the construction of socialism in the Soviet satellites as an authoritarian bureaucratic organization which I consider incompatible with authentic socialism. Let me give you another example: he says that I envisage the Communist Party as authority after the revolution. I have equally consistently criticized the Communist Party as repressive of any genuine development towards socialism.

[Here Marcuse denies his own words. At the conclusion of his book "An Essay on Liberation", he discusses the kind of life which is to follow a successful revolution. He gives particular attention to the role of anarchy and anarchists in the revolutionary processes and in the post revolutionary situation. He states:

> "The anarchic element is an essential factor in the struggle against domination: preserved but disciplined in the preparatory political action, it will be freed and *aufgehoben* in the goals of the struggle. Released for the construction of the initial revolutionary institutions, the antirepressive sensibility, allergic to domination, would militate against the prolongation of the 'First Phase,' that is the authoritarian bureaucratic development of the productive forces."*

N. B. Aufgehoben is a German term which means fulfilled and negated. [The phrase "authoritarian bureaucratic development of the productive forces" reads like an academic synonym for the Marxist-Leninist Dictatorship of the Proletariat. I ask Marcuse, "What authority will appoint the bureaucrats during this *First Phase?*"]

---

*Marcuse, *op. cit.*, p. 89.

KEEN: Now you have also been quoted as saying that self-indulgence should be mobilized for political purposes like sexual license, general rebelliousness of youth, absurdity, and obscenity.

MARCUSE: Well, I must tell you I find it funny, and I just don't see how self-indulgence can in any imaginative way be political. It seems to me that the two are contradictory to each other. I did point out that a sexual revolution as it prevails among the youth is and cannot be in itself a revolutionary force, and that unless the individual protest becomes political protest, it remains simply a private escape.

[In his POLITICAL PREFACE, 1966, to "Eros and Civilization" Marcuse writes:

"It was the thesis of 'Eros and Civilization,' more fully developed in my 'One Dimensional Man,' that man could avoid the fate of a Welfare-Through-Warfare State only by achieving a new starting point where he could reconstruct the productive apparatus without that 'innerworldly asceticism' which provided the mental basis for domination and exploration . . . 'Polymorphous sexuality' was the term which I used to indicate that the new direction of progress would depend completely on the opportunity to activate repressed or arrested *organic,* biological needs: to make the human body an INSTRUMENT OF PLEASURE RATHER THAN LABOR."*

[Marcuse teaches that the revolution must start with this "polymorphous sexuality", but he emphasizes that it must develop a political program if it is to be successful. He is critical of the hippies who merely drop out of society, and commends the yippies who try to enlist the hippies into political programs to destroy society.]

KEEN: Such as the present Women's Liberation Movement for instance?

MARCUSE: Women's Liberation Movement? I can even give you a better example from among my own students. The development of the San Diego commune is to me a typical case where a rebellion, which began on the private personal level, has been

*Marcus, *op. cit.,* pp. xiv-xv.

transformed into political action. Now you may not like this political action, but in any case it is certainly something very different from self-indulgence as he says as mobilization of the body—I don't know what.

KEEN: The typical "Marcusian" was described by Dr. Schwarz as "Yippies" such as Abbie Hoffman or Jerry Rubin, two of the "Chicago 7". Is that correct?

MARCUSE: I don't feel qualified to say what the typical Marcusian can possibly mean. Abbie Hoffman and Jerry—well, I don't know. I think one of them certainly doesn't like me. I like both of them, and there again I think it is a case where you can refute what he says. I mean, these kids risk years of their lives in jail for a political cause. It certainly cannot be called self-indulgence or simply interest in sexual revolution or whatever.

KEEN: There is an impression from your well-know essay "Repressive Tolerance" that you oppose freedom of speech for anyone who is against your views or anyone who is opposed to socialism, and only those who are for communism or socialism should have outright freedom of speech and assembly.

MARCUSE: Well, I think I could put a rather high reward on anyone who could show me that I said or wrote or implied that anyone who was opposed to socialism or communism should be prevented from speaking. In my essay on "Repressive Tolerance", I have clearly confined the notion of a withdrawal of tolerance to demonstrably destructive and aggressive movements. This means, for example, that the vast majority of liberal and conservative thought in this country, certainly would be and should be entitled to toleration.

KEEN: Could you give examples of what forces you believe should not be allowed freedom of speech or assembly?

MARCUSE: Yes, for example, a Nazi Party, any party or organized group coming out and propagating racism, anti-Semitism, the escalation of the war, the prolongation of the war, and so on.

KEEN: Now in our society, today, we permit these groups freedom of speech.

MARCUSE: That's right. I think it's a mistake; as I think back to Weimar Germany, as I always say if at that time the Hitler Party would have been prohibited, we may have been spared a second World War and the extermination of 6 million Jews.

KEEN: Should these antisocial views, those you consider antisocial views, be physically stopped?

MARCUSE: I have nowhere said that they should be physically

stopped. They should be stopped exactly the way they are being stopped now, namely by the decision of the courts.

[In his essay "Repressive Tolerance", Marcuse writes:

"Liberating tolerance, then, would mean intolerance against movements from the Right, and toleration of movements from the Left ... it would extend to the state of action as well as of discussion and propaganda, of deed as well as of word.*

[He also advocates:

"The withdrawal of toleration of speech and assembly from groups and movements which promote aggressive policies, armament, chauvinism, discrimination on the grounds of race and religion, or WHICH OPPOSE THE EXTENSION OF PUBLIC SERVICES, SOCIAL SECURITY, MEDICAL CARE, etc. (emphasis added) Moreover, the restoration of freedom of thought may necessitate new and rigid restrictions on teachings and practices in the educational institutions which by their very methods and concepts, serve to enclose the mind within the established universe of discourse and behavior."†

[Will Marcuse pay the "high reward" he mentions?]

KEEN: Would you encourage heckling or disruption of such speakers as Dr. Schwarz?

MARCUSE: I have in my long experience found out that heckling is spontaneous and the business of the students. I wouldn't think of organizing heckling, and I don't think it has ever been necessary.

KEEN: Are you in agreement with the general views of communists in the U.S. and abroad?

MARCUSE: I am not. I already mentioned that I have for years criticized communist policy. I may add here that to my knowledge, the communist countries today are the only countries in the world where my books are not published, and they probably know why.

*Marcuse, *op. cit.*, p. 109.
†*Ibid.*, pp 100–101.

[Marcuse has commended the actions of the communist dictatorships in Cuba, China, and North Vietnam. He has been critical of the bureaucracy in the Soviet Union but blames it on the necessity to coexist with the capitalist United States.]

KEEN: Summarizing as a Marxist, Dr. Marcuse, are you against the presentation of conservative views at UCSD, a campus that many people in this community believe is already too liberal?

MARCUSE: I am most certainly not against it. In fact I would favor a real and good course on conservative and traditional thought.

KEEN: Would you debate a conservative scholar, having already refused to debate Dr. Schwarz?

MARCUSE: I would certainly debate a conservative scholar of whom I can assume that he knows the facts and is willing to analyze and evaluate the facts as objectively as possible. I would be very glad to do so.

KEEN: Your contract at UCSD expires this June. What are your plans after that?

MARCUSE: I have no plans. I like it very much here, and, if I can, I would like to stay in La Jolla. I definitely will stop teaching at UCSD, and I must say I am rather happy that the taxpayer is at least relieved of this role.

As the time of the lecture drew near, tensions rose. Rumors of protest demonstrations circulated. The big question was, "Would there be violence?"

200 "radical" students gathered outside the Scripps Auditorium where the session was to be held. They were not protesting my appearance, but rather their exclusion from the lecture. This was an official University function and an admittance fee of $4 had been set by the University. The students outside claimed they could not afford the admittance fee.

I suggested that these students be admitted and was informed that the officials could not break the rules established by the University. I then said that the Christian Anti-Communism Crusade would pay the $4 fee for each student. Administration authorities approved the proposal and the students were admitted on a first-come, first served basis to fill up the 44 vacant seats.

Behavior during the lecture was perfect with no heckling or

disturbance. Attention could not have been better. During the question time that followed the lecture, all questions asked by the students were pertinent and searching. There was no hostility evident from students, though there was some from adults.

Frankly, I cannot applaud the conduct of Herbert Marcuse as revealed in these episodes. They appear to reveal intellectual arrogance, intolerance and deceit. If his conduct exemplifies the New Morality he and his supporters are working to create, the old morality would seem preferable.

# PART IV:
# OVERVIEW

# THE WEATHERPEOPLE                    10

The three revolutionary streams—communism, anarchism, and sensualism—merge in the remarkable movement of terrorists known as Weatherman or Weatherpeople.

The "Weatherman" organization evolved from the leadership of Students for a Democratic Society (SDS). At its inception in 1960, SDS adopted an anti-totalitarian constitution and excluded communists and fascists from membership. The emphasis was on participatory democracy. But in less than ten years, SDS had produced bands of urban guerrillas, operating underground and practicing armed robbery, arson, bombing, and murder.

By the late 1960's the Students for a Democratic Society had become an organization immobilized by various revolutionary forces contesting for control of the group. Communists had infiltrated the organization and transformed SDS into something quite different from what it had once been.

The steps that led to communist control and ultimately to the disintegration of SDS were:

1. Anti-authoritarianism. Totalitarians were not accepted as members. This excluded the communists.
2. Non-exclusion. Membership was open to all.
3. Communists were allowed to become leaders.
4. Communists capture leadership.
5. Communist leaders fight and SDS disintegrates into three fragments:
   a. Weatherman
   b. Revolutionary Youth Movement II (RYM II)
   c. The residual SDS dominated by the Progressive Labor Party (PL).

During 1968 and 1969, Progressive Labor, a communist sect, was threatening to capture SDS.

On one side were members of Progressive Labor Party, a communist party which had proclaimed its fidelity to Mao Tse-tung. On the other side was the reigning SDS leadership, which was radical also, but they wanted to avoid domination by the Progressive Labor Party crowd. To show that their communist militancy was equal to, if not greater than, that of the Progressive Laborites, the SDS incumbent leaders produced a document in 1969 to spell out their specific positions. It was called "You don't need a Weatherman to know which way the wind blows."

The title was taken from a line in a song by Bob Dylan entitled, "Subterranean Homesick Blues." Apparently it was chosen to suggest that since everyone was experiencing the oppression of the American establishment, theory was not necessary to convince people that the system was evil.

The fight for control of the SDS organization shattered the organization's national convention which commenced on June 18, 1969, in the Chicago Coliseum. The Progressive Labor faction had organized well and its delegates at the convention formed a well-disciplined block of voters. They were able to outvote the other delegates during the early convention procedures. Most of the leaders of SDS were antagonistic to the Progressive Labor Party and when they saw how the votes were going, they walked out of the convention to reconvene in another building. (The incumbent leadership held the keys to the office and the safe.)

The reconvened "SDS convention" then proceeded to elect three secretaries, all associated with the "Weatherman" position.

They were Mark Rudd, leader of the revolt at Columbia University, as National Secretary; Bill Ayers of Michigan and Jeff Jones of San Francisco.

The message of the document, "You don't need a Weatherman to know which way the wind is blowing," contains these major features:

1. The major conflict in the world today is between U.S. Imperialism and the national liberation struggles against it. Consequently friends or enemies are identified by whether they help national liberation struggles or vice versa.

2. The goal is world communism, and the U.S. will be defeated by the people of the world.

3. The blacks in America form an oppressed black colony.

4. The black battle for independence is the most important fight within America in the battle against U.S. Imperialism and is a battle for socialism.

5. Blacks could, if necessary, win the battle alone.

6. White revolutionaries must regard themselves as auxiliaries in the black struggle.

7. The international strategy is the creation of many Vietnams.

8. The white working class is corrupted by being paid some of the profits of imperialism.

9. Youth rebellion is due to the internal decay of the U.S.

10. Young people will be part of an International Liberation Army.

11. Schools must be closed, not reformed.

12. Demands for impossible objectives must be made.

13. Black caucuses must be encouraged in factories.

14. Military organizations of women must be formed.

15. Women must repudiate the role of wife-mother.

16. The police must be fought.

17. A Marxist-Leninist Party must finally be formed to win the war.

18. Revolutionary collectives on communes must be formed immediately.

19. These collectives should work to create a mass revolutionary movement which will become a division of the International Liberation Army.

While the Weatherpeople were not successful in carrying out

their whole program, they did set up "affinity groups." Such groups consisted of 5 to 25 individuals who knew each other well. These groups sought at least three goals:

1. Deepening the knowledge of and trust among individuals in the group.

2. Learning various medical, legal, self-defense and propaganda skills.

3. Internal political education.

The organization was directed by a committee of the top leadership called the Weather Bureau. The organization was democratic centralist and the leadership exercised control over political policy and published the newspaper, FIRE.

Tiers of leadership existed within the collectives and competition was fierce. Members of a collective debated ideological questions, learned various skills, worked on political projects, fought in the streets, shared their clothes, food, money; danced; turned-on; tripped out; and slept together. Political thought and activity dominated their lives.

The turnover among members of the rank and file was high. Many found the going too tough and dropped out. But the toughest, strongest-willed, least sensitive, stuck.

Weatherpeople declared war on monogamy and male supremacy which it termed male chauvinism. This attitude was explained in an article entitled "Weather Letter," published July 15, 1970 by "Rat Women's Collective:"

> "Much internal struggle centered on male chauvinism and monogamy, both of which we attacked, not as abstract principles, but as counterrevolutionary practices. We saw how male chauvinism set up men as machismo leaders who developed a politics around proving their masculinity. It held women back from being leaders and denied them the ability to struggle politically. We attacked monogamy because we saw it as a central form of male chauvinism which reinforced women's political dependence on men.
>
> The collective was conceived of as an arena for struggle and transformation, a form in which people could be open about their past lives and struggle over what it meant now to be a revolutionary. Machismo prevented men particularly from being open about their fears and weaknesses. Monogamy was a dependency relation-

ship in which people held on to each other rather than pushed each other."*

All did not go smoothly. The authors confess:
"Too often we forgot that criticism was meant to build and not to smash. In their anger against chauvinism, women often attacked men rather than struggling with them. We understood a great deal about sisterhood and revolutionary love, but we still found it difficult sometimes to believe that men could change."†

The situation in the collectives was described by four ex-Weatherpeople, Inessa, Victor Camillo, Lelina Jones and Norman Reed:

> Weatherman's practice of 'smashing monogamy' closely paralleled the way the state affects all close relationships. Anyone familiar with divorce and separation figures in the U.S. knows most marriages are 'smashed' before they are a few years old. This does not, of course, eliminate the oppression of women nor does it eliminate male chauvinism.
>
> Neither did the Weatherman 'solution.' In fact, Weatherman attacked couples and close relationships (at least among the lower level cadre; for in truth there was double standard within the organization—a concrete example of elitism) which they erroneously labeled as 'smashing monogamy.'
>
> What did Weatherman substitute for forcing couples to break up, some of whom have been together for years? 'Sex, dope, and violence.' There was no mention of love. Perhaps this is why we hear so much about love in the 'Weather Letter.' Attempts were made to force sexual relationships between people who 'struggled' with each other. This was labelled building communist relationships. Women in particular were supposed to be freed from male chauvinist men by engaging in sexual activity with women, many of whom were as chauvinist as any of the men. People literally hid from each other to avoid having sex with comrades for whom they had no sexual desire.§

Even after the final split between Progressive Labor and the old leaders of the Students for a Democratic Society, all was not harmony among the P.L. opposition. A sharp disagreement devel-

*Jacobs, *op. cit,* p. 458.
†*Ibid.,* p. 459.
§*Ibid.,* p. 431.

oped between the Weatherman leadership and a group known as Revolutionary Youth Movement #2 (RYM2) led by outgoing National SDS Secretary, Mike Klonsky, and supported by a West Coast group known as the Revolutionary Union. The argument centered on the possibility of organizing the white revolutionary class and the nature of desirable violence. RYM 2 believed that the white working masses could and should be organized while the Weatherpeople tended to regard them as a lost cause. RYM 2 believed violence should be Leninist, or mass violence, carried out by a mob in pursuit of some objective while Weatherites were preparing for anarchist terror. These ideological differences led to a split over the nature of preparations being made from demonstrations in Chicago, October 8–11, 1969. Klonsky wanted to recruit the support of the blacks, the welfare recipients, strikers and workers, while Weatherman proposed to bring a trained army to Chicago to commence civil war.

Klonsky accused the Weatherpeople of being a group of rich kids indulging their bourgeois penchant for violence. He said the real purpose of the demonstration was not to influence people against the war in Vietnam but to attract violent individuals into Weatherman ranks. Klonsky accordingly disassociated himself and RYM 2 from the demonstrations.

Meanwhile the Weatherpeople planned for civil war in Chicago and published their plans in the old SDS publication, New Left Notes. Undergoing "Red Army" training in Cleveland, Ohio, the Weatherpeople chanted such slogans as "Bring the war home," and "The time has come for fighting in the streets."

The purpose of their "Civil War" was to support a litany of radical demands ranging from release of "political prisoners" to independence for Puerto Rico, but they focused on the Vietnam War. An article in a Weatherman publication reported that the Chicago "Civil War" action would be:

> An action not only for immediate withdrawal of all U.S. occupation troops, but also in support of the heroic fight of the Vietnamese people and the National Liberation Front for freedom and independence. An action not only to bring peace to Vietnam, but beginning to establish another front against imperialism right here in America—to 'bring the war home'. . .

When we move with the people of the world, against the interests of the rulers, we can expect their pigs to come down on us. So we're building a fighting force to struggle on the side of the Vietnamese, the blacks, and oppressed people everywhere. There's a war we cannot 'resist'. It is a war in which we must fight. We must open another front against U.S. imperialism by waging a thousand struggles in the schools, the streets, the army, and on the job, and in CHICAGO, OCTOBER 8 – 11.*

The Weatherpeople group finally reached Chicago in early October. But instead of the thousands they had predicted, only a few hundred came. In fact most of their allies had, along with Klonsky, repudiated them because of what they considered to be the Weatherman preference for suicidal violence.

But the Weatherpeople soon proved they meant business about civil war regardless of how few they numbered. They emerged from their barracks at Garrett and McCormick Theological Seminaries wearing helmets and boots and armed with lead pipes, wooden staves, and bricks. They engaged in an orgy of violence that left a trail of wrecked automobiles, smashed windows, and maimed bodies, as they moved through Chicago. They tried to isolate individual police so that one could be attacked by many.

Newsmen and others familiar with previous demonstrations were amazed at the frenzied violence practiced. The whole action was popularly named the "Days of Rage", but the rage was planned, not spontaneous.

To an observer, the violence may have seemed purposeless. There was however, method in the madness; for the rioters saw themselves as an elite bent on destroying a corrupt society. They believed that violence was a magnet that would attract other destroyers into their ranks. They knew that violence would be portrayed widely on television screens, and those with aggressive and destructive urges would be stimulated. Through publicized violence, the process of the natural selection of potentially violent personalities would be promoted.

Because of my interest in the Weatherman phenomenon, I sent two representatives to Chicago to observe the activities. They were armed only with cameras and tape recorders. They were in the

* *New Left Notes,* September 20, 1969

front of the Weatherman group when the initial violence burst forth on Wednesday, October 8.

My two young representatives were sickened as they observed one policeman being hit in the stomach with a bottle by one Weatherman, and over the head with a stick by another. They were fearful that the police might lose control, but they were filled with admiration for the manner in which the police conducted themselves. The police exercised great patience and resisted provocation and restored order with a minimum of force, even though this cost casualties in their own ranks.

Since the Weatherman group had announced in advance its intention to engage in mass violence, the role of the seminaries and churches which granted them sanctuary was questioned by numerous people. Many even accused the churches and seminaries of being accessories in the maiming of Richard Elrod. On the other hand, some of those involved tried to justify their actions in the name of Christian love.

The Evanston Methodist Parish which had housed part of the Weatherman contingent, produced the following statement:

> The Evanston United Methodist Parish responded to the request for housing of members of the Students for a Democratic Society. We did so out of our understanding of the nature of the church, not out of our understanding of the SDS. In fact, we explicitly reject their political program.
>
> By nature the church is open to all. Such openness does not carry with it approval of what those who come are or do. This is the unique nature of Christian love. Christians are committed to the coming of a new society. We hope for its coming through a nonviolent witness. We do not approve of any violent action of the S.D.S. in the streets nor of the police in forcing entry to church doors which would have been opened to them.
>
> By nature the church is especially sensitive to the alienated and the dispossessed. A "Cup of water" given because "You bear the name of Christ" is the tradition of the church. In a time when we too easily call our brothers enemy, the church lives her life under command: 'You have heard that it was said, You shall love your neighbor and hate your enemy. But I say to you Love your enemies.'
>
> The role of the church, therefore, is to offer itself as a link of

communication between those sectors of society alienated from each other. The response of our churches this week is offered as the best effort we could make to fulfill the ministry of reconciliation in a badly divided world.

The call today is to all who love the church and her Lord to strengthen the ties of love: to love the unlovable to express confidence in the sincerity of one another; and to search together in our many conversations for a new commitment to a true and relevant mission of Christ's Church in this present moment.

However, the Administrative Board of Chicago Temple First United Church had a different viewpoint. They published this statement:

Last Saturday afternoon multiple crimes were committed within the area—and against the people of—this parish. Those directly responsible for these crimes will be dealt with by the law.

Of greater concern to us is the complicity of the United Methodist Church in these crimes as some of our pastors and churches became accessories both before and after the fact as they aided and abetted these criminals while knowing of their intent and purpose.

We want to believe that this complicity was the result of good, if totally irresponsible, intention.

However, our credulity is strained in this as we read of the attempts of those involved to use adapted theological arguments to not only excuse what they have done but to try to make virtue of it. We find it unbelievable that a leader of those directly responsible could proudly announce in the public press that what was done was 'the greatest moment for Evanston Methodist Churches in recent history—the fact that they were becoming involved in society rather than staying on the fringes.'

We find this calloused and irresponsible. If the church is to learn anything from this tragedy, it cannot be left unchallenged.

Those directly involved state that they were seeking to 'open a door, build a bridge,' to those alienated from society. They admit that they failed in both purposes.

But it should be carefully noted that they did not fail in closing dozens of doors to thousands of people, in the destruction of hundreds of bridges painfully and responsibly built by the church.

Those involved are partly responsible for injury to the cause of reasonable dissent, and this is a society where significant dissent is desperately needed. They are in part responsible for the blunting of protest as a weapon for justice. Hundreds of thousands of minority peoples, who know little of these events, have been set back in their search for justice by what has been calculatedly and deliberately done.

In view of the seriousness of this matter—and of the extended attempt of apologists to make virtue of irresponsibility and error —and of the need of the church to learn a lesson from this experience, the Administrative Board of the Chicago Temple—First United Methodist Church, in session October 12, 1969, unanimously adopted, and directed the undersigned committee to convey to our Bishop, the following resolution:

'We call upon our Bishop to provide that discipline which shall clearly indicate the censure which the United Methodist Church of the Northern Illinois Conference must accept—clergy and laymen—for the Church's part in aiding and abetting those revolutionists involved in the violence that took place in Chicago last week, through providing them with food, shelter and a meeting place in which to arrange, and from which to stage, their attacks upon our people and our community. Further, we ask our Bishop to make it clear that unilateral use of the good name of The United Methodist Church indicating support of demonstrations and actions that lead to violence will not again be permitted.'

The President of Garrett Theological Seminary published this statement:

The Garrett community—faculty, students, staff—during the past week has been reviewing recent events on our campus and asking ourselves some pointed questions. The review of the events is a simple matter; how the SDS got on our campus and what took place after they came. Enclosed is a statement of these facts as they relate to Garrett.

Our discussions have turned spontaneously toward searching theological questions arising out of the difficult, disturbing experiences of these days. Students and faculty have opened their hearts to each other. I want to share with you the essence of our concerns, for none of us can escape them. Let me pose three questions.

First, does the church have any responsibility for redemptive communication with that segment of our society made up of mostly young (some in their middle teens), alienated, angry, violence-prone, perplexed human beings. Many of them are idealistic, but confused and distorted in their thinking—willing to go to revolutionary extremes in the destruction of life and property (including their own) to bring in what they would describe as a 'more humane society'. Does the church have a responsibility to try to bring to them some ministry marked by redemption and reconciliation?

The weight of opinion among us as we searched our hearts on that question was that responsible Christian discipleship requires that we answer in the affirmative.

That leads to a second question: If the church has such a responsibility, how does it go about doing it? And that is a very difficult question. For the people with whom you must deal are tough (though many of them are terribly afraid and are held in line by the almost military discipline of their group), their scale of values may be diammetrically opposed to your own, their social practices and language often are repugnant. But here they are—human beings, bent on shaping the future, and inescapable in their presence. How do you reach them?

It may well be that the answer is not found in allowing a few of them in your midst. But we are convinced of one thing: to ignore them, to hate them isn't the answer either. In obedience to the mandate of our Lord, our task is to seek the alienated. A number of our students and faculty engaged in this ministry with SDS students while they were here.

The third question is a difficult one also: If you should try to make some redeeming reconciling approach to these people, are you willing to take the risks and pay the cost? Maybe that is the question, for it is not theoretical but intensely personal and practical.

In God's mission to 'reconcile the world unto himself' the road led to a cross.

If Lee Harvey Oswald had announced in advance that he was going to Dallas to shoot President John Kennedy, would a church on the route have had a Christian duty to provide him with a seat near a window so that he could take good aim? Is not this a perversion of the doctrine of reconciliation? Does not reconciliation embrace the victim as well as the criminal?

For their part, the Weatherman took particular delight in the plight of Richard Elrod, chief counsel of Chicago, who lay in bed paralyzed from the neck down, the result of injuries incurred during the violence. Here is their version of what happened:

> They're trying to frame Brian Flanagan on a charge of attempted murder in the paralyzing of tricky Dick Elrod—Pig Daley's top legal oinker. The pig press reported that Brian had attacked pig Elrod with a club, a brick, a lead pipe, and his fists. What they didn't report was the true story—Pig Elrod, living up to his role, trying to attack demonstrators and help finger leadership, saw Brian running through the streets and tried to tackle him, breaking his own neck when he hit the pavement. Elrod is now paralyzed —*hopefully for life*. He won't be so quick to play pig next time.'*

The Weatherpeople even composed a song to sing in their collectives as well as during the demonstrations celebrating Elrod's injury:

> LAY ELROD LAY
> (to the tune of "Lay, Lady, Lay")
>
> Lay Elrod lay
> Lay in the street for a while
> Stay Elrod stay
> Stay in your bed for a while
>
> You thought you could stop the Weatherman
> But up-front people put you on your can
>
> Stay Elrod stay
> Stay in your iron lung
> Play Elrod play
> Play with your toes for a while
>
> You thought the Weatherman was mighty green
> But we were the heaviest that you'd ever seen
>
> Lay Elrod lay
> Lay in the street for a while
> Stay Elrod stay
> Stay in your bed for a while

*\*New Left Notes,* October 21, 1969

The final public appearance of the Weatherman group was in Flint, Michigan, December, 1969. About 400 young people attended the session. A story from the Liberation News Service reported that:

> The meeting hall was decked with large banners of revolutionary leaders—Che, Ho, Fidel, Malcolm X, Eldridge Cleaver—hanging from the ceiling. One entire wall of the ballroom was covered with alternating black and red posters of murdered Illinois Panther leader, Fred Hampton. An enormous cardboard machine gun hung from the ceiling . . .

The opening speech was given by Weatherman leader Bernadine Dohrn:

> She began by admitting that a lot of Weatherman's actions have been motivated by 'a white guilt trip.'
> Dohrn characterized violent, militant response in the streets as 'armed struggle' against imperialism.
> Part of armed struggle, as Dohrn and others laid it down, is terrorism. Political assassination—openly joked about by some Weatherman—and literally any kind of violence that is considered anti-social were put forward as legitimate forms of armed struggle.
> "Honkies are going to be afraid of us," Dohrn insisted. She went on to tell the war council about Charlie Manson, accused leader of the gang which allegedly murdered the movie star and several others on their Beverly Hills estate. Manson has been portrayed in the media as a Satanic, magnetic personality who held near-hypnotic sway over several women whom he lent out to friends as favors and brought along for the murder scene. The press also mentioned Manson's supposed fear of blacks—he reportedly moved into rural California to escape the violence of a race war.
> Weatherman, the 'Bureau' says, digs Manson, not only for his understanding of white America—the killer purportedly wrote 'pig' in blood on the wall after the murder—but also because he's a 'bad _____.'

> 'Dig it, first they killed those pigs, then they ate dinner in the same room with them, then they even shoved a fork into a victim's stomach! Wild!' said Bernadine Dohrn.

Following the National War Council, Weatherman went underground. Public attention was called to their continued existence and activity when an explosion rocked a luxurious $250,000 town house in Greenwich Village. Three people were killed in the explosion—Ted Gold, Diana Oughton, and Terry Robbins. All were Weatherman leaders.

The house was a bomb factory and an accidental explosion had occurred. Since then, hundreds of Weatherman bombs have shattered buildings all across the country. While all bombings are not the work of Weatherman, many undoubtedly are.

The typical member of the Weatherpeople comes from a family of wealth and a university of stature. Ted Gold, one of those killed in the Greenwich Village blast, came from a typical Weatherite family background, though many came from families much wealthier than his. He was born in New York City on December 13, 1947 an only child. His parents were liberals living in a pleasant apartment in Manhattan, comfortably well-off if not exactly rich. His father, Dr. Hyman Gold was a highly respected internist. His mother, Dr. Ruth Gold, was an associate professor of education at Columbia University's Teachers College. Coming from such a background, why did Ted Gold turn to revolutionary terror?

Some contend that Weatherpeople are seeking to expatiate a sense of guilt. They say that young radicals tend to feel guilty about the comfortable, privileged homes from which they come— especially when they try to take their message into the desperate homes of the poor. The Weatherites feel guilty about what they regard as their own middle-class racism and that of the society that has showered its benefits on their parents. They feel guilty because of their initial fear of violence and envy which blacks and others have confronted from infancy. And they feel guilty because their brains, money, or influence has kept them safe on university campuses while others are sent to Vietnam.

This sense of guilt turns into anger and they experience an emotion of rage against society associated with an overwhelming need to prove their renunciation of that society. They are willing to become martyrs for their cause.

So intense is their rage against their background and society that the Weatherpeople have even talked of promoting a "kill your parents" week. The tragedy is that some susceptible youth will undoubtedly be influenced and commit the outrage.

In the final analysis, their outrage is a protest against a life that has showered material blessings upon them, but which has robbed them of their spiritual heritage. Having lost faith in God, they conjure up a god of revolution to whom they dedicate both body and mind and to whom they sacrifice themselves.

The anarchist violence of the Weatherpeople has resulted in its virtual isolation from the community. This illustrates the foresight of Lenin who warned revolutionaries that individual violence could lead nowhere else. Their activities seem to have diminished during the past year and many trapped in the coils of Weatherpeople violence may be regretting the day they cut themselves off from society. The way back will be difficult if not impossible.

# SEMANTIC QUICKSANDS     **11**

The communists and their allies are engaged in a war to destroy the United States. This war knows no frontiers and uses many weapons. The use of words has been one of the revolution's most effective weapons.

Marcuse urges the left to break "The conformist and corrupted universe of political language."* Whatever the cause, this has been done, and it is now very difficult to engage in rational discussion on political issues, because words have been subverted and no longer have an accepted meaning. The same words convey different and even contradictory meanings to different audiences. It is no longer possible to agree with a simple statement such as "Christianity is the answer to Communism", unless the hearer knows what the speaker intends to convey by the words: "Christianity", "Answer", and "Communism".

Communication is very difficult. Even when two people agree

*Tedori, *op. cit.*, p. 471

completely on the meaning of the words used, the hearer may receive a message very different from that given by the speaker. The interpretation depends upon the universe of experience of the listener. This is illustrated by a simple story: "The temperance lecturer announced with great indignation and pride, 'There are 190 taverns in this county, and I'm proud to say that I have never been in one of them'. An alcoholic voice questioned, "Which one was that?"

Much of the time we think we're communicating a message but we would be surprised if we knew what message was being received. Communication is difficult enough if we agree on the meaning of the words used. When there is no agreement on the meaning of the words, it is impossible.

During my debate with Greg Calvert, former National Secretary of SDS, to which I've previously referred, he asked me, "Do you believe in the resurrection of the body?" I thought I knew what he meant by his question but decided not to expound upon it and answered simply, "yes".

One of the students who had been following the argument, stood up and said, "Will Dr. Schwarz please discuss what he thinks Greg Calvert meant by the expression 'resurrection of the body' and what he meant by his reply?"

I said that I assumed that Calvert meant sexual license and drug indulgence by "Resurrection of the Body." Norman O. Brown and others argue that the "Puritan Ethic," by denying gratification of carnal bodily appetites, had killed the body. Feeding these appetites would resurrect it.

On the other hand, I said that I meant the resurrection referred to by St. Paul when he wrote "If we die with Christ, we will also live with Him."

It is difficult to imagine two meanings more different.

I spoke at a meeting in Columbus, Ohio. During question time, a young man stood up and said, "I notice from your literature that your organization is called the Christian Anti-Communism Crusade. Isn't that a contradiction in terms? You cannot be both Christian and anti-communist because Christianity and communism are similar."

By a series of questions I endeavored to discover what the words "Christianity" and "Communism" meant to him. He had private definitions of these terms. His Christianity and communism were unrelated to any existing organizations or systematized doctrines. Christianity had nothing to do with God or the continuity of life. He surprised the audience by saying that he was a Christian atheist. To him Christianity was merely an attitude and a program designed to help your brother, to distribute this world's goods more equitably and to abolish discrimination on the basis of race and social origin. It was, in essence, a program of social action based on sharing wealth and equalization of opportunity.

Communism to him meant something very similar. It meant common ownership and the sharing of this world's goods.

Since Christianity and communism were both programs for the more equitable distribution of this world's goods, he believed you couldn't be for one and against the other.

The problem was (and this is a common problem on the campuses) that he had a private definition of the terms. His thoughts were outside the realm of common agreement. Christianity and communism are not mere abstract concepts. They are labels attached to large organizations with systematized doctrines.

Since the same label is attached to a variety of organizations and doctrines, some agreement in advance concerning the organizations and doctrines designated by the words is essential for meaningful discussion to take place. Such agreement is often sadly lacking.

The business of defining terms can be carried to extremes. Any debate can be reduced to absurdity by one participant repeatedly demanding what his opponent means by such and such a word or phrase. Each explanation can be questioned further. Finally the ultimate question can be reached, "What do you mean by mean?"

Definition is essentially the process of describing the less familiar in terms of the more familiar. When the most familiar is reached, definition becomes impossible as there is nothing more basic in terms of which it can be described. How could the color red be defined to a color-blind person except by enumerating the objects that possess that color.

The existence of a common culture and language assumes there is agreement concerning basic words and phrases. Without this, any community would be impossible. But this agreement is being shattered to a considerable degree. The slogan, "Do your own thing," is extended to the realm of vocabulary and syntax. As a result, society disintegrates.

It is important to try to use words with precision. Only thus can confusion be diminished. Words which confuse rather than clarify include: right, left, and extremist. Many times I have been called a "right wing extremist." This enables opponents to pigeonhole me and absolves them, they think, from the obligation of examining my arguments. But the term is pejorative and insofar as it has any meaning, the classification is unmerited. However, it is very seldom that those using the words attempt to define them. Since the accusation is not rational, it is difficult to refute.

I've been asked at many a press conference, "Dr. Schwarz, are you an extremist?" I usually reply this way: "I suppose, in some areas, I am. For example, I would prefer to be extremely healthy rather than just moderately healthy. I would prefer to have my car repaired by a mechanic who was extremely honest rather than by one who was only moderately honest. The extreme is not undesirable in all situations. Have we totally discarded the quest for excellence? When the coach is selecting his athletes, does he seek the extremely fast or the moderately fast runners? The champion of the world in any realm is an extremist; the valedictorian is an extremist; the Heisman trophy winner is an extremist."

The term extremist has no moral significance unless the quality to which it is applied is specified. Extreme in what? The unqualified use of the term "extremist" is a confession of inadequacy in the use of English language. There are much more specific terms to use. If an individual supports violence, he may be called "violent". If he practices falsehood, he may be called "dishonest"; if he uses exaggeration and oratory to excite crowds, he may be called a "demagogue."

Consider the terms "right" and "left" as used in the political sense. These are approximate synonyms for the words "conservative" and "radical." Their use dates back to the French National Assembly of 1789. In that assembly, nobles who were largely conservative, took the honored seats to the king's right while the radicals ranged to the left.

The terms "right" and "left" have been corrupted. In the popular mind, the Nazis and Fascists are considered to be far-right while the communists and anarchists are considered far-left. This division confuses instead of clarifying.

A more rational use of the terms is shown by the following

graph. Select the two variables—Governmental Authority and Individual Liberty. Let the scale of authority run vertically, and that of liberty, horizontally. Societies can then be located on the graph:

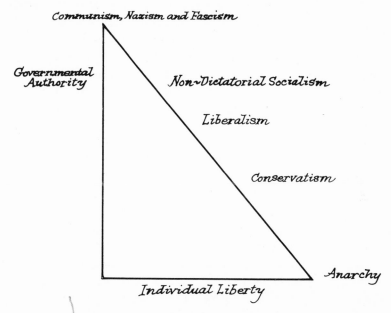

At the left of the scale would be those systems with maximum governmental authority and minimal individual liberty, while on the right there would be minimal authority and maximum liberty. On the left there would be totalitarianism and on the right, anarchy. Between there would be the gradations of limited government—from democratic socialism to liberalism, conservatism and, finally, anarchism.

Thus on the far left, there would be Communism, Nazism and Fascism, on the far right would be anarchy.

While this scale would be rational, it does not harmonize with common usage since the anarchists are usually considered as part of the New Left. However, it does show the close association between Communism, Nazism and Fascism. These systems are similar, not opposites. They have identical historical roots and similar organizational structures. They are all species of Leninism. The difference that private capitalists continue to own industrial enterprises under fascism while the state owns them under communism is not a major one. The government dominates the economy in both systems.

Mussolini was a Leninist Socialist before he formed the Fascist Party of Italy. He discarded some of the economic concepts of Marx while he adhered to the organizational ideas and revolutionary techniques of Lenin. He substituted the mystique of nationalism for that of Proletarian Internationalism.

Hitler organized the Nazi Party in accordance with Leninist principles. The name he chose is significant, The German Nationalist Socialist Workers' Party. At one stage in Berlin, serious consideration was even given to a union of the Communists and Nazis.

The problem for any society is to find the correct balance between authority and liberty. This is not easy to discover and a considerable amount of trial and error is essential. A system which allows for orderly, not violent, change is imperative. This is only possible where government is limited by law and when government and governmental acts are reversible.

The reversibility of government is one of the guarantees of freedom. Government is power and one restraint on its abuse is that the one who exercises power may be called to account. This is difficult while he is in power, but is easier when he has relinquished power. The limitation on the period an individual can exercise power and the periodicity of elections is a restraint on the arbitrary use of power.

Some governmental authority is necessary to enable individuals to exercise liberty. The question is "How Much." Too much of anything is evil. Water is essential to life but too much can destroy it.

Through the exercise of democratic rights and an informed electorate though, authority will hopefully be exercised so as to provide maximum liberty for the citizenry.

One semantic bog that should be avoided is the argument whether actions should be positive or negative. Often it is said, "We must not be against things, we must be for something." This statement poses false alternatives. How can you be for health without being against illness? Surely, because the medical profession concentrates on the diagnosis and treatment of disease, this does not make it a negative force.

What would be the use of a fire-fighting force if it did not act against fires? Who would want a police force that was not against crime? The most effective slogan for environmental cleanliness is "don't be a litterbug." Six of the ten commandments begin with "Thou shalt not . . ." Christ was against many things.

Every positive action is simultaneously a negative act and vice versa. To be against the forces that would destroy life is to be for life; to be against tyranny is to promote freedom; to be against communism is conduct consistent with humanity and Christianity.

Some years ago, I was arguing with a man who claimed it was essential to be positive. I tried to indicate the difficulty in deciding whether a course of action was positive or negative. I said, "If my house catches on fire and I call the fire brigade, is that a positive or a negative act?"

He said, "If you call the fire brigade, that's negative; if you put the fire out yourself, that's positive." His answer seemed to me to typify the rationality of those who claim it is impermissible to be against anything.

Some of the arguments used against anti-Communism and anti-Communists may be helpful in clarifying the discussion.

## THE GOOD IN COMMUNISM

Should we not emphasize the good in communism? When faced with the question, "Won't you acknowledge that communism has done good things for some people?" my reply is something like this:

"I can't deny it. Take Stalin for example. What a good thing it was for him. He could murder at will, he could use the entire property of Russia, he could do anything he liked."

Communism may have seemed a wonderful thing for Joseph Stalin, but it was a tragedy for the Russian people.

Most things have some good in them. I am told that the most toxic snake venom contains nutritive elements. Only a small percentage of the fluid causes death. The value of the entity cannot be measured by balancing the good against the evil. The addition of good to a unit of evil may magnify rather than dilute the evil. Consider an unbaited hook. As far as the fish is concerned, it is pure evil. Consider a piece of succulent bait. It is pure good with no evil in it. Now add the bait to the hook. The danger of the hook to the fish is increased many times. We now have a magnified unit of evil, not a diluted one.

A system must be considered as a unity, not merely as the sum of its constituent parts.

Opposition to communism need not be muted because there is some good in it. It is also legitimate to oppose communism even though areas of injustice remain in democratic societies. There are degrees of tyranny, and a system with greater tyranny should be condemned. When that system threatens to impose itself on a society enjoying greater freedom, it should be resolutely opposed. You do not need to be perfectly healthy to be justified in being immunized against poliomyelitis.

## THE USE OF ANALOGY

Is not the use of analogy in argument dangerous?

It is. Analogy is permissible to illustrate truth but it can never prove it. Sometimes an analogy can clarify one point. The temptation is to extend the use of the analogy beyond the purpose of illustration. Analogy is only valuable when the truth can be sustained by other means. A simple analogy, however, can often bring out a truth that would otherwise require a complex argument for its substantiation.

## "THE OPEN MIND"

"You must always keep an open mind." "Education should not indoctrinate." These statements are quoted as though they were self-evident truths.

However, a mind that's open at both ends is empty. Unless it is closed at one end, it cannot retain and digest information; it cannot think. History has taught certain lessons and a capital of knowledge and morality has been arduously accumulated. This includes language and techniques of calculation. It is represented by the three R's—reading, 'riting, and 'rithmetic. This capital should be given by the process of education so that the individual can invest it. "A fool learns by his own experience; a wise man by the experience of others." If each individual had to commence from scratch and devise his own language and method of computation, civilization would remain unborn.

This common capital of knowledge should be given to the young as efficiently as possible. They should be taught to read and write, to speak and spell, to add and subtract; to divide and multiply. If this is indoctrination, so be it.

Certain moral values can also be taught affirmatively. These include such concepts as: 1) Life is preferable to death, 2) Health is preferable to disease, 3) Freedom is preferable to slavery, 4) Kindness is better than cruelty, 5) Knowledge is preferable to ignorance.

Sophisticated arguments may be developed to question all of these maxims. Nevertheless, is it not permissible to teach them dogmatically before the critical faculties have fully developed? Let the mature individual renounce them later if he so decides. It is unwise to wait until he is fully capable to judge for himself before teaching basic moral values.

In Boston, an intellectual called on one of the radio talk shows and questioned the right of a teacher to indoctrinate pupils by teaching the basic mathematical tables dogmatically. She said, "You might inhibit the genius of an Einstein." My reply was, "Let him learn the mathematical tables first; let him develop and display his genius later."

## "TREAT THE CAUSE—NOT THE SYMPTOMS"

This is the "right" thing to say whenever a riot occurs in a ghetto, a school or a prison. The trouble is that the symptoms are obvious and painful while the cause is often obscure. The cause must be known before it can be treated. The assumption usually is that the cause is social injustice and that an attempt to eliminate social and economic injustice will promote harmony.

This is the modern manifestation of the old doctrine that communism is caused by bad economic conditions. Old delusions die hard. There are still people who believe the world is flat, just as there are still people who believe that the fever of malaria is caused by the stench emanating from swamps. And there are still people who believe that communism, racial unrest and riotous conduct are caused by bad economic and social conditions. Actually rebellion is more likely when conditions are improving than when they are stationary at a low level. This has been called the revolution of rising expectations. An improvement in social conditions may increase the probability of riot or rebellion.

The cause of mass violence is complex, but generally speaking, at least two factors are involved: 1) The environment that creates an aggrieved constituency susceptible to agitation, and 2) The agitators who organize the aggrieved constituency. Both elements are generally necessary for a riot or revolt, and both elements must be treated.

Changing the environment is a difficult, long, and arduous process. While work proceeds to do this, it is also necessary to observe, isolate and expose the agitators seeking to exploit the situation. Those working on the environment often feel themselves superior to those seeking to expose the agitators. Their cry is, Why don't you join us? However, the two approaches are complimentary.

The final answer to malaria was the draining of the swamps to eliminate the malarial mosquitoes. While this was being done, drugs were needed to protect the workers from malaria and to treat them if they succumbed.

Environmental factors contribute to the spread of tuberculosis. Malnutrition and overcrowding favor the spread of the disease. But while some work to improve the quantity and quality of the food supply and provide better housing, others must work to treat the disease itself. The tubercular bacillus which invades and destroys the weakened tissues must be studied and attacked with specific drugs.

Until conditions are so perfect that no group has any grievance and therefore no agitator can be effective, study of the doctrines and techniques of agitation and programs to defeat agitation will be necessary. Such an era cannot be realistically expected in the immediate future. Intelligent and effective programs of anti-communism are therefore imperative at present.

If poverty caused communism, the world would have been communist ages ago. Until this era, poverty has been the universal characteristic of human society. Until we know the cause, it is better to treat the symptoms than to do nothing.

## "VIOLENCE IS NECESSARY FOR CHANGE"

"Change can only come about through violence." This statement is as false as it is popular. At a symposium at Long Beach State College in Southern California, I attempted to refute this doctrine. I pointed out that two great changes that had affected the lives of those present had come about without violence. These were: 1) Survival through childhood and adolescence. Infectious diseases had decimated previous generations. This survival was due to medical research which had produced the life-saving drugs and vaccines to treat and prevent infectious disease. And 2) The availability of educational institutions which had enabled the student population to multiply dramatically in two decades. This was due to a productive economic system and technology which had produced enough material wealth to build the institutions and to support the army of educators needed and, to a considerable degree, the students.

One man tried to sustain the thesis of the necessity of violence as follows: He said, "Death itself is a form of violence. The fear of death has stimulated medical research. Medical research has discovered the life-saving drugs. We could say, in a sense, that the discovery of these drugs is due to violence." Could semantic sabotage proceed further?

In passing, it is interesting to note that every life-saving drug discovered in the past three decades was developed in the capitalist world. Not one was discovered in the socialist world.

## "FREE ALL POLITICAL PRISONERS"

This slogan makes great propaganda, but there are few, if any, political prisoners in the United States. A political prisoner is one who is imprisoned because of political acts or opinions. However, the radicals have extended the definition to include anyone they consider disadvantaged, whatever his crime may have been. To them, a black man who shoots a teller while robbing a bank and is convicted and imprisoned is a political prisoner because blacks are a politically oppressed minority. This is the rationale for Plank No. 8 in the platform and program of the Black Panther Party.

"We want freedom for all black men held in federal, state, county and city prisons and jails."

Bobby Seale was not a political prisoner. The crime of which he was accused was very real. The mutilated, murdered corpse of Rackley was real. The executioners of Rackley had confessed to the crime. They testified that they acted on the orders of Bobby Seale. They were tried and convicted. To call Seale a political prisoner was semantic sabotage.

Angela Davis was not a political prisoner. The crime again was very real as four men had been killed with guns and others grievously wounded. The evidence that she was a close associate of the individual who had initiated the crime and that her guns had been used was undoubtedly sufficient to indict and try her. The facts that she is black and a communist were incidental. A white noncommunist, in similar circumstances, would undoubtedly have been indicted, arrested and tried. A verdict of not guilty by the jury does not indicate that the trial was unjustified.

Examples of the subversion of words could be multiplied. Looters stealing goods from a store are "liberating" the goods. The radicals and the tiny majority who support them comprise the "people" to whom all power belongs. Kidnaping, disruption and bodily harm are "dissent" or even "peaceful" acts.

Words do kill. They should never be dismissed with a shrug as "Just rhetoric". If the driver of a car receives false directions and as a result drives the car over a cliff, the words were responsible for his death.

The concept that words are not subject to restraint by law whereas actions are, is a cherished American concept. Nevertheless, it should be questioned. In this dangerous age in which we live, words can destroy lives in a very literal sense. In other democratic countries such as England and Australia, crimes can be committed with words. There, speech and action are considered appropriate areas for legislation.

The borderline between words and deeds can be very obscure. There is no natural right to advocate murder and to teach the techniques of murder. Punishment for the act of murder does not bring the victim back to life. Prevention is better than cure.

# THE UNPERFECT SOCIETY --
# AMERICA ON TRIAL          **12**

**T**he United States is far from being a perfect society. To some
this fact justifies attempts to destroy it. The assumption is that
destruction will lead to improvement, which does not necessarily
follow.

The most recent book of Milovan Djilas, a disillusioned Yugo-
slavian communist, titled, "The Unperfect Society—Beyond the
New Class," makes the points that society is not merely imperfect
in the present, it is also not perfectible in the future. Djilas reached
this conclusion after many years of bitter and frustrating experience. The intellectual and sociological evolution of Djilas is instructive. As a radical student, he joined the communists and
dedicated his life to the perfection of man and society. He fought
heroically as a partisan during the war against Germany and
became Vice-President of Communist Yugoslavia and President
of the Federal Assembly under Tito. He witnessed the emergence
of a new class under communism, protested, wrote a book entitled

"The New Class", was expelled from the Communist Party in 1954 and was sentenced to three years in prison. On his release he wrote "Conversations With Stalin" and was recommitted to prison. In 1969 he published "The Unperfect Society" to express his conviction that man must seek the better and avoid the worse as the best is unattainable. Since the individual is imperfect, society must be so.

This does not mean that because all societies are imperfect they are necessarily equal. It does mean that no society should be judged by comparison with an unattainable ideal. It should be judged by whether its progress is towards or away from that ideal. It should also be judged in relation to available alternatives. Since society in the United States is far from perfect, it is possible to reach the conclusion that this society is evil by concentrating on the areas of obvious imperfection. It is only a short step to the conclusion that this "evil society" should be destroyed. The reason for the destruction is the supposed nature of existing society, not the vision of the society to replace it.

The same glass of water can be viewed in two ways. One person may see it as ¾ full; another as ¼ empty. By concentrating on the one quarter that is lacking, the impression may be given that the actual contents are of no value.

The picture of America portrayed throughout the world is an ugly picture. When I am in Australia, the question is frequently asked, "Are things in America as bad as reports make them out to be." Do you see much rioting and crime? How far off is open race war and complete collapse?"

There is much wrong with America. Volumes are being published constantly which document this view. Everyone hears of poverty, racism, militarism, crime, juvenile delinquency, drug addiction, corruption in high places, and the harassment of dissenters. Hovering over all is the grim hand of something called the "Establishment." Responsible for all evils is something called the "System."

Most discussion concerns that part of the American cup of happiness which is empty. For the purposes of this discussion, all that which is wrong is taken for granted. I wish to turn the spotlight on that part of the cup that is full; the admirable features of American Society.

America is criticized, often by the same people, for: 1) Creating material abundance, and 2) Failing to create material abundance.

The first criticism charges that America exalts material values at the expense of spiritual values and that the material needs of most of the people are oversupplied. Large cars, color television, central heating and air-conditioning; these are taken as a substitute for higher artistic and spiritual values. Some say it is possible to be comfortable in America but not happy. An abundance of material goods, to be sure, has not solved the problem of human alienation and produced happiness, but these same critics are often most irate because America has failed to supply these material comforts, which they condemn, in sufficient quantity to the racial minorities and the poor.

## POVERTY

It is charged that poverty is endemic in America and ten percent of her people live in poverty. In absolute figures, the situation looks even worse. More than 20 million live below the poverty line. In a society as wealthy as America, this is surely undesirable.

However, the corollary to this is often overlooked. Ninety percent of the American people enjoy relative abundance. This is a unique achievement in human history. At the turn of the century, ninety percent of the American people lived in poverty, if we use today's standards while allowing for inflation. Think of it— American society has lifted 80 percent of its population from poverty to abundance in 70 years. What an achievement!

The poverty line is drawn arbitrarily at an income of $3500 for a family of four. This definition of poverty is unique for America. An income of $3500 per year for a family of four would be wealth in most countries of the world.

America could, with some justice, be called the overfed society. More people are concerned with keeping to a diet that restricts food intake than with securing enough to eat. In the United States more deaths are caused by overindulgence in food and drink than by starvation.

Poverty is a relative term—yesterday's luxury is often today's necessity. Eldridge Cleaver, the militant black revolutionary, sees the poverty situation in the world in perspective. In his published conversations with radical journalist Lee Lockwood, he says:

> Now when you start talking about what's wrong with the United States, you also have to take into consideration the fact that everything that happens in the United States happens on a level far beyond what's happening in the rest of the world. Take poverty, for instance. Poverty in the United States cannot be talked about in the same sense that poverty can be talked about in India. I mean, you don't have people in the United States literally, and by the thousands, just starving to death. You have other forms of dehumanization of the individual. You have other forms of the poverty of individuals.
>
> Lockwood: Well, we also have Appalachia.
>
> Cleaver, "Yes, but you don't have people in Appalachia like you have people in New Delhi. There's no place in Babylon that can be equated with the poverty in the rest of the world."**

Cleaver can hardly be classified as a friendly witness.

There are, of course, individual cases of starvation in the U.S. Examples would be: children who are neglected by their parents; old people living alone who become immobile; and alcoholics who depend almost entirely on alcohol for nourishment. There is no group starvation, however.

The charge remains that there is widespread malnutrition. This is true, but malnutrition is qualitatively different from starvation. The causes for malnutrition are many and include ignorance, alcoholism, and food faddism as well as poverty.

The idea of a society with adequate food, clothing, and shelter for all has been the "impossible dream" of man since the dawn of history. Ironically, now that this condition has been realized in great degree, it tends to be despised.

During my first visit to the U.S. in 1950, I met a New Zealand radical who was about to be deported to New Zealand. We discussed life and its values.

He said, "I am not interested in God and spiritual values. I am interested in food, clothing and shelter." I replied, "I will meet you on your own chosen battlefield. The U.S. has provided more

**Lee Lockwood, "Conversation with Eldridge Cleaver", (New York, Delta Books, 1970) pp. 74–75.

food, clothing and shelter for each of its citizens than any other system in the world." He answered, "I have to admit, you are right."

This relative abundance creates by-products. Twenty years ago, the hippie cult could not have existed. They would have starved. They consume without creating. Their existence is a tribute to the system they condemn.

On the Sunset Strip in Los Angeles, the hippies survive by panhandling. Sometimes they diluted their panhandling with a dash of primitive capitalism. They tried to sell some hand-made objects such as strings of beads. Hippie girls were talking to me one evening when a young boy interrupted and tried to sell me something. But one of the girls said crossly, "He's ours." Even embryonic capitalist competition exists.

During another evening on Sunset Strip, a young girl said to me, "This is our street."

I asked, "So you poured the concrete, did you?"

"Oh, I don't mean that," she replied.

"Well, sombody poured the concrete, it didn't just drop down from the sky. The people who worked to build this street spent a lot of energy and lost a lot of sweat. How has it come about that you now own it?"

In an effort to drive my point home, I continued to question her, "How did you get here?"

"I thumbed it," she said.

"I've heard of people riding a broomstick, but never a thumb. What actually transported you?"

"Oh, we came in an automobile, of course."

"Where did that automobile come from? Did it drop down from the skies in a rainstorm or did somebody work and build it?"

"They worked and built it of course," the young girl observed.

"You acknowledge then that you're a parasite living off the labors of others." She made no reply.

The system in America has constructed such abundance that it can now maintain a substantial parasitic class. The existence of dropouts from society is a tribute to the efficiency and compassion of American society. Judged by its ability to provide and distribute the basic necessities of life, the American system of capitalism must be judged a success.

This success is even more apparent when the achievements of competing systems are compared. Most of these systems emphasize government control and direction of the economy. Of course, the major competing system is dictatorial socialism with the dictatorship exercised by the Communist Party.

Is communism a success or a failure? Success or failure in what? In some areas it is a great success and in others a dismal failure.

As a technique of tyranny, communism is a great success. Communism has devised the most efficient form of tyranny mankind has known. There has been no successful internal revolution against the communist dictatorship once it has been established.

Communism is also very successful in devising and distributing propaganda. Their literature and radio programs are effective indeed.

As a system to provide economic well-being for its subjects, communism is a dismal failure. This is illustrated by the political joke: "What would happen if the communists conquered the Sinai Desert?" Answer: "Well nothing much for a year or two; then there would be a shortage of sand."

Communism has an unusual ability to turn an agricultural surplus into a deficit within a very few years. This seems to be a general characteristic of communism. Yugoslavia is often regarded as the showcase of communism, yet more than 1 million Yugoslav workers have to work outside Yugoslavia to earn money, much of which they send home.

Conditions in Yugoslavia are described by a young Yugoslav in the September 1, 1971, issue of a British Trotskyite publication, the "Red Mole":

1. The growing number of workers abroad is now close to 1¼ million.

2. The situation for most peasants and workers is getting worse. Sixty per cent of the population receives minimum wages at which only bare subsistence is possible.

3. A report on Factory Wages in 1969 in South Serbia, which is not one of the poorest regions, reveals:

    a. 20% of salaries about $30 per month.
    b. 20% of salaries about $45 per month.
    c. 50% of salaries about $60 per month.
    d. 10% of salaries about $90 per month.

Is it any wonder many of the Yugoslavs who leave their country never return? The American economic system with its production and distribution of abundance, compared to the available alternatives, stands out like a beacon of success.

Communist propaganda accuses America of favoring the wealthy while socialism favors the poor, yet despite all the talk of tax loopholes, the taxation structure of the U. S. is loaded in favor of the working man and the poor, whereas the taxation structure in the socialist countries operates against the working man and the poor.

When Khrushchev was in America, he made a great point by boasting that they were on the point of abolishing income tax within the Soviet Union. This did sound like glorious achievement. However, there would be no difficulty in abolishing income tax in the United States if a hundred percent sales tax was added. A graduated income tax discriminates against the rich in favor of the poor. Sales tax is indiscriminate, and it hits the poor harder than it hits the rich. The communist countries operate on the basis of an enormous sales tax. They call it a use tax. The obvious conclusion is that the American system serves the poor better than the communist system.

When judged by progress being made towards the elimination of poverty and when compared with available alternatives, America emerges with credit.

## MILITARISM

The charge is constantly made that America is a militaristic nation. It is true that America has military might, but this does not prove devotion to militarist adventures. Certain facts contradict the contention that America is militaristic:

1. I know of no responsible American who contends that war is good. At best they regard it as a regrettable but necessary evil. On the other hand, Mao Tse-tung, the great communist leader, teaches the beneficence of war. His maxim, "Revolutionary War is an antitoxin which not only eliminates the enemy's poison, but also purges us from our filth," may be accepted by some students

and professors but finds no vocal advocates in the so-called military—industrial complex.

2. If America desired to conquer other countries by military might, she could have done it easily at the end of World War II when she had a monopoly of the atom bomb. Instead of doing that, America withdrew her forces, disarmed, and offered to share atomic secrets with the Soviet Union provided mutual inspection was allowed. This project collapsed because of the unwillingness of the Soviet Union to allow inspection.

3. America's neighbors have no fear of American military might. Each share a long border with the U.S.A. and these borders are among the most open in the world. The Mexican border does present some problems because the U.S. is a magnet to many Mexicans. There are so many Mexicans trying to enter the U.S. illegally that certain border problems result.

The military power of the U.S. is a protection to the sovereignty of free nations.

As an Australian, I am sometimes asked, "Why don't you stay in Australia and fight communism?" I reply by asking, "If you were Prime Minister of Australia and you received a phone call informing you that submarines of a Communist power were located off Brisbane, Sydney, Melbourne, Adelaide, Perth and Hobart and that these submarines were equipped with missiles with thermonuclear warheads, and you were instructed to prepare the welcoming speeches and lay out the red carpet for the communists, what would you do?" You would know that more than one-half of the Australian population lives in those cities. You would know that every one of those cities was located on the coast and was defenseless against any missiles that would be fired from submarines. You would know that there was not one thing that you could do to prevent those missiles being fired nor one thing you could do by way of retaliation if they were fired.

The only course of action that would present itself as an alternative to surrender would be to rush to the telephone and call the President of the U.S. If the U.S. were either unable or unwilling to help, there would be no alternative to surrender.

This is a hypothetical situation, but all the elements required to make it real, exist. The communists possess the missile firing submarines, and these could be placed within missile range of Australia's major cities.

The continued existence of a sovereign Australia depends upon the protective umbrella of the U.S. forces. The security of Australia is inextricably interwoven with the power and the will of the U.S. Whether the U.S. likes it or not, it has become the custodian of national sovereignty and human liberty throughout the world.

The world communist movement exists and it possesses massive military power. Communist doctrines teach the desirability and inevitability of world communist conquest. American military might is not evidence of militarism but of defensive prudence.

Again we should compare America with the visible alternatives. The AFL-CIO pamphlet, entitled "Who is the Imperialist?", compares the countries annexed and the peoples enslaved by the communists since World War II with the colonies liberated by the western powers. (See chart next page.)

## RACISM

America is racist to the core. This is accepted without question by many people. The accusation cannot be brushed aside. It would be surprising if America were not a racist society since racism seems to be a universal characteristic of human nature. Wherever there are people of different races living in quantity in proximity in this world, there are potentials of trouble. In Malaysia the conflict is between Malays and Chinese; in Indonesia, between Indonesians and the Chinese; in Ceylon it's between the Cingalese and the Tamils; in the Near East it's between the Jews and Arabs; in Pakistan, it's between the Bengali and the Punjabi; in Cyprus between the Greeks and the Turks; in Yugoslavia between the Serbs and the Croats; in the Sudan between the Arabs of the North and the blacks of the South; in Guyana between the Africans and the Indians; in Fiji between the native Fijians and the Indians, and in Canada between the French and the English. Racial conflict is almost universal. It would be surprising if there were no racial problems.

The U.S. is the land of minorities. The largest and most obvious national minority is black, and the accusation of racism usually

# THE THREE FACES OF REVOLUTION

Here is the Soviet and Communist Chinese
Record as of 1970

| TERRITORIES ANNEXED | AREA (Square Miles) | POPULATION (Before Annexation) |
|---|---|---|
| Romanian Provinces | 19,446 | 3,700,000 |
| Estonia | 18,353 | 1,122,000 |
| Latvia | 25,400 | 1,951,000 |
| Lithuania | 22,059 | 2,957,000 |
| Northern East Prussia | 5,418 | 1,187,000 |
| Eastern Czechoslovakia | 4,900 | 731,000 |
| Eastern Poland | 70,000 | 11,800,000 |
| Finnish Provinces | 18,000 | 450,000 |
| Tannu Tuva | 64,165 | 65,000 |
| Japanese Possessions | 17,850 | 433,000 |
| Tibet | 560,000 | 1,200,000 |
| TOTAL | 825,591 | 25,596,000 |
| **"SOCIALIST CAMP" DEPENDENCIES** | | |
| Albania | 11,100 | 2,019,000 |
| Bulgaria | 42,845 | 8,370,000 |
| Cuba | 44,218 | 8,074,000 |
| Czechoslovakia | 49,370 | 14,362,000 |
| Eastern Germany | 41,500 | 16,100,000 |
| East Berlin | 155 | 1,100,000 |
| Hungary | 35,919 | 10,284,000 |
| Poland | 120,632 | 32,207,000 |
| Romania | 91,660 | 19,721,000 |
| Outer Mongolia | 604,090 | 1,174,000 |
| North Korea | 46,814 | 13,100,000 |
| North Vietnam | 63,360 | 20,000,000 |
| TOTAL | 1,151,663 | 146,511,000 |
| **TOTAL ANNEXATIONS AND DEPENDENCIES** | 1,977,154 | 172,107,000 |
| **UNDER ATTACK** | | |
| Cambodia | 69,898 | 6,557,000 |
| Laos | 91,429 | 2,825,000 |
| South Vietnam | 66,263 | 17,404,000 |
| TOTAL | 227,580 | 26,786,000 |
| GRAND TOTAL | 2,204,834 | 198,893,000 |

New Independent Nations Since World War II

| COUNTRY | AREA | POPULATION | YEAR OF INDE- PEND- ENCE | FORMER CONTROL |
|---|---|---|---|---|
| Algeria | 919,352 | 12,943,000 | 1962 | French |
| Barbados | 166 | 251,000 | 1966 | British |
| Botswana | 238,605 | 629,000 | 1966 | British |
| Burma | 261,721 | 26,389,000 | 1948 | British |
| Burundi | 10,744 | 3,406,000 | 1962 | Belgian |
| Cambodia | 69,898 | 6,557,000 | 1949 | French |
| Cameroon | 183,381 | 5,562,000 | 1960 | French |
| Central African Republic | 241,000 | 1,518,000 | 1960 | French |
| Ceylon | 25,332 | 11,964,000 | 1948 | British |
| Chad | 495,624 | 3,361,000 | 1960 | French |
| Congo (Brazzaville) | 132,000 | 826,000 | 1960 | French |
| Congo (Kinshasa) | 905,328 | 16,730,000 | 1960 | Belgian |
| Cyprus | 3,572 | 621,000 | 1960 | British |
| Dahomey | 44,685 | 2,571,000 | 1960 | French |
| Equatorial Guinea | 10,830 | 286,000 | 1968 | Spanish |
| Fiji | 7,055 | 519,000 | 1970 | British |
| Gabon | 103,000 | 480,000 | 1960 | French |
| The Gambia | 4,003 | 357,000 | 1965 | British |
| Ghana | 92,100 | 8,376,000 | 1957 | British |
| Guinea | 97,000 | 3,702,000 | 1958 | French |
| Guyana | 83,000 | 710,000 | 1966 | British |
| Iceland | 39,758 | 200,000 | 1944 | Danish |
| India | 1,261,483 | 523,893,000 | 1947 | British |
| Indonesia | 735,268 | 112,800,000 | 1949 | Dutch |
| Israel | 7,992 | 2,813,000 | 1948 | British |
| Ivory Coast | 127,520 | 4,200,000 | 1960 | French |
| Jamaica | 4,411 | 1,900,000 | 1962 | British |
| Jordan | 37,738 | 2,071,000 | 1946 | British |
| Kenya | 225,000 | 10,209,000 | 1963 | British |
| South Korea | 38,012 | 30,400,000 | 1948 | Japanese |
| Kuwait | 6,178 | 555,000 | 1961 | British |
| Laos | 91,429 | 2,825,000 | 1949 | French |
| Lebanon | 4,015 | 2,367,000 | 1943 | French |
| Lesatho (Basutoland) | 11,716 | 1,000,000 | 1966 | British |
| Libya | 679,182 | 1,869,000 | 1951 | Italian |
| Malagasy | 228,000 | 6,643,000 | 1960 | French |
| Malawi | 48,443 | 4,285,000 | 1964 | British |
| Malaysia | 128,430 | 11,835,000 | 1957 | British |
| Maldive Is. | 115 | 104,000 | 1965 | British |
| Mali | 478,640 | 4,900,000 | 1960 | French |
| Malta | 95 | 319,000 | 1964 | British |
| Mauretania | 397,850 | 1,120,000 | 1960 | French |
| Mauritius | 720,000 | 810,000 | 1968 | British |
| Morocco | 171,843 | 14,816,000 | 1956 | French/Span. |
| Nauru | 8 | 6,053 | 1968 | Australian |

| | | | |
|---|---|---|---|
| Niger | 489,062 | 3,909,000 | 1960 | French |
| Nigeria | 356,574 | 62,650,000 | 1960 | British |
| Pakistan | 365,432 | 109,520,000 | 1947 | British |
| Philippines | 115,800 | 35,993,000 | 1946 | American |
| Rwanda | 10,170 | 3,306,000 | 1962 | Belgian |
| Senegal | 76,104 | 3,685,000 | 1960 | French |
| Sierra Leone | 27,625 | 2,475,000 | 1961 | British |
| Singapore | 225 | 2,004,000 | 1965 | British |
| Somalia | 246,000 | 2,500,000 | 1960 | Ital./British |
| Southern Yemen | 111,080 | 1,146,000 | 1967 | British |
| Sudan | 967,275 | 14,979,000 | 1956 | British/ Egyptian |
| Swaziland | 6,705 | 375,000 | 1968 | British |
| Syria | 71,228 | 5,738,000 | 1944 | French |
| Tanzania | 362,820 | 12,926,000 | 1961 | British |
| Togo | 22,000 | 1,818,000 | 1960 | French |
| Tongo | 270 | 81,000 | 1970 | British |
| Trinidad & Tobago | 1,980 | 1,010,000 | 1962 | British |
| Tunisia | 63,379 | 4,533,000 | 1956 | French |
| Uganda | 93,981 | 8,133,000 | 1962 | British |
| Upper Volta | 105,946 | 5,278,000 | 1962 | French |
| S. Vietnam | 66,263 | 17,414,000 | 1954 | French |
| West'n. Somoa | 1,097 | 137,000 | 1962 | N. Zealand |
| Zambia | 290,586 | 4,144,000 | 1964 | British |
| | 13,223,124 | 1,153,452,053 | | |

refers to the treatment of the blacks, though it also includes discrimination against other minorities such as American Indians, Mexican-Americans and Orientals.

It is indisputable that the black minority has suffered and continues to suffer from discrimination and injustice. Nevertheless, the sincere efforts to abolish discrimination and injustice are unique in history. Legislation to abolish the cruder manifestations of discrimination has been written and enforced. The battle against cultural and social discrimination has been joined. The black community has made remarkable social and economic progress during the past decade.

The economic standards of black people are higher in the U.S. than anywhere else in the world. Equal rights for blacks are written in the laws. Progress towards the goal is being made.

The onlooker sees most of the game. A French journalist, Guy Sitbon toured the U.S. in 1969 to observe black misery and investigate black power. Here is his report:*

> The facts and data showing their misery are numerous and convincing. One has only to consult the tons of documents put out by official U.S. organs. The only thing which is generally omitted is that their misery is for the most part less than ours. A black American may be poor, but he is still richer than a Frenchman. Though the black American has an income 40 percent lower than the average white, the average Frenchman has an income smaller still. The black American eats better, lives better, in general gets more consumer benefits than a Frenchman.
>
> And this is not simply a matter of material goods. Black Americans study at universities in greater proportion than the citizens of any European country. In Europe one in ten get to a university; 1.5 in ten blacks go on to college. What does this mean? It means that they are richer, better educated, more cultivated, better trained, stronger than we are in all areas. But I am persuaded that if a charity organization in France had the idea of collecting blankets for the relief of black Americans, they would get boatloads full. The black American is mixed up in most Frenchmen's minds with the rest of suffering humanity: the Biafrans, the lepers, the Indians of Brazil and the starving men in the streets of Calcutta.

*Guy Sitbon, (His report was published in LeNouvel Adam of Paris, France and reprinted in Atlas, June 1969, p. 43).

> We stuff everything in the same bag of injustices, from the bad conscience all Westerners inherit about the victims of capitalism and imperialism. In the main, we are right to feel guilty. But to feel this for the American Negro is pointless.

The following personal experience shows the bright side of relations between blacks and whites in America. On September 1, 1967, I accompanied my son, John, to see a football game between the Los Angeles Rams and the Kansas City Chiefs in the Los Angeles Coliseum. Los Angeles was in the throes of a heat wave and we perspired freely as the car slowed to a crawl in the dense traffic near the coliseum. We solved the parking problem by driving through a narrow drive-way into a parking lot behind a residential building in a lane off Hoover Avenue. We were in a Negro area or "ghetto." As we walked the few blocks to the grounds, the streets were lined with drugstores and storefront churches. Black children played everywhere.

At the Coliseum, both the football teams and the crowd were thoroughly integrated. To reach our seats, we had to clamber over about a dozen Negro fans. They submitted to this misfortune cheerfully. Seated next to me was a black man with a small beard. He was an enthusiastic expert on American football, and throughout the match he courteously kept us informed of the records of the players and the finer points of the game. The densely-packed crowd all around us, consisting as it did of black and white, old and young, male and female, was the epitome of smiling good will.

As we walked from the grounds, John said, "A visitor from another country could not believe there is any racial problem in the United States."

I immediately thought of American visitors to Moscow, Hanoi and Peking and how irrelevant their observations must be and what little significance should be attached to their reports. Even if an individual moves around freely throughout a country, judgments are superficial in the extreme.

We walked back to the place where we had parked the car and found a crowd of 30 or 40 people waiting patiently and chatting amiably. Every inch off space had been utilized for parking and this included the narrow drive way leading from the street to the parking lot behind the residence. The front car in the driveway was locked and the driver had failed to arrive so all the other cars were trapped.

The crowd waited patiently until midnight. Approximately half were black and half were white. They talked and laughed together as a group. I did not hear one angry or bitter word spoken.

Finally someone managed to insert a hook, made from a wire coat hanger, above the window and unlocked the car door. We pushed it to a safe parking area on the street. We entered our cars, waved good-bye to each other, and dispersed.

There is an enormous reservoir of good will between black and white in the United States. Friendship is the companion of shared interests. Driving home I felt a warm glow of optimism for the future. Racial violence is not inevitable.

## PARTICIPATORY DEMOCRACY

Bigness brings problems. The individual feels isolated and powerless in the face of the Leviathan of Impersonal Government. A longing to participate and experience a sense of community and of control over one's own destiny is natural. This feeling was behind the original devotion of SDS to participatory democracy. The enemies were big, distant, impersonal government and the big impersonal computerized multi-versity. The words, "The Establishment" and "The System" specify the hated enemy.

But as a matter of fact, there is more participatory democracy in America than in any other large nation. The individual can exercise far more influence over his government for instance than can a citizen in Australia or England. In those countries democratic activity is restricted to periodic elections. The representatives elected are usually subject to party discipline and letters from their constituents have little effect on their votes. In America however elected legislators are primarily responsible to their constituency. There are sensitive to the opinions of the voters. Letters from the voters can be very influential.

Voters can write to the President, a Senator or a Congressman without fear. This is unusual in this world. A major from the Mexican army attended an anti-communist school conducted in New Orleans, Louisiana. He heard speaker after speaker urge the audience to write letters of protest to the President, to their congressmen to their senators. He said, "I broke up when I heard people being urged to write the President or their Senators. Nobody in Mexico urges you to write to the President. You would get action, but not exactly the action you had in mind."

Participatory democracy is a reality in the United States. Countless thousands write to the President or their Representatives. Some complain that their letters do not produce the requested policy. However, the essence of democracy is the right to express, not enforce, an opinion. Democracy entails a willingness to submit to the will of the majority when that will is determined legitimately. Still, there is evidence that letters affect legislation. This is supported by the fact that all sorts of organizations urge their constituency to write and petition the President and Congress.

Despite this it is easy to lose patience because the process is slow. In most circumstances, that may be an advantage as it prevents precipitate action based on temporary impulse. This slowness is particularly irritating to the young who are naturally opinionated and impatient.

Participatory democracy in America extends from local to national issues. It is expressed by the election of school boards, voting on bond issues, referenda and the right of recall. It is actual and not merely formal. Those who condemn the system because their opinions do not prevail, pay only lip-service to democracy. There are essentially totalitarian.

## LAND OF OPPORTUNITY

"The individual is powerless against the system." "You can't fight city hall." Such statements are quoted as axioms but are they true? Consider Ralph Nader. Was he powerless against General Motors? The American system allowed Ralph Nader to develop national influence. You may consider this influence good or bad, but the fact is that one lone and unknown individual confronted mighty General Motors and prevailed. Ralph Nader is no Don Quixote tilting at windmills. He is a force no institution can ignore. He offends powerful corporations; the powerful unions and powerful governmental departments with impunity. The Ralph Naders can flourish in America.

The Rev. Robert Schuller, a humble minister of the Reformed Church of America began conducting services in the drive-in theater of Garden Grove, California, in 1955. He had a keen mind, buoyant personality, a vision and faith. His material assets were minute. Today the Garden Grove Community Church is one of the wonders of Southern California. A magnificent glass-walled church building seats 1600. Adjacent to this is a drive-in sanctuary which accommodates 600 cars. The glass wall alongside the pulpit is electrically controlled and slides aside so that Bob Schuller can speak to those within the auditorium and in the cars simultaneously. Accessory buildings include a 13-story administration and prayer tower which is topped by a magnificent, illuminated cross which can be seen for many miles around. The grounds are beautifully landscaped with fountains, statuary and a carillon adding an environment of beauty.

Five services are conducted in the auditorium each Sunday. One Sunday morning service is even televised over many TV stations. The church provides a 24-hour counseling service and anyone with problems can contact a trained counselor at any time by dialing the letters of NEW HOPE, area code 714. The church is a beehive of activity. Young people abound. The property is worth millions of dollars.

This is a living example of genuine freedom of religion. How different from the caricature of freedom of religion which exists in the Soviet Union. There, the constitution grants "Freedom of Religious Worship" and "Freedom of Anti-Religious Propaganda." The right to worship in an established church is the sole right the individual possesses. The church cannot conduct Sunday School, evangelistic services or youth activities. It cannot build; it cannot publish; it cannot televise; and it cannot conduct public counseling. Growth is inhibited while the children of the church are taught atheism in school.

Freedom of religion is meaningless without the freedom to persuade. America is still the land of opportunity.

## THE RIGHT TO LEAVE

American citizens have the right to emigrate. No one need risk death by fleeing across an armed border. No one can be denied a passport because of his political, religious or racial characteristics.

Millions in the communist world would give everything they possess for this right. The plight of the Jews in Russia dramatizes this. The refugee flood from communist countries is eloquent.

## DISSENT

The right to dissent is guarded diligently. The most heretical ideas can be taught and the most outrageous activities advocated. Such solicitude is shown for the right to dissent that often criminal activity successfully masquerades as dissent.

Such latitude is allowed to the dissenter that America has been called the permissive society. Those who protest the ills in America often possess in super-abundance the freedom which they deny. There is something incongruous about an individual calling a radio talk show, articulating controversial ideas and complaining that he has no freedom of speech.

Those who accuse America of being a repressive society are usually the first to take advantage of its permissiveness. They are the living refutation of their own argument.

As an Australian, I have been privileged to spend much time in America. From my personal experience, three things are typical of the American character: Energy, Generosity, and Compassion.

## ENERGY

America exudes energy. America is energy in motion; Things are happening. Cars jam the highways 24 hours a day. Workers commence work at 7:00 a.m. instead of 8:00 a.m. or later as usually happens in England or Australia. Businessmen meet for breakfast. Groups form clubs of every conceivable variety. Inventors invent; new products are conceived, produced and marketed; new ideas

232

proliferate. America is active, vivid, and somewhat boisterous. Plainly, this energy is not due to genetic factors but to the political and economic climate that prevails. Individuals are not terrorized and inhibited but instead are stimulated by the prospect of reward and by competition and the result is achievement.

## GENEROSITY

The American people are generous with their friendship and with their money. They are lavish in their hospitality and in their support for their chosen cause. They converse easily and do not hesitate to talk to the stranger in their midst. There is an almost complete absence of caste or class. The boss is addressed by his first name by the janitor. The taxi-driver advises the statesman and the professor. Truly the United States approaches the true egalitarian society.

Despite heavy taxation, Americans donate voluntarily and generously to a multitude of causes. Most major cities have their community funds. Churches, hospitals, schools, and a variety of charities all exist because of this generosity.

The American system encourages individual generosity by making gifts to charitable, educational, and religious organizations tax-deductible. Foundations to channel private fortunes into service to mankind are also encouraged.

## COMPASSION

A child wanders away from home. The whole community ceases its activities and all combine in the search for the child. The question of money does not arise.

A seaman is stricken with an attack of appendicitis at sea. A warship changes its course and arranges for a helicopter to fly the man to a hospital on shore.

A disaster strikes anywhere in the world. America reacts with food, medicine, blankets and personnel.

There are many fine commendable features in the complex society known as the United States of America. This society is presently in an unfinished state—It is still changing and growing. But the future is not predetermined, so it can be influenced by the character and activity of individual citizens.

America is an "unperfect" society, but it is also among the very best to be found in the world. Surely, it is worth defending.

# THE INHERITORS

# 13

If the activities of the groups promoting the destruction of the
United States are successful, who will inherit the chaos? If they
can produce the breakdown of our governmental system and create anarchy, the job of the destroyers will be complete. The enforc-
ers will then take charge.

The breakdown of government will be a reality once it is unable
to fulfill its three basic functions: 1) Protection against external
enemies, 2) Protection against internal enemies, and 3) The administration of justice.

## PROTECTION AGAINST EXTERNAL ENEMIES

The breakdown of the power to protect against external enemies
could come about in a number of ways.

One way would be the reduction of America's military power

in relation to that of the communist forces, particularly the Soviet Union, so that, by blackmail, the communists could engulf the independent nations one by one till the United States was isolated and its military situation hopeless. All responsible authorities agree that the balance of military power has been moving in the direction of the communists, particularly of the Soviet Union. This imbalance seems to alarm even the Chinese Communists who are depending on the U.S.A. to protect them from Soviet might until their own military establishment is adequate.

A second way in which the American government could lose the power to defend the people against external enemies would be the moral disintegration of the armed forces. Many factors are contributing to this: racial conflict, drug indulgence, and indecisive leadership. Groups organized and led by communists exploit these disintegrative forces.

## PROTECTION AGAINST INTERNAL ENEMIES

The second function of government is protection against internal enemies or the preservation of law and order. The ability of the government to guarantee the security of its citizens has diminished during the past few years. Many people hesitate to walk on the streets of many major cities at night.

The locations where an individual can feel safe are diminishing. Crimes are committed in government buildings, public parks, and homes. This is the era of the lock and key as few people dare to leave their homes or cars unlocked.

## ADMINISTRATION OF JUSTICE

The third function of government is the administration of justice. This includes the conduct of the courts and the correctional institutions.

Administration of justice is becoming more difficult. This is due in part to the conduct of lawyers and defendants and the techniques of delay. At times it is impossible to secure an unbiased jury. The government found it impossible to administer justice in the trial of the Black Panther Party leader, Bobby Seale, for the murder of Rackley. He was not tried and found guilty or innocent. The jury could not agree. The verdict was: We cannot try you; we are unable to administer justice in your case; you may go free.

The administration of justice is hampered by violence and the threat of violence in the courtroom. The 1970 events in the San Marin, California, courthouse where the judge and prosecuting attorney were kidnapped by Jonathan Jackson and the prisoners on trial and which led to the death of the judge and some prisoners, and the wounding of the prosecuting attorney, are well known.

The correctional institutions are also becoming increasingly more difficult to administer. Murder, riot, and potential rebellion characterize the conditions in many prisons. San Quentin and Attica are household words.

The conditions of law and order in America are deteriorating. If the descent into anarchy is not halted, the government will lose its legitimacy and drastic actions will be taken by those awaiting their chance to seize power.

If legitimate government disintegrates, what organizations could exercise power? We can eliminate the sensualists and the anarchists, as their skills are limited to the art of destruction. They have neither the vision nor the organization to direct society. The Marcusian slogan, "All power to the imagination," does not help much. Obviously more than imagination is needed for the complex task of government in modern society.

I appeared on a television show in Chicago and criticized the message of the book, The Greening of America, by Charles Reich.* I was particularly critical of its repudiation of excellence and its glorification of self-indulgence. I called it the "Cult of the slob."

A young man spoke up: "You don't understand. This is a carefully worked out program to destroy this society and to replace it by," he hesitated for a moment, "we don't quite know that yet."

The sensualists do not know what is to follow destruction, but others do. These others include the communists. They are ready to move into the vacuum the sensualists and the anarchists create.

The anarchists are efficient destroyers, but they have yet to

*Charles Reich, "The Greening of America", (New York, Random House, 1970).

demonstrate any constructive skill. They assume society will flourish by people "doing what comes naturally." Bakunin gave little attention to the society that would follow the destruction of the revolution, and he considered it wrong to inquire since it was liable to siphon energy from the urgent task of destruction.

The anarchists mouth a few slogans such as, "The peasants will own the farms and the workers will own and operate the factories." How the produce of the farms would be transferred to the workers in the factories while the products of the factories were made available on the farms was never specified. This involves such things as exchange or money and raises the question of economic justice. This inevitably leads to the consideration of adjudication and authority or government, and this is taboo.

However, the communists know exactly what to do once the government collapses and they have the organization to do it. The Communist Party is a durable organization. It can operate openly or underground if this is necessary. It can retain its structure and function under intense persecution. Musssolini tried to destroy the Communist Party of Italy. Yet, when Mussolini was killed, the Party emerged from the underground, functioning and apparently healthy. Today, the Communist Party of Italy is the largest Communist Party in Western Europe and commands the largest following in the democratic world. Clearly the Communist Party has the organization and the will to impose order on chaos.

Subjectively, both the sensualists and the anarchists repudiate Marxism-Leninism and the socialism of the Dictatorship of the Proletariat. Objectively they are working for it. If their efforts to destroy the democratic state are successful, the communists will inherit. Fittingly, among the first to feel the lash of the communist whip will be their erstwhile allies, the anarchists and sensualists.

Censorship will replace license in literature; the rule of force will replace the rule of law and "Do as you are told" will make "doing your own thing" a nostalgic memory. The quiescence of the grave will end both the dreams and anguish of the anarchists.

The communists will not have to exercise authority through their own resources. They will be able to count on the fraternal aid of the international communists; particularly the Soviet Union. This aid could take the form of military force as in Hungary and Czechoslovakia, economic assistance as in Cuba or secret police as in the East European satellites between 1945 and 1953 when the Communist Parties of those countries were purged.

## FASCISM

If anarchy develops, it is not certain that the communists will restore order. Another possibility is the rise of a national dictatorship or noncommunist fascism.

In his book "Points of Rebellion," Supreme Court Justice William O. Douglas quotes Adolph Hitler as saying in 1932:

"The streets of our country are in turmoil. The universities are filled with students rebelling and rioting.

"Communists are seeking to destroy our country. Russia is threatening us with her might and the republic is in danger. Yes, danger from within and without.

"We need law and order."*

Considerable controversy has arisen over this quotation. The controversy has centered around the question of whether Hitler actually said this. This argument is irrelevent.

If Hitler did not say it, he most definitely could have said it, because the situation described in the quotation is true. He almost certainly said something like it many times. It was the truth embodied in this statement that helped Hitler ascend to power. That is why those who create such conditions are providing ammunition for tyrants.

The inference that anyone who states the truth concerning the riotous and anarchic conditions in America must have aspirations similar to those of Hitler is logically fallacious and morally contemptible. The truth remains true independently of the motives of the one who draws attention to it.

When a thief cries, "Stop, thief," it does not mean no theft has taken place. The important thing is to correct the conditions that grant plausibility to the argument of the tyrant. It is utterly shortsighted and irresponsible to ignore cries of alarm without first determining whether there is substance to the charges.

During the Second World War, I was a teacher in Australia. In one of my classes, there was a migrant from Austria. He told me

*William O. Douglas, "Points of Rebellion", (New York, Random House, 1970), page 58.

of the student riots organized by the Nazis in the schools of
Austria. In his school, the principal had been held captive by
rioting primary students. He also told me of the attitude of his
German aunt, a widow of a German army officer who was killed
in the early stages of the Second World War and a mother of two
girls. The conditions in the early 30's were so anarchic that it was
unsafe to walk in the streets. There were roaming bands of Nazis
and communists. She had to walk miles to meet her two daughters
at the conclusion of work each day and to escort them home. She
said, "When Hitler came to power, and we had law and order once
again, it was heaven."

Anarchy very clearly creates the conditions that lead to tyranny. The promise of authority and order becomes irresistibly
seductive. Those who are rioting in the name of liberty are objectively contributing to the establishment of total authority.

I tried to make this point to a young man following a lecture
in San Diego, California. I said, "You should be careful. You will
create a police state."

He said, "We have a police state now."

I replied, "This is the most permissive society in the history of
mankind, and you call it a police state. How long do you think
your revolution would last if the authorities did what they did in
Mexico City before the Olympic games?"

He said, "Not very long."

It is unpleasant but instructive to recall what happened in
Mexico City prior to the 1968 Olympic games. Many thousands of student-led rioters were protesting and threatening to
stop the famous sporting games from being held. Shortly
before the Olympics were due to start, however, the authorities
turned the Mexican Army loose and they shot many rioters. It
is difficult to obtain an accurate report of how many were
killed, but estimates range from scores to hundreds or even
thousands depending on who gives the figures. The leaders
who were not shot were arrested and kept in prison. A strange
calm descended on the scene and the Olympic games were
held without a murmur of external protest.

It is alarming that when I relate these events to large audiences,
there is often a spontaneous burst of applause. This shows the
mood of many people. They fail to see that when such actions

occur, the cause of freedom and justice has been defeated. The rule of law has been replaced by the rule of force.

A free society is fragile and must be nurtured tenderly. Waiting to burst out are the caged aggressive impulses of imperfect man. Anarchy breaks the bars of the cage and lets loose unrestrained brutality. At first the brutality may be exercised only against those who contribute to the anarchy but later it turns and attacks all. Thus we have two possibilities if legitimate government collapses: communist or fascist dictatorship. Both of these are left-wing authoritarian tyrannies.

How could a home-grown fascist dictatorship develop in the U.S.? What organizations can be considered as potential rulers?

I think we can eliminate the openly fascist organizations in the United States. They have nuisance value but little popular support. Such organizations as the American Nazi Party and the White Peoples' Party have no popular base of support so cannot be compared with parties that have seized power in other countries. Hitler had great popular support, and he was elected to office. The Ku Klux Klan has some local support and political power, but it is inconceivable that it could prevail on a national scale.

If a non-communist authoritarian government is to be established in the U.S., the most likely instrument is the military. Military dictatorships are commonplace throughout the world since the military forces have the weapons and the personnel needed to impose authority. However, the American military forces have a tradition of submission to civilian authority. The President of the U.S. is Commander-in-Chief of the Armed Forces. The military never has seized power in this country although this does not mean it never will do so.

If the nation descends into anarchy, it is conceivable that certain military men would consider it their patriotic duty to take over and establish order. Civil liberties tend to be suspended when there is a threat to public order. Events in neighboring Canada during 1970 illustrate this. Pierre Trudeau was one of the founders of the Canadian Civil Liberties Union, but when the Quebec Liberation Front kidnaped and killed the Quebec Labor Minister and kidnaped a British diplomat, Trudeau, as Prime Minister of Canada, reactivated the War Crimes Act and suspended the basic civil liberties of the Canadian people. Arrest and confinement without trial were permitted.

In the light of American military tradition, provocation would need to be great before extra-legal action was taken. If the military did seize power, it would almost certainly be represented as a temporary expedient necessary to deal with disrupters and establish an orderly society after which constitutional government would be restored. However, American democracy would never be the same again and a precious heritage of liberty would have been lost. Such a development would be tragic.

Another possibility is the establishment of a communist dictatorship. This would result from a combination of internal disintegration and external pressure. It could be camouflaged at first by some form of international agreement and it would probably not come suddenly but as the result of a series of concessions, each one of which would leave the United States weaker in relation to the communist world. The dismantling of the democratic state would be a comparatively slow process as basic liberties were progressively whittled away. Each step in the process would be insufficient to provoke massive resistance and once each step was successfully completed, massive resistance would become more difficult till finally it was impossible. The end result would be the naked dictatorship of the Communist Party.

How can both of these possible eventualities be avoided? The essential prelude to either is anarchy. The prevention of anarchy is the prevention of totalitarian dictatorship; thus, the decline into anarchy must be stopped.

The obvious first step toward avoiding anarchy is to support the police and peace officers. The police constitute the thin blue line standing between law-abiding citizens and anarchy. When this line is ruptured, the results are devastating. The aggressive forces within human nature would strike with lightning rapidity. There are many historic illustrations of what happens when the dikes of police power break.

On September 9, 1919, 1,400 men out of a total of 1,544 on the Boston police force went out on strike. Within hours after the police turned in their badges and guns, all hell broke loose in Boston. Looting, window smashing—all sorts of anarchic action was the order of the day. The city had seemingly gone mad. Order was reinstated and the roaming crowds brought under control only after Gov. Calvin Coolidge sent in National Guard troops on September 10. Anarchy ceased after but a day's reign. Brief though the existence of anarchy may have been, the city of Boston paid dearly for the experience. Besides the untold property damage, nine people died and 58 were wounded. Two deaths occured as National Guardsmen attempted to restore order.

"Forty years later, the world witnessed a repeat performance. The site was Montreal, Canada instead of Boston but the results were the same. On October 7, 1969, the entire Montreal Police force of 3,700 men walked off the job. The strike lasted only 17 hours but in that time 456 burglaries occurred—350 a week was the average when the police were on duty. Rioters, using whatever they could get their hands on, ran amuk through the downtown area, smashing and stealing at random. More than $2 million worth of property was destroyed. At least two people were killed. After 16 hours the Montreal police voluntarily returned to their jobs and quickly restored order.

The borderline beween order and anarchy is a very thin line and that line is manned by the police. Without the police, all would be in serious trouble. If I were asked where I would sooner live —in a community without doctors or in one without police, I would reluctantly reply, "Let the doctors go, I'll keep the police. We'll live longer without the doctors than we would without the police."

The police have a very difficult job which grows more complex every day. They need the patience of Job, the wisdom of Solomon, and the compassion of St. Francis. If the policeman does not use force to restrain the violent, he is not doing his job. If he does use force, he is being brutal. The dividing line between necessary force and brutality is arbitrarily drawn by the critics after the fact.

Supporting the police does not mean that corruption and brutality should be condoned. These weaken the police and render them less efficient in serving society, but all police should not be condemned because of the faults of a few.

Police are people subject to passions and temptations. It would be surprising if corruption and brutality did not exist to some extent. Some mothers are brutal towards their children, but, of course, this does not mean that motherhood is brutal or brutalizing.

The profession of a policeman is honorable and should be honored. But supporting the police involves more than lip service. Wearing the badge, "Support your local police" is not enough. True support involves avoiding non-essential activities that would make the task of the police more difficult. This may involve refraining from activities in which we may very well have a perfect right to indulge. Things that are lawful are not always expedient.

In order to diminish the possibility of anarchy and to help the police I am prepared to refrain from exercising two of my rights. They are the rights to participate in mass demonstrations, and to own a gun for self-defense.

## DEMONSTRATIONS

Every group has the right to demonstrate peacefully. However, mobs on the street pose certain dangers. Mobs generate counter-mobs and, thus, the possibility of violence always exists. However sincere leaders may be in desiring and working for peace, there are always individuals who desire violence and who strive to take advantage of a potentially explosive situation. A spark may ignite a mob.

Other methods are available and preferable to solve complex problems. Avenues of persuasion remain open to all. The substitution of mass pressure for reasoned argument is traumatic to democracy.

The power of person to person persuasion is great. Supporters can expand geometrically. When these approach a majority, their political power is unlimited. I have often used the illustration that if a person recruits one supporter each week, and each supporter in turn recruits another who likewise recruits weekly, everyone in the world could be recruited in 32 weeks.

Counter demonstrations merely help demonstrations. No argument can be settled reasonably by determining which side can raise the largest mob. To react to one mob by forming another is like trying to extinguish a flame by pouring gasoline on it.

To say the least, mass demonstrations impose great strains on the police and at times may become intolerable.

244

## GUNS

Few subjects generate more emotion than the question of whether citizens should own guns for the protection of family and self. Women are particularly susceptible to attack on the streets or at home, and it would seem prudent to have a weapon available to deal with such a contingency.

It is questionable, however, whether the security of citizens is increased by the availability of guns. More people in the U.S. are killed each year by impassioned members of their families or by friends than by criminals. Many of these would live if the presence of a gun did not coincide with the moment of passion.

The widespread distribution and easy availability of weapons also increases the personal danger to each policeman. Every call to a domestic dispute becomes a potential death-trap.

It is difficult to reconcile maximum support for the police with advocacy of the easy availability of lethal guns. If every individual has to protect himself, or herself, by owning a gun, we have taken a giant step towards anarchy.

For my part, in order to give the police full support, I am willing to renounce my right to own and use a gun for self-protection. This discussion does not refer to guns used for hunting and sporting purposes. Such guns can be locked away unloaded, whereas guns for self-protection to be effective must be loaded and readily available.

The slogan, "If guns were outlawed, only outlaws would have guns" sounds convincing but it is untrue. The police would also have guns. They should be provided with the most efficient weapons available to do their duty. The greater their superiority in weapons, the less likelihood they will be called upon to use them.

## CIVIL DISOBEDIENCE

Laws should be obeyed. Unless the majority of the people are prepared to obey the law voluntarily, democracy is unworkable. Only the massive coercion of the totalitarian state can coerce a majority of the people so that they obey unwillingly.

What about civil disobedience? Is it permissible to disobey unjust laws? Many contend that it is not only permissible but obligatory to disobey unjust laws in order to generate momentum to change them, and that civil disobedience is moral provided the one who breaks the law is willing to accept the penalty.

This raises many questions. Who decides that a particular law is unjust? The answer usually given is the individual's conscience. This assumes that the conscience is invariably a just judge. Many individuals are convinced that abortion is murder. Would an individual who believed this sincerely be justified in killing an abortionist in order to save many future lives? This example shows that the relation of the individual conscience to the law is far from a simple one.

Civil disobedience should never be undertaken lightly. If widely practiced, it would produce anarchy with the consequence already described. Where legal channels are open, it must be condemned.

The price of freedom is high. Not long ago, I witnessed a young man stand up and say, "I can conceive of no circumstance in which I would be willing to die." This is the attitude which the communists believe assures their success. Once it prevails on a sufficient scale. All they will need to do is to create a series of crises in which the choice is to make a concession or risk possible death. The thinking might proceed like this: the concession is unpleasant, but the risk of death is unthinkable. You have only one life, and nothing else can equal it in value, so it should not be exchanged for anything else. Therefore, the concession is made. Obviously, a series of such concessions would equate surrender.

If the Jews of Israel were not prepared to die, their nation could not live and the tragedy of the gas chambers would be repeated. The willingness to die in certain circumstances is one of the conditions for continuing to live. Those who love freedom must be willing to sacrifice as much to retain it as the totalitarians are to destroy it. Jesus said, "Greater love hath no man than this; that a man lay down his life for his friends."

# INDEX

# INDEX

248

# INDEX

# INDEX